A FIELD GUIDE TO THE WATERBIRDS OF ASIA

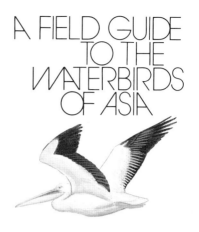

W0010506

The Wild Bird Society of Japan is a private, non-profit organisation founded in 1934 which has over 42,000 members and 80 chapters throughout Japan. It aims to promote the co-existence of human beings and nature. To meet this objective, the Society is actively involved in the conservation of wild birds and their habitats; encourages more people to be aware of the importance of nature conservation through birdwatching, and carries out research on the status of wild birds and their natural habitats in Japan. Recognising that no international boundaries exist for birds, the Society is aware of the importance of international cooperation and has been working with other national organisations in Asia to conserve birds and their habitats — especially important areas for migratory birds.

Wild Bird Society of Japan
Aoyama Flower Bldg., 1-1-4 Shibuya, Shibuya-ku,
Tokyo 150, Japan

The Tokai Foundation was founded by The Tokai Bank, Ltd., in 1975 in commemoration of its 100th anniversary. The objective of the Foundation is to promote and support projects which will contribute to the preservation of a healthy natural environment. Some of the activities conducted by the Foundation are: production of a film on the Birds in the Tokai District, construction of Tokai no Mori Woods (a collection of plants from the Tokai District), publication of a guide book series "Tokai Nature Trail", and financial support for research on the ecological system of whales in the seas surrounding Japan.

Tokai Foundation
3-21-24 Nishiki, Naka-ku,
Nagoya 460, Japan

The Asian Wetland Bureau is an international non-profit organisation which aims to promote protection and sustainable utilization of wetland resources in Asia. The Bureau's work is divided into 4 major programmes: 1. Wetland Monitoring, 2. Wetland Management, 3. Information and Training, 4. Institution Building and Awareness. The Bureau is a registered charity in Britain, and operates offices through formal arrangements with the University of Malaya, in Malaysia, and the Ministry of Forestry, in Indonesia. The Bureau currently channels about US$1,600,000 a year into projects in the region and is keen to cooperate with or provide technical assistance to other institutions or individuals who have an interest in wetlands.

Asian Wetland Bureau
Institute of Advanced Studies, University of Malaya,
Lembah Pantai, 59100 Kuala Lumpur, Malaysia

A FIELD GUIDE TO THE WATERBIRDS OF ASIA

Text by
Bharat Bhushan
Graham Fry
Akira Hibi
Taej Mundkur
Dewi M. Prawiradilaga
Koichiro Sonobe
Shunji Usui

Illustrations by
Takashi Taniguchi

Editor in Chief
Koichiro Sonobe
Editor
Shunji Usui

WILD BIRD SOCIETY OF JAPAN
in collaboration with ASIAN WETLAND BUREAU
with the assistance of a grant from
TOKAI FOUNDATION

KODANSHA INTERNATIONAL
TOKYO · NEW YORK · LONDON

Distributed in the United States by Kodansha America, Inc., 114 Fifth Avenue, New York, N.Y. 10011, and in the United Kingdom and continental Europe by Kodansha Europe Ltd., Gillingham House, 38-44 Gillingham Street, London SW1V 1HU.

Published by the Wild Bird Society of Japan, Aoyama Flower Bldg., 1-1-4 Shibuya, Shibuya-ku, Tokyo 150, Japan, in cooperation with Kodansha International Ltd., 17-14 Otowa 1-chome, Bunkyo-ku, Tokyo 112, and Kodansha America, Inc.

Publication of this book has been done in collaboration with the Asian Wetland Bureau, and was assisted by a grant from the Tokai Foundation.

Copyright © 1993 by the Wild Bird Society of Japan. All rights reserved. No part of this book may be reproduced in any form without written permission from the publishers.
Printed in Japan by Sanyo Printing Co., Ltd.
Book Design by Minoru Imai.

First edition, 1993
93 94 95 4 3 2 1

Reference: Sonobe, K. and Usui, S. (editors) 1993. A Field Guide to the Waterbirds of Asia. Wild Bird Society of Japan, Tokyo.

Library of Congress Cataloging-in-Publication Data
A Field Guide to the Waterbirds of Asia/text by Bharat Bhushan...
[et al.]: illustrations by Takashi Taniguchi; editor in chief,
Koichiro Sonobe; editor, Shunji Usui, — 1st ed.
     p.   cm.
  Includes bibliographical references and index.
  "Wild Bird Society of Japan in collaboration with Asian Wetland Bureau..."
  ISBN 4-7700-1740-5
  1. Water birds—Asia—Identification. I. Bhushan, Bharat.
II. Taniguchi, Takashi. III. Sonobe, Koichiro. IV. Usui, Shunji.
V. Nihon Yachō no Kai. VI. Asian Wetland Bureau.
QL691. A1F54 1993
598.295—dc20
                                        93-18482
                                          CIP

Systematic List by

Bangladesh	Anisuzzaman Khan
Bhutan	Prakash Gole
Brunei	Clive F. Mann
Cambodia/Viet Nam	Le Dien Duc
China	Lu Jian Jian
D.P.R. Korea	Chung Jong Ryol
Eastern Russia	Alexander Yo Kondratyev
Hong Kong	Peter Kennerley
India	Bharat Bhushan/Suhel Quader
Indonesia	Yus Rusila Noor
Japan	Sanae Maehara/Koichiro Sonobe
Laos	Richard E. Slater
Malaysia	David R. Wells
Mongolia	Ajurzanyn Bald
Myanmar	U Saw Han
Nepal	Taej Mundkur
Pakistan	Abrar Husain Mirza
Philippines	Perla Magsalay
Rep. of Korea	Won Pyong-Oh
Singapore	Clive Briffett
Sri Lanka	Thilo W. Hoffmann
Taiwan	Tsai Hong-Ye
Thailand	Bubphar Amget

Contents

Preface by Nagahisa Kuroda

Wetlands comprise some of the most valuable and important natural environments for living creatures, including man. And yet, like tropical forests, they are one of the most threatened habitats in the world, under pressure from human activities and development.

In Asia there has been tremendous interest in wetland conservation in recent years. A great deal of research has been carried out, especially on the ecology of shorebirds — one of the best indicators of the current status of wetland habitats. However, in the absence of any comprehensive and authoritative field guide to waterbirds throughout the region, it has been difficult to use this research to develop an integrated conservation strategy.

With this in mind, the Wild Bird Society of Japan, in collaboration with the Asian Wetland Bureau, resolved to publish a comprehensive field guide to waterbirds which could be used for field research, and as a source of information for wetland conservation projects in the region.

In compiling the guide, we have worked closely with many researchers and conservationists from all countries in Asia, and it is a great honour to publish this book, which is the collaborative effort of so many people throughout the region.

On behalf of the Wild Bird Society of Japan, I should like to offer thanks and congratulations to the seven authors; to Takashi Taniguchi for his excellent illustrations; to the editors, and to all contributors for their knowledge and skill which collectively make this such a comprehensive field guide. I would also like to express my sincere appreciation to the Asian Wetland Bureau for their great contribution, and heartfelt gratitude to the Tokai Foundation, whose financial support made the project possible.

Finally, I would like to thank all those whose continuing effort helps to expand our knowledge of wetlands and waterbirds, and I hope that this publication encourages more people to develop new conservation projects in the region, which WBSJ will be happy to support.

President
Wild Bird Society of Japan

Foreword

Birds do not recognise national boundaries. This is the principal basis of co-operative international activities carried out by bird conservation organisations. Since birds migrate from north to south, and from south to north, often passing through numerous countries on the way, it is essential to collaborate at international level to conserve birds and their habitats throughout the world.

This principle has led the Wild Bird Society of Japan to pursue its international activities based on working closely with people and organisations in each country, and to build networks in the Asian region. Based on these concepts, WBSJ international projects include: donating binoculars to Asian conservation organisations; collaborating with the Taiwanese to publish the "A Guide to the Birds of Taiwan"; helping Taiwanese and Philippine organisations to develop plans for bird sanctuaries; organising international meetings etc. All these projects have encouraged people and governments in each country to conserve birds and their habitats, and WBSJ hopes to continue developing similar projects to improve bird conservation in the region.

The publication of this field guide is also based on the same principle, and we hope it will encourage people throughout the region to think about the importance of protecting wetland environments, and to develop new conservation projects to this end.

In conclusion, I would like to thank all those who have been involved in this project who have helped to make this field guide so authoritative.

Noritaka Ichida
Director
Wild Bird Society of Japan

Acknowledgements

This field guide is published in the hope that it will promote conservation of waterbirds and their wetland habitats in Asia. More than most books, field guides are works of collective effort and enthusiasm. In particular, this one was made possible by the cooperation and contributions of many people from 24 countries and areas in Asia and also from countries outside the region, who generously volunteered their time and expertise.

First of all, we would like to express our deep appreciation to the Asian Wetland Bureau for their generous support and valuable contributions to articles and for editing the field guide, and to the Tokai Foundation for their sponsorship which made the project possible.

In AWB, Taej Mundkur played the most important role as a coordinator. Useful contributions have been made through AWB from Andrew Cockburn, Phil Moors, Christian Perennou, Derek Scott, Mike Smart, David R. Wells and Tunku Mohd Nazim Yaacob. We would like to thank the following present and former staff of AWB for their help: Scott Frazier, John Howes, Ross Hughes, S.A. Hussain, Roger Jaensch, Brett Lane, Yus Rusila Noor, Faizal (Duncan) Parish and Marcel J. Silvius. David Bakewell advised on accuracy of colour plates and M. Nagarani did all the typing. Mr. Hidehiro Satake, the Tokai Foundation, understands the project well and gave his generous support.

Takashi Taniguchi dedicated his time to draw all the illustrations to such a high standard and all authors collected the most up-to-date information in order to write accurate text on each species. Per Alström and Urban Olson gave useful advice on the species for which K. Sonobe and S. Usui wrote the text. Graham Fry translated into English text by Sonobe and Usui as a coauthor. Woo Yong Tae, introduced by Woo Han Chung, gave helpful information on the Relict Gull, including some unpublished measurement data. Shinichi Takeda advised on the plumage of the Ruddy Shelduck, and thanks to Minoru Tomiyama for the use of the photograph of Lake Poyang. We wish to thank all contributors representing each country and area, for the information contained in "Systematic List of Waterbirds of Asia".

We give heartfelt thanks to Peter Kennerley for his advice and comments on both text and illustrations, and to Taej Mundkur for sparing his time while in Japan to check all illustrations. Akira Hibi and Debbie Macklin kindly helped with proofreading. We are grateful to Kilian Mullarney for permitting the use of topography by the late Peter Grant and himself, and would like to mention that we use the Peterson system devised by Roger Tory Peterson for indicating field marks with arrows on the plates.

K. Sonobe, as the Editor in Chief, and S. Usui, as the Editor, were involved in all stages of the field guide's production and Sanae Maehara gave support throughout as Assistant Editor. Book design by Minoru Imai.

Introduction

   In the recent years considerable awareness and interest has been created in wetlands and their importance in Asia — thanks mainly to two important publications that came out during the 80's. First of these has been "A Directory of Asian Wetlands", which, not only provided a compilation of information on wetlands in the region but also, in the process, focussed attention on values of the wetlands as well as the need to monitor them. The second publication, "A Directory of Wetlands of International Importance", underlined the importance of "Ramsar Sites" and provided a basis for future action in these areas.
   In the meantime, the Asian Waterfowl Census which started on a region-wide basis in 1987 caught the imagination of hundreds of birdwatchers in the Asian region who enthusiastically took up the task of conducting annual midwinter waterfowl counts. In a short span of seven years, the

exercise metamorphosed into a large scale annual movement, creating in its wake, ever increasing legion of converts to birdwatching who combined their ornithological interest and conservation zeal to provide an effective tool for monitoring and protection of wetlands and waterbirds. However, with so many variations in plumage colours and patterns during breeding and non-breeding periods as well as among adults and juveniles of waterbirds, it is sometimes difficult to identify species viewed from a distance or under poor light conditions. Therefore, a well illustrated field guide, together with appropriate information on plumage description, behaviour, distribution etc will help both rank beginners, amateurs as well as seasoned birdwatchers to identify them correctly in the field.

Asia is one of the largest continents covering diverse ecological, socio-economic, multi-racial and geopolitical regions with natural barriers as formidable as political ideologies. The many ethnic groups speaking a variety of languages and the heady mixture of religions, cultures and traditions provide a challenging task of any attempt to bring out a comprehensive information document. It is hoped that this field guide will provide a basic tool for understanding one aspect of the biological resource of the region and we also hope this comprehensive and up-to-date field guide could be used for field research and as a source of information for wetland conservation projects in the region.

This book covers 327 species of birds, resident as well as migrants occurring in Asia. Some of the species breed in one part of their range and move to another part during the non-breeding period. All of the species are illustrated in 82 plates arranged according to their sequence in the main text. A systematic list is appended at the end of the book.

Range

The geographical scope extends from Pakistan in the west through Central Asia and South Asia and the areas immediately north in Russia (C.I.S.), the whole of China and Mongolia and south through Japan, South-East Asia up to Indonesia (excluding Irian Jaya). Many of the species have overlapping ranges and are dealt as such. Some have restricted ranges within the region.

Georgraphy, Climate and Habitat

The Asian realm has a wide range of geographical, climatic and vegetational entities covering most extremes. The world's highest mountain ranges; the largest and most extensive deserts, expansive steppes and tundras, elevated plateaus; Arctic and sub-arctic regions; as well as humid tropical oceanic islands are represented in the region, making it the most diversified conglomerate of bio-geographic area. The climate ranges from Arctic to temperate and tropical humid with rainfall from almost zero to in the cold desert to very high in the tropics. The bio-climatic zones are sharply divided north to south with Palaearctic zone covering much of mainland Asia while the sub-tropical and tropical regions dominate in the south. Wetland regimes of the Palaearctic are characterized by the vast tundras, bogs and marshes where most of the migrant waterbirds breed during the period from May to July, to the vast steppes and boggy grasslands of southern Siberia and large, plateau of Tibet. The whole area is interspersed with lake systems, both brackish and freshwater, and areas in adjacent bogs and marshes which provide excellent breeding grounds for waterbirds.

The great Himalayan Mountain range dominates the mainland, a great physical barrier which sharply divides bio-climatic zones of the north and south. Several great river systems drain mainland Asia, sustaining vast floodplain systems and maintaining a constant energy flow to wetland systems of the region.

However, the conditions differ in the southern part of mainland Asia where land masses are represented by chains of large and small islands. Most of the areas here are predominated by estuarine systems with mangroves and mudflats dominating the ecosystems; while freshwater regimes are reduced to small widely scattered pockets often replaced by low inundated rice-fields.

Order of Presentation

The order of presentation generally follows "A Complete Checklist of the Birds of the World" by Howard & Moore 2nd ed. (1991). However, in order to make it easier for quick reference in the field, species are grouped according to their basic groups and field characteristics.

Identification

A. Species' and Scientific Name   The book follows Howard & Moore (1991) for common and scientific names of the species. Alternative common names widely used in the region follow the common name. These are mainly based on King & Dickinsen, "*A Field Guide to the Birds of South East Asia* (1975)", Ali & Ripley, "*A Handbook to the Birds of India and Pakistan* (1983)" and Cheng, "*A Distribution List of Chinese Birds* (1976)".

Genuine marine species, in particular ducks and gulls, are excluded, and some species, though recorded in the area, have been excluded. Notable among these are: White Pelican *Pelecanus roseus,* it is widely accepted as Great White Pelican *P. onocrotalus;* Sri Lanka Stilt *Himantopus ceylonensis,* which is widely accepted as the Black-winged Stilt *H. himantopus* (Hayman *et al,* 1986); Cox's Sandpiper *Calidris paramelanotus,* whose validity as a species has not been established (Cox, J.B., "The enigmatic Cooper's and Cox's Sandpipers", *Dutch Birding* 12: 53-64, juni 1990); Black-fronted Plover *Charadrius melanops*, record unconfirmed and doubtful (Hayman *et al,* 1986), and Greater Black-backed Gull *Larus marinus*, record is only on collected specimen (Harrison 1983), and is a truly western Palaearctic species. Three subspecies of Herring Gull are described (Grant, 1986).

B. Size   It is often difficult to judge size in the field, especially when a bird is wading or swimming in the water. The size of the species is measured from the tip of the bill to the tip of the tail at maximum stretch, and is the total approximate length of the birds.

C. Age and Sex   Distinguishing features which differentiate between sexes as well as between adult and juveniles are listed with a stress on salient features easily visible in the field both at rest and/or in flight.

D. Similar species   The species that are more or less similar in appearance and which belong to the same family, are described for one key speices and further distinctions between them are discussed briefly under this heading for appropriate similar speices. The point to be noted is to make sure that these minor differences are sufficently well noted in order to make proper identification.

E. Voice   Most of the waterbirds are vociferous, especially while they are feeding or when flushed/alarmed or sometimes flying over head. Some secretive species skulking in vegetation can be identified by their characteristic calls/voices. The calls are described with appropriate descriptions and/or with appropriate similar sounding examples.

F. Habitat The appropriate habitat they are associated with are described under this heading.

G. Distribution The entire region has been roughly divided into South Asia, Central Asia, North Asia, South-East and East Asia in the following map.

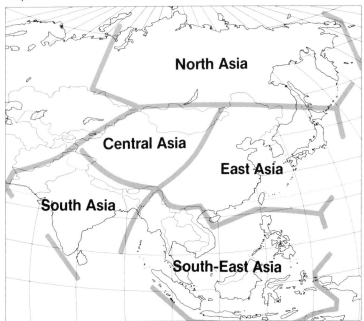

H. Authors Initials at the end of each text indicates the author of it; BB, Bharat Bhushan; AK, Akira Hibi; TM, Taej Mundkur; DMP, Dewi M. Prawiradilaga; KS, Koichiro Sonobe; and SU, Shunji Usui. Each text may differ slightly because of this collaborative work.

Topography

UPPERPARTS

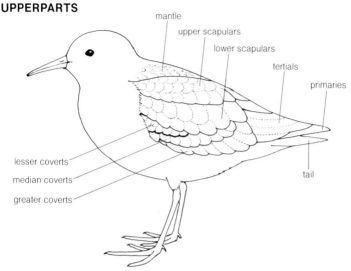

mantle
upper scapulars
lower scapulars
tertials
primaries

lesser coverts
median coverts
greater coverts

tail

HEAD, UNDERPARTS AND LEGS

* = areas mostly concealed by overlaying scapulars and wings

forehead
crown
lore
ear-coverts
bill
nape
back*
chin
throat
rump*
breast
uppertail-coverts*
flank
thigh
belly
tibia
ankle
knee
inner-toe
tarsus
middle-toe
hind-toe
outer-toe
sole
vent
undertail-coverts

UPPERWING

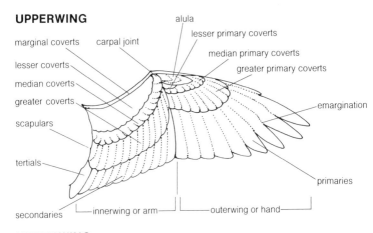

- marginal coverts
- lesser coverts
- median coverts
- greater coverts
- scapulars
- tertials
- secondaries

carpal joint

alula
lesser primary coverts
median primary coverts
greater primary coverts

emargination

primaries

— innerwing or arm —   — outerwing or hand —

UNDERWING

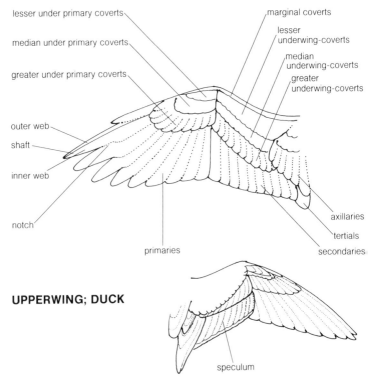

- lesser under primary coverts
- median under primary coverts
- greater under primary coverts
- outer web
- shaft
- inner web
- notch
- primaries

marginal coverts
lesser underwing-coverts
median underwing-coverts
greater underwing-coverts

axillaries
tertials
secondaries

UPPERWING; DUCK

speculum

FEATHERS

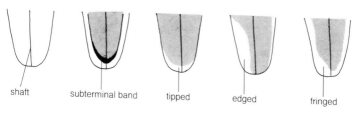

shaft subterminal band tipped edged fringed

HEAD

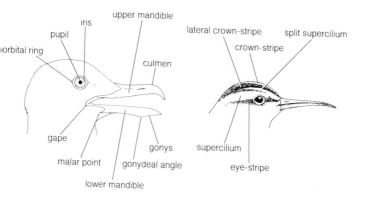

pupil
iris
orbital ring
upper mandible
culmen
gape
malar point
gonys
gonydeal angle
lower mandible

lateral crown-stripe split supercilium
crown-stripe
supercilium
eye-stripe

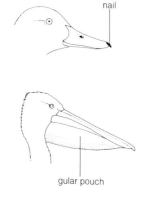

nail

gular pouch

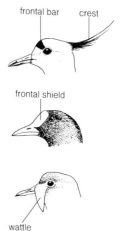

frontal bar crest

frontal shield

wattle

Terms and Abbreviations

♂ : male
♀ : female
Adult: a bird which has attained its definitive plumage.
Altitudinal migrant: a species which breeds in high mountains and moves to foothills in the non-breeding period.
Breeding plumage: a different plumage acquired by many species during the breeding season.
Colonial: used to describe species which form colonies when they breed. Cormorants, herons etc are the main examples.
Crepuscular: used to describe a species which is active at dawn and/or dusk.
Diurnal: used to describe a species which is active during the daytime.
Eclipse plumage: a dull-coloured plumage stage of short duration that alternates with the bright breeding plumage and occurs in some species, most notably male ducks.
Endangered: a bird that is internationally endangered or threatened.
Endemic: used to describe a species which is restricted to a certain area or region.
Eye ring: feathered ring immediately surrounding the orbital ring.
Flight-feathers: the primaries and secondaries of wings.
Gregarious: used to describe a species which is often found in flocks when feeding, in non-breeding period etc.
Immature (imm.): a bird in a plumage in between juvenile and adult.
1st imm. non-breeding: a bird in a plumage which still retains juvenile feathers in its first year. It is observed in gulls and terns etc.
2nd imm. non-breeding: a bird in a plumage which is different from the adult non-breeding plumage in its second year. It is observed, mainly, in large gulls.
Juvenile: a bird in its first plumage which replaces the downy one.
L: length from the tip of the bill to the tip of the tail with neck stretched.
Leading edge of wing: the forward edge of an extended wing.
Moult: the process of shedding of feathers and replacing them with new ones. All birds moult at least part of their plumage once a year.
Nocturnal: used to describe a species which is active at night.
Non-breeding plumage: the plumage worn by birds when they are not breeding; refers to those species which have a different plumage in the breeding season.
Orbital ring: bare, fleshy ring immediately surrounding the eye.
Passage migrant: a bird which regularly passes through a country/area on its migration without remaining there for either the breeding or the non-breeding period.

Primary projection: used to describe that the tip of primaries that project beyond the longest tertial.

Leg projection: used to describe that the tip of legs that project beyond tail when a bird is flying.

Race: a subspecies; a population of a species the members of which can be distinguished morphologically from the members of all other populations of that species. In this field guide, races which are clearly distinguished from others in the field are described.

Resident: a bird which remains in the same region throughout the year.

Speculum: a patch of distinctive colour on secondaries; notably metallic glossy patch seen on the wings of marsh ducks.

Trailing edge of wing: the rear edge of an extended wing.

Underparts: under surface of body from throat to undertail-coverts.

Upperparts: upper surface of body including wings and tail.

W: length from the tip of one wing to the tip of the other when stretched.

Wing-bar: a line across the wing contrasting in colour with the rest of it.

Wing projection: used to describe the projection of the tip of the primaries beyond the tail when a bird is at rest.

Waterbirds in Asia

Introduction — Asia as a waterbird habitat

Asia is the world's largest continent, stretching from the Ural mountains eastwards to the Pacific Ocean and from north of the arctic circle southwards to the equator and beyond. It also supports over half of the world's human population and is the fastest growing region of the world in economic terms.

Asia contains all the major environments found on earth, from the frozen landscapes of the arctic to the highest mountains, and from deserts to tropical rainforests and coral reefs. As would be expected, the wetland habitats for waterbirds are almost equally diverse.

Climate plays a fundamental role in determining both the nature of wetlands and the movements of waterbirds. The long northern winter forces millions of breeding waterbirds to leave for warmer regions in the southern part of the continent. On the other hand, the warm tropical climate of equatorial regions of Malaysia and Indonesia so encourages tree growth that extensive peat swamp and mangrove forests form, effectively excluding many types of waterbirds. In between, lie desert and mountain lakes, coastal mudflats, freshwater marshes and river deltas, all of which support vast numbers of waterbirds.

Migration — Globe-trotting waterbirds

For many centuries people have observed the regular, seasonal arrivals and departures of birds. It has not been until recently that some of the mysteries of this annual coming and going have been uncovered. Asia and the western Pacific are a vast route-map of waterbird migration paths, covering tens of thousands of kilometres. This brief account describes the migration of the large proportion of waterbirds in Asia which do so. It also examines the implications of long distance migration for conservation efforts to protect Asia's waterbirds. The map shows the approximate location of known waterbird migration routes within Asia. These are generalised as there are almost as many migration routes as there are species of migratory waterbirds.

In the northern summer (June – July), migratory waterbirds breed in northern Asia. They build their nests, lay their eggs and raise their young during the short arctic and boreal summer while the day lengths are long and food is abundant. They occur in low densities across the vast tundra, forest and steppe zones of north-eastern and north-central Asia, in habitats which bear little resemblance to their wetland non-breeding habitats.

As autumn approaches, the many millions of waterbirds in this area depart on long journeys southwards. They pass through many Asian countries between August and November to spend the cold northern winter in milder climates on the tropical and warm temperate wetlands of

Waterbirds migration routes

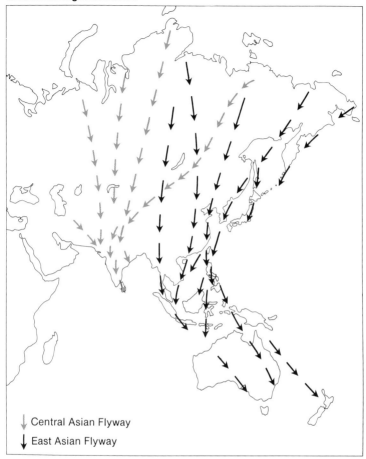

↓ Central Asian Flyway
↓ East Asian Flyway

eastern and southern Asia, Australia and New Zealand. They live here for up to eight months before returning northwards again in March, April and May as the northern Asia warms up again.

The most spectacular examples of migratory waterbirds are ducks, geese, cranes, and shorebirds and terns. Some species fly only short distances between stops while others fly vast distances over deserts and oceans in order to reach their destinations. Migration flights of any distance require the use of much energy in a very short time. For this reason, there must be wetlands at either end of the flight which can provide sustenance for waterbirds on the move. An example illustrates the global scale of waterbird migration.

After breeding in the highland arctic tundras of eastern Siberia, the

Great Knot, a sandpiper, migrates southwards to the coast of the Korean peninsula and north-eastern China. Here, flocks spend several weeks feeding and they accumulate large reserves of fat just under the skin and around the internal organs. Just before southward departure, this fat can represent as much as 50% of their body weight. The fat is burned up in only three or four days as they fly south non-stop for 6,500 kilometres across the vast expanse of the south-western Pacific Ocean to northern Australia, where most of the world's population spends the non-breeding months. Flocks of waderbirds, probably including this species, have even been spotted by radar overflying the island of Guam, 2,000 kilometres east of the Philippines. The return journey is equally spectacular and an individual marked with a metal band (ring) in north-western Australia in late March has been re-trapped near Shanghai in China only seven days later!

Migration is an expensive way of life. It requires very energetic feeding, the accumulation of fat reserves and long flights, often at altitudes of several kilometres and lasting several days. The waders for example are thought to have elevated metabolic rates in order the generate the energy needed to do the hard work of migration. To reduce the high cost of migration, most species of migratory waterbirds only fly under a particular set of weather conditions. The earth's atmosphere is constantly in motion but patterns in weather systems create favourable winds for a particular migratory flight.

Most birds migrate with a good tail wind. Although this tail wind may not be evident at ground level before departure, many waterbirds seem to know that several hundred meters aloft, winds are favourable. A migratory flight is commenced when winds are favourable. Although such winds can last for several days at a time, most migratory departure occurs at dusk, in the hours either side of sunset. Afternoon and early morning departures are not unknown, especially for those species which depend on rising thermals and gliding to cover the distance while saving energy (e.g. pelicans, cranes).

Departure can be a spectacular sight as flocks of several hundred birds fly up, slowly circling, gradually sorting themselves into a shallow "V" formation before fixing on their preferred direction then disappearing up into the sky. Much has been written about how birds know which direction to fly. Many clues are probably used by birds, from the position of sunset, to the moon and stars, even to sensing the earth's magnetic field. At a smaller scale, simple geography seems to play a part. It is likely that different species of waterbirds use their own unique mix of these simple environmental clues.

Many newly-fledged birds of some waterbird groups (e.g. waders) depart the breeding grounds several weeks after their parents, indicating that the general patterns of migration are probably inherited, rather than learnt. In other groups (e.g. cranes), the young depart on their first flight southwards with their parents. A common phenomenon among migratory waterbirds is the tendency for the same individual birds to stop at the same places and use the same wetland as a non-breeding site each year. This is thought to be related to the better chances of survival associated with knowing a habitat well: where the good food is; where the safe roosts are; and the types of predators present and ways of avoiding them.

Banding was briefly mentioned earlier. This is one of the most important tools which scientists have in uncovering some of the many mysteries of migration. Banding involves placing an individually numbered metal band on the leg of a bird. Many species of waterbirds are regularly banded in Asia and nearby regions. Given how extensively waterbirds

Generalised pattern of usage of sites during the annual cycle of a migratory waterbird

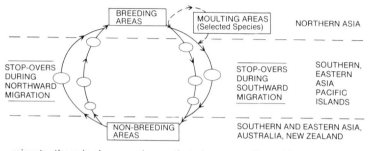

migrate, there is always a chance that observers will see birds with bands on their legs.

In Asia, an increasingly frequent means of investigating waterbird migration is colour marking. This involves placing conspicuous coloured markers on birds, either in the form of plastic coloured leg bands and flags, neck collars or wing tags. In some cases, more than one coloured plastic band is placed on the leg. These can often be very conspicuous and sightings, including details of the species, date, location and colour combination should be sent to Asian Wetland Bureau (see address elsewhere in this book) which is the Asia-wide clearing house for such sightings. Details will be sent to finders on the original place and date where the bird was marked.

Asia's waterbirds are such international travellers that the efforts of one country alone to protect them and their wetland habitats are pointless. Cooperation between Asian and Pacific countries is needed if waterbirds are to continue to fly unhindered up and down their flyways. The migration of waterbirds throughout the world has stimulated the emergence of the "Convention on Wetlands of International Importance, especially as Waterfowl Habitat", or the "Ramsar" Convention (after the town in Iran where it was first signed). Seventy countries are party to this convention which encourages governments to protect their best waterbird habitats. The Ramsar Convention provides the forum for international cooperation to protect migratory waterbirds.

Moult — The importance of being well dressed

A bird's plumage gradually wears and fades with use and exposure to sunlight. Consequently, it is necessary for birds to replace their plumage at least annually. This is done by moult, where old feathers are lost and replaced by new ones. It is one of the most important annual functions which must be incorporated into the life history of a bird. There are examples of species postponing breeding but still moulting if climatic conditions are exceptional and environmental conditions become difficult. A bird can always wait until the following year to breed but it cannot survive to do so without moulting.

Moult requires energy, both for making new feather material and for compensating for the temporary loss in plumage insulation which moult causes. Moult of the wing and tail feathers can also reduce the efficiency flight. Therefore, moult of the flight feathers generally does not occur when birds are migrating and they need maximum flight capacity.

It is not unusual however for body plumage moult to occur during migration, especially among those species which moult into a distinctive breeding plumage, such as the shorebirds.

Moult can occur at varying speeds, depending on the species and its other life history characteristics. For example, many of the ducks, geese and swans undergo a simultaneous moult of the wing feathers, rendering them completely flightless for several weeks. In this situation, they require large, open and undisturbed water bodies on which to rest where they are safe from predators and have abundant food. Other species moult in stages. In some waterbirds, such as the herons, egrets and shorebirds, this can be seen when they are in flight. A narrow gap appears and slowly moves along the wings as feathers are successively lost and replaced. Moult can last for a few weeks to several months. In this way, the birds are able to continue their daily routine unhindered.

In some waterbird species, the moult of the flight feathers is commenced immediately after breeding. In some of these species, it is completed, usually rapidly, before birds migrate. In others, it will be stopped and resumed once the bird has reached its destination. The latter strategy is called suspended moult and it can be seen as a difference in wear pattern between new and old feathers. Still other species moult half way between their breeding and non-breeding areas. Once again, such a moult must be completed rapidly so that migration can proceed.

Other species do not moult until they reach their non-breeding grounds where they undergo a leisurely moult lasting up to five months. Such a long moult minimisies daily energy costs, requiring much less effort on the bird's part to compensate for extra energy demands.

In non-migratory waterbirds, moult usually occurs just after breeding and it can commence in adults before the young have left the nest or fledged.

Young waterbirds moult from a downy juvenile plumage into their first full set of feathers from the age of about one to three weeks. Often, their first plumage will look quite different from that of the adult. There are many examples where annual moults in the first few years of life produce plumages which increasingly resemble that of the adults, but which nonetheless are still distinctive.

The timing, habitat choice and nature of moult are collectively referred to as the moult strategy. Understanding the moult strategy is critical in knowing how to protect waterbird populations. For example, large scale movements of ducks occur to some wetlands which can sustain and protect them during the short period of flightlessness associated with simultaneous wing moult. Such wetlands are critically important to the survival of waterbird populations and need to be protected. Not to do so could remove a link in the chain of habitats used for all the necessary parts of the annual cycle of waterbirds.

Wetlands — Asia's natural restaurants, hotels and airports

The survival of waterbirds cannot be viewed in isolation. No amount of legal protection or hunting prohibition will ensure the survival of waterbirds without adequate habitat protection. Waterbirds are generally very mobile, often moving vast distances each year. Just as a person travelling around the world needs hotels, restaurants and airports, so waterbirds need the natural equivalents: wetlands. This section briefly examines how waterbirds use wetlands.

The diversity of waterbirds reflects the many ways of life possible for birds in wetlands. Waterbirds exploit a range of different parts of a wetland, or microhabitats. Each of these microhabitats can support a variety of different food sources. Different waterbird species specialise in a range of food types: from fish, crustacea and mud-dwelling invertebrates, to water plants and tiny plankton. To do so, waterbirds display a surprising range of feeding behaviours: from probing and sweeping, to diving and grazing. The many different shapes of bill, body and legs in waterbirds reflect the range of food and feeding behaviours possible in wetlands.

Many waterbirds feed during day and night, others feed only during the day. In coastal wetlands, many waterbirds follow the rhythm of the tides rather than the days, feeding on mudflats while they are exposed at low tide. When not feeding, waterbirds need somewhere to stay where they can preen and rest, free from the threat of predators. At night, day-feeding waterbirds often move to large communal roosts, sometimes numbering tens of thousands of individuals. Similar communal roosting occurs at high tide in species which feed at low tide on mudflats. The roost sites can be within or near wetland feeding areas.

The richness of a wetland for waterbirds depends on the diversity of microhabitats and food sources available. The number of waterbirds a wetland can support depends on its size and, most importantly, its biological productivity. This is the rate at which organisms in the wetland reproduce and are available for "harvesting" by waterbirds.

Most wetlands do not have all microhabitats and food sources possible and not all provide appropriate safe roosting sites. Furthermore, the physical and biological nature of wetlands differ geographically, depending on factors such as climate (especially rainfall), tidal range, soil and vegetation. Therefore, different wetland types support different species of waterbirds. This is reflected in different waterbird distribution patterns.

A generalised classification of wetlands in Asia is provided below, together with an indication of the groups of waterbirds which inhabit them. The relative importance of these wetland types for each waterbird group is also indicated. This table will be useful in enabling observers to predict which groups of birds they are likely to encounter during a visit to any of the wetland types listed.

A generalised classification of wetlands in Asia

1. Swamp Forest: This wetland type includes freshwater flooded forest. This is either seasonally or permanently inundated. It is dominated by forest trees adapted to waterlogged soils. In many parts of Asia, extensive peat deposits have accumulated under swamp forests.

2. Non-forested Swamp: This wetland type includes overflow wetlands (such as occur in the floodplains of rivers) and other freshwater swamps with open water and/or emergent aquatic vegetation.

3. Coastal Marshes: This wetland type includes mangroves, mudflats and supratidal marshes. The mangroves occur exclusively in the tropical parts of Asia and they are normally inundated by the tide each day.

4. Coral Reefs: This wetland type consists of intertidal reef flats, atolls and associated beaches. It is inundated by the tide each day. Coral is restricted to the tropical regions of Asia.

5. Seagrass Beds: These areas consist of intertidal and subtidal flats clothed in a dense growth of seagrass and/or seaweed. They are found in both tropical and temperate regions of Asia.

6. Lakes: These include large and small lakes, permanent, seasonal or ephemeral, and from freshwater to hypersaline. They include small mountain tarns and large, ephemeral desert salt lakes. Reservoirs are also included in this category.

7. Estuaries: These wetlands are where rivers meet the sea. They can be large or small, narrow or extensive. They are often fringed by mangroves and their beds will often hold areas of seagrass.

8. Rivers: This category covers rivers from high mountain streams and torrents to meandering, lowland rivers. In dry parts of Asia, rivers can dry at certain times of the year, leaving shrinking river pools.

9. Rice-Fields: Although not a natural wetland, these can at times support large numbers of waterbirds. They can occur in areas influenced by the tide or in non-tidal areas. They can be rain-fed or irrigated.

10. Aquaculture Ponds: This type of wetland consists of artificial ponds of either fresh-, brackish- or sea-water. They are used primarily for culturing fish and crustacea and they can vary from extensive, low-input systems to intensive, high-input systems.

11. Salt Ponds: These artificial coastal wetlands consist of very shallow pans from which sea-water is evaporated to form salt. They are widespread in Asia, especially in coastal areas with a dry or seasonally dry climate.

Table showing waterbird usage of different wetland types in Asia
(Wetland type as in foregoing classification; waterbird usage —
* occasional ** regular *** abundant)

WATERBIRD GROUP	WETLAND TYPE										
	1	2	3	4	5	6	7	8	9	10	11
Divers & Grebes		*	**	*		***	*	**			
Pelicans & Cormorants		*	**	*	*	***	***	***			**
Herons & Egrets	*	**	**	***	***	***	***	***	***	**	**
Bitterns						***					
Storks	*	**	**	**		**	**	**	***	**	**
Ibises & Spoonbills	*	**	**	**	*	***	***	***	**	**	**
Flamingos						**	**	**			***
Whistling Ducks	*	**	**			***	**	***	***	*	*
Swans						***	***	**	*		*
Geese						***	***	***	*		*
Ducks	*	***	**		*	***	***	***	***	*	***
Cranes						***	***	***	**		**
Rails & Crakes						***	**	**	***	*	*
Finfoot			**			*	*	**			
Jacanas		**				***			**		
Painted Snipe		**				***		**	***		
Crab Plover			***	***			**				*
Oystercatchers			***	***			**				*
Ibis Bill								**			
Stilts & Avocets						***	**	**	**	**	***
Stone Plovers				**		**	*	**			
Pratincoles		**				***	**	**	***	*	*
Lapwings		**				***	**	**	**		*
Plovers			**	***	**	***	**	**	*	**	***
Sandpipers & allies			**	***	**	***	**	**	**	**	***
Snipes		**				***	**	**	***	*	*
Gulls			***	***	**	***	***	***	**	***	***
Terns		**	**	***	**	***	***	***	***	***	***

Divers

Family *Gaviidae* (World: 5 species; Asia: 4 species) Medium to large waterbirds. Streamlined body, with legs set far back, is well adapted to dive and catch fish underwater. Flight direct, with long, thick neck extended and shallow wing-beats. Swim low in water. Sexes similar.   KS

RED-THROATED DIVER *Gavia stellata* L 61cm. Smallest diver. Slender bill; lower mandible uptilted. **Breeding:** face and sides of neck pale-grey; clearly marked stripes on hindneck; large reddish-brown patch on foreneck. **Non-breeding:** head paler than other divers, less sharp division between light and dark on side of neck. White usually extends to front of eye. Small white spots on brown mantle/scapulars. **Juvenile:** crown and nape darker than non-breeding. White spots on mantle/scapulars less bold. Some have trace of reddish-brown foreneck patch. **Similar species:** see other divers and non-breeding Great Crested Grebe. **Habitat:** sea coasts, large lakes, estuaries. **Distribution:** breeds from North Asia to the Arctic; mainly off coasts of North-East Asia in non-breeding period.   KS

BLACK-THROATED DIVER *Gavia arctica* L 72cm. Straight bill. White on rear flanks shows usually above water-line and conspicuous even far away. **Breeding:** foreneck black with metallic-green sheen. Black and white stripes on chin and sides of neck are thicker than on Pacific Diver. Also, hindneck is darker and contrasts less with blackish face. **Non-breeding:** clear dividing line between light and dark on side of neck. Forehead often darker than hindneck. Upperparts blackish. Almost identical to non-breeding Pacific Diver; but no dark line on chin, though a few birds do have incomplete line. **Juvenile:** pale fringes to feathers on mantle/scapulars. Crown and hindneck paler than non-breeding. **Similar species:** see Pacific Diver. Pale area sometimes visible on rear flanks of Red-throated, especially during moult, but usually greyish. **Habitat:** seacoasts, large lakes, estuaries. **Distribution:** breeds in east part of North Asia; off coasts of north part of East Asia in non-breeding period.   KS

PACIFIC DIVER *Gavia pacifica* L 65cm. Straight bill is slightly shorter, more slender than Black-throated. White on rear flanks missing or indistinct. **Breeding:** black foreneck with metallic-purple sheen. Pale head and hindneck contrast with blackish face. **Non-breeding:** many birds have dark line on chin. **Juvenile:** pale fringes to feathers on mantle/scapulars. Crown and hindneck paler than non-breeding. **Similar species:** see Black-throated Diver. **Habitat:** seacoasts, large lakes, estuaries. **Distribution:** breeds in north-east part of North Asia; off coasts of north part of East Asia in non-breeding period.   KS

WHITE-BILLED DIVER *Gavia adamsii* L 83cm. Largest diver. Forehead usually has pronounced 'lump'. Thick neck. Large pale bill; uptilted lower mandible. **Breeding:** head and hindneck black. **Non-breeding:** pale around eye. Often has dark patch on ear-coverts. Crown and hindneck brown; no sharp dividing line from white foreneck. **Juvenile:** crown darker than non-breeding. Pale fringes to feathers on mantle/scapulars. **Similar species:** 1st imm. non-breeding Japanese Cormorant has yellow patch of bare skin around base of bill. **Habitat:** seacoasts, estuaries. **Distribution:** breeds in extreme north of North Asia; moves to coasts of north part of East Asia, but less far south and in smaller numbers than the other 3 species.   KS

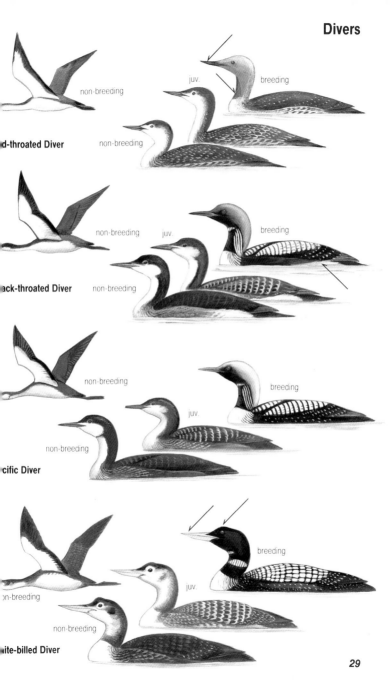

Divers

non-breeding

juv.

breeding

d-throated Diver

non-breeding

non-breeding

juv.

breeding

non-breeding

ack-throated Diver

non-breeding

juv.

breeding

non-breeding

cific Diver

n-breeding

juv.

breeding

non-breeding

ite-billed Diver

Grebes
Family *Podicipedidae* (World: 21 species; Asia: 6 species) Small to medium compact body with very short tail and legs set far back. Expert at diving. Flight direct with neck extended.   KS

LITTLE GREBE [Dabchick] *Tachybaptus ruficollis* L 27cm. Smallest grebe. Often fluffed-up tail. Iris yellow. Some races have white part on secondaries. **Breeding:** chestnut from cheeks to sides of neck. Yellow gape patch conspicuous. **Non-breeding:** brown above, sandy-buff below. **Voice:** high-pitched whinnying trill "wi-i-i-i-i-i-i-i" in breeding season. **Similar species:** Eastern Indonesian race of Little Grebe has dark-red iris and white wing-patch on secondaries only; Australian Dabchick has yellow iris, white bar extending full length of wing. **Habitat:** ponds, lakes, marshes, rivers. **Distribution:** resident from South to East and South-East Asia. Northern breeders drift south in non-breeding period.   KS

AUSTRALIAN DABCHICK *Tachybaptus novaehollandiae* L 28cm. In flight, broad white wing-bar. **Breeding:** narrow chestnut stripe on sides of neck only and conspicuous yellow gape patch. **Non-breeding:** upperparts grey-brown, underparts whitish. **Juvenile:** paler than adult. **Voice:** trilling call in breeding season. **Habitat:** mainly in freshwater (dams, lakes and marshes) with some fringing vegetation. **Distribution:** Resident from Lesser Sundas, Indonesia, to Australia and New Zealand.   DMP

RED-NECKED GREBE *Podiceps grisegena* L 45cm. Yellow base of bill. White bars visible in flight on forewings and secondaries. **Breeding:** black crown with short crest, white cheeks. **Non-breeding:** Dark cap comes down to eyes. Rear crown rounded. **Similar species:** see Great Crested Grebe. **Habitat:** lakes, marshes, estuaries, sea-coasts. **Distribution:** breeds in North and East Asia; in East/South Asia in non-breeding period.   KS

GREAT CRESTED GREBE *Podiceps cristatus* L 49cm. Largest grebe. Black line from eyes to base of bill. In flight white visible on forewings, scapulars and secondaries. **Breeding:** pointed black crest; long orange-red ear-coverts bordered with black. **Non-breeding:** pink bill. Sharp contrast between white and black on sides of long neck. **Habitat:** lakes, marshes, estuaries, seacoasts, salt pans. **Distribution:** breeds in Central and East Asia; from East to South-East Asia in non-breeding period.   KS

SLAVONIAN GREBE [Horned Grebe] *Podiceps auritus* L 33cm. Red iris. Straight bill with white at extreme tip. Pale stripe from base of bill to eyes. In flight white wedge visible on inner forewing and white secondaries. **Breeding:** golden ear-tufts sweeping back from eyes. **Non-breeding:** clearly defined black cap comes down to eyes but not below. Most have white foreneck, dark hindneck. **Similar species:** see Black-necked Grebe. **Habitat:** lakes, marshes, estuaries. **Distribution:** breeds in Central/North Asia; moves to North and East Asia in non-breeding period.   KS

BLACK-NECKED GREBE [Eared Grebe] *Podiceps nigricollis* L 30cm. Often fluffed-up tail. Red iris. In flight white extends to inner primaries and secondaries. **Breeding:** Fan-shaped golden ear-tufts. **Non-breeding:** ill-defined dark cap comes down to cheeks. Dark upper foreneck between white breast and throat. **Similar species:** see Slavonian Grebes. **Habitat:** lakes, marshes, estuaries. **Distribution:** breeds in North and East Asia; moves to East and South Asia in non-breeding period.   KS

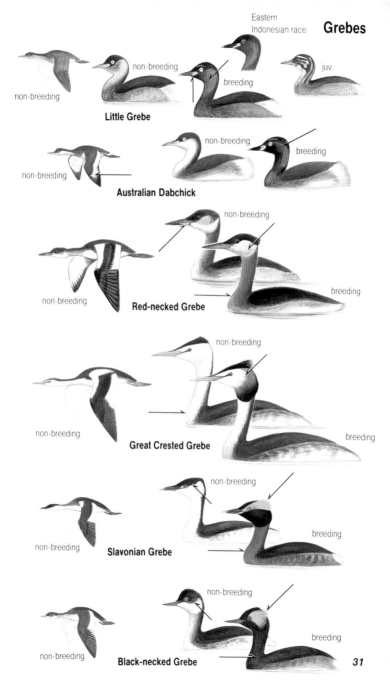

Grebes

non-breeding

non-breeding

Little Grebe

Eastern Indonesian race

breeding

juv.

non-breeding

non-breeding

breeding

Australian Dabchick

non-breeding

non-breeding

breeding

Red-necked Grebe

non-breeding

non-breeding

breeding

Great Crested Grebe

non-breeding

non-breeding

breeding

Slavonian Grebe

non-breeding

non-breeding

breeding

Black-necked Grebe

31

Pelicans

Family *Pelecanidae* (World: 8 species; Asia: 4 species) Large waterbirds. Long and large bill with large gular pouch. In flight flap their long, broad wings slowly, retract necks in S-bend; regularly soar, glide. Gregarious. Sexes similar. KS

GREAT WHITE PELICAN [Rosy Pelican, White Pelican] *Pelecanus onocrotalus* L 157cm. W 315cm. Bare skin around eyes pinkish-yellow. Gular pouch yellow to orange. Nail reddish, pointed forehead feathers over culmen. Legs pink. Iris dark. In flight underwing has primaries and secondaries black; upperwing has primaries black, secondaries grading from black to near-white inwards. **Breeding:** white body tinged pink. Short crest. Yellow area on foreneck. **Non-breeding:** upperparts buffy; bill/gular pouch duller. **Juvenile:** upperparts brown with pale edges to feathers. Bill yellow with grey base. Legs grey. In flight underwing has primaries/secondaries dark-brown; dark bands on underwing-coverts. **Similar species:** Grey and Dalmatian Pelicans have smaller patch of bare facial skin, different wing-patterns in flight. **Habitat:** lakes, marshes. **Distribution:** localised breeding in Central and South Asia; stays across South Asia in non-breeding period, but not numerous. KS

GREY PELICAN [Spotted-billed Pelican, Spot-billed Pelican] *Pelecanus philippensis* L 140cm. W 250cm. Smaller than Dalmatian Pelican. Row of dark spots on upper mandible (visible at close range). In flight, black primaries and dark brown secondaries above and below. Slight crest on rear crown. **Breeding:** whitish bare skin around eye, dull pinkish-grey bill with distinct lines of spots; lower back, rump and undertail-coverts pinkish. **Juvenile:** upperparts pale brown; underparts whitish tinged brown. **Similar species:** See Great White and Dalmatian Pelicans. **Habitat:** Large lakes, reservoirs, seacoasts, marshes and rivers. **Distribution:** resident on South Asia and South-East Asia but not numerous. BB

DALMATIAN PELICAN *Pelecanus crispus* L 170cm. W 327cm. Largest pelican. Bare skin around eyes yellow to purple, not extensive. Gular pouch yellow to orange. Legs lead-grey. Iris pale yellow. In flight underwing has primaries dark-grey, secondaries dusky-white, only tips are dark; upperwing has primaries and a few outer secondaries black, grading to white on inner secondaries. **Breeding:** upperparts slightly silvery. Short, untidy, curly crest. **Non-breeding:** upperparts greyer. **Juvenile:** upperparts tipped greyish brown. Bill/gular pouch grey. In flight underwing like adult's. **Similar species:** see Great White and Grey Pelican. **Habitat:** lakes, marshes, rivers, sea-coasts. **Distribution:** localised breeding in Central and South Asia; stays from India to southern part of East Asia in non-breeding period, but rare and declining. KS

AUSTRALIAN PELICAN *Pelecanus conspicillatus* L 167cm. W 252cm. White pelican with black-and-white wings and pale bill. Back white with black V across rump; tail black. Iris pale yellow; legs blue-grey. **Breeding:** washed-yellow on neck, yellow tip on bill, gular pouch pink with blue stripe from proximal edge to the centre. Iris orange-yellow. **Non-breeding:** gular pouch pink-yellow with pale-red stripe. **Juvenile:** similar to non-breeding with white and brown plumage; head greyish-white, throat pink, legs brownish-grey. **Voice:** hoarse "orrh-orrh-orrha". **Habitat:** lakes, ponds, estuaries. **Distribution:** resident from Indonesia to Australia. DMP

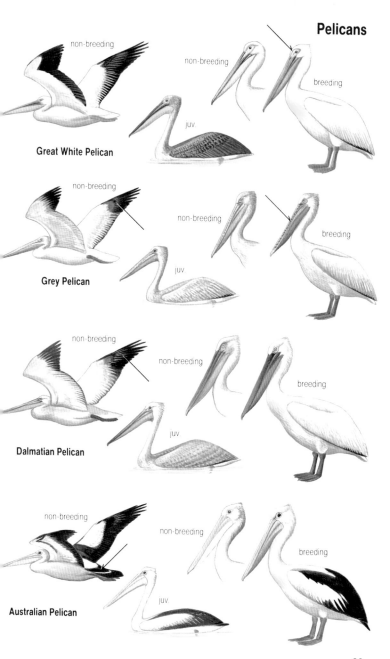

Pelicans

Great White Pelican

non-breeding

non-breeding

juv.

non-breeding

breeding

Grey Pelican

non-breeding

non-breeding

juv.

non-breeding

breeding

Dalmatian Pelican

non-breeding

non-breeding

juv.

breeding

Australian Pelican

non-breeding

non-breeding

juv.

breeding

Cormorants and Darters Family *Phalacrocoracidae* and
Anhingidae (World: 36 species; Asia: 11 species) Medium to large waterbirds with slender bills, long necks and bodies; long wings and short legs.
Found in marine and freshwater habitats, typically swim with body low in
water or even partly submerged with only head and neck visible. Often
seen sitting with wings outstretched to dry. Sexes similar.   DMP

LITTLE BLACK CORMORANT *Phalacrocorax sulcirostris* L 60cm.
Slender dark cormorant with very thin and slightly hooked bill, dark facial
skin and long tail. **Breeding:** entirely black with glossy sheen except for
thin buff or white line on throat; white nuptial plumes over eye in patches
on side of neck and sparsely on head and hindneck. Wings black with
glossy purple sheen; tail black; legs black. **Non-breeding:** plumage dark-
brown; throat fades to grey-blue and no nuptial plumes. **Juvenile:** silky
dark-brown. **Voice:** a series of ticks, whistles and croaks given at rest.
Similar species: Javanese and Pygmy Cormorants are smaller. Little Pied
Cormorant has white face and underparts. **Habitat:** inland and coastal
waters. **Distribution:** resident from Indonesia to Australia.   DMP

INDIAN CORMORANT [Indian Shag] *Phalacrocorax fuscicollis* L 63cm.
Black with bronze-brown upperparts. Head and bill much less heavy than
Great Cormorant. White border to gular pouch highly variable in extent.
Breeding: white tuft behind eye and white speckles on head and neck.
Juvenile: upperparts dark-brown with black scales on mantle; underparts
dusky-white. **Similar species:** Great Cormorant is larger with yellow gular
skin and white-speckled throat. Javanese Cormorant is smaller with shorter
bill and rounded head. **Habitat:** rivers, reservoirs, tidal creeks, marshes,
lakes. **Distribution:** resident mainly in South Asia.   BB

LITTLE PIED CORMORANT *Phalacrocorax melanoleucos* L 59cm. Upperparts black, underparts white. Stout bill, brownish above and yellow below.
Iris grey-brown, orbital ring black. Head white with black crown. Small
erectile black crest during breeding season. Little seasonal variation.
Juvenile: similar to adult with duller upperparts. **Voice:** normally silent,
"uk-uk-uk" at nest. **Similar species:** see Little Black Cormorant. **Habitat:**
mainly freshwater, also coasts, mangroves. **Distribution:** resident from
Indonesia to Australia.   TM

JAVANESE CORMORANT [Little Cormorant] *Phalacrocorax niger* L 51cm.
Small black cormorant, bill short and head rounded. **Breeding:** forehead,
sides of head and neck with narrow white feathers. **Non-breeding:** chin
and upper throat white. **Juvenile:** upper- and underparts dark-brown; chin
and throat dusky-white. **Similar species:** See Pygmy Cormorant. **Habitat:**
rivers, reservoirs, tidal creeks, mangroves, marshes, lakes. **Distribution:**
resident in South and South-East Asia.   BB

PYGMY CORMORANT *Phalacrocorax pygmeus* L 51cm. Browner than
Javanese Cormorant. **Breeding:** blackish-brown head tinged with red short
crest. Narrow white feathers on head, neck, underparts. **Non-breeding:**
brownish head with white chin and throat. **Juvenile:** body dark-brown,
whitish chin; throat and breast grey-brown. **Habitat:** prefers standing or
slow-flowing freshwater; rice-fields, marshes. **Distribution:** East European
species; a few records in South Asia.   BB

Cormorants

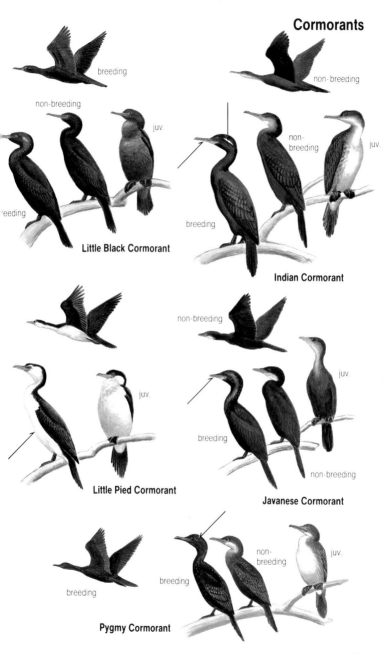

breeding

non-breeding

non-breeding

juv.

breeding

Little Black Cormorant

non-breeding

juv.

breeding

Indian Cormorant

non-breeding

juv.

breeding

Little Pied Cormorant

non-breeding

juv.

breeding

non-breeding

Javanese Cormorant

breeding

breeding

non-breeding

juv.

breeding

Pygmy Cormorant

GREAT CORMORANT [Cormorant, Common Cormorant] *Phalacrocorax carbo* L 90cm. Black body with bronze-brown tinged upperparts. White part behind eyes relatively small; border with yellow bare skin straight just behind gape. Yellow throat conspicuous. **Breeding:** narrow, white feathers grow densely on rear crown, hindneck and thighs. Reddish spot appear on bare facial skin. **Non-breeding:** white feathers absent on rear crown, hindneck and thighs. **Immature:** body brown except for white patch of variable size on breast and belly. **Similar species:** Japanese Cormorant has yellow bare skin on face which is less extensive in size but just encloses the eyes; line separating yellow and white areas comes to a point behind gape. Some juveniles cannot however be distinguished. See Indian Cormorant. **Habitat:** lakes, marshes, rivers, sheltered bays. **Distribution:** resident from East to South Asia; some move south in non-breeding period.   KS

JAPANESE CORMORANT [Temminck's Cormorant] *Phalacrocorax capillatus* L 92cm. Black body, greenish gloss on upperparts. Yellow bare area at base of bill is relatively small; border between the two comes to a point behind gape; white area behind eyes large, often extends almost to the back of head. **Breeding:** narrow, white feathers on rear crown, nape and thighs. Many small black spots develop in white area behind eye. Orange spot on bare skin below eye. **Non-breeding:** no white feathers on head or thighs. **Immature:** body brown except for white of variable size on breast and belly. Bare skin sometimes extends just above eyes. **Similar species:** see Great Cormorant. Immature Pelagic and Red-faced Cormorants have more slender necks, no yellow at base of bill, and no white part on breast/belly. **Habitat:** rocky coasts and islands; during migration occasionally seen on inland lakes/marshes. **Distribution:** breeds on sea-coasts of East Asia; stays in East Asia in non-breeding period.   KS

PELAGIC CORMORANT [Sea Cormorant] *Phalacrocorax pelagicus* L 68cm. Body black with greenish gloss. Slender neck; no white on face; bill dark greyish-yellow. **Breeding:** short crests on forehead and hindneck. Small bare patch of skin at base of bill is reddish. White patch on each thighs. **Non-breeding:** facial skin dark; no crests or white on flanks. **Immature:** whole body plain brown, but underparts slightly paler. Facial skin dark; bill brown. **Similar species:** Red-faced Cormorant is larger with bigger head, whitish bill; bare facial skin extends to forehead; in breeding plumage bigger crest and bluish base of bill. Japanese Cormorant is larger; adult has yellow and white on face. **Habitat:** rocky coasts, islands. **Distribution:** breeds on coasts from east part of North Asia to north part of East Asia; stays in north part of East Asia in non-breeding period.   KS

RED-FACED CORMORANT *Phalacrocorax urile* L 84cm. Body black with metallic gloss. Neck thinner than Japanese, thicker than Pelagic Cormorant. Bare facial skin extends to forehead. No white on face. Bill mainly yellowish with dark tip, bluish base. **Breeding:** floppy crest on forehead and rear crown. Facial skin bright-red. White patch on each thighs. **Non-breeding:** body duller. Bare facial skin dull red. No crest or white on thighs. **Immature:** generally dark-brown, underparts slightly paler. Bill pale; facial skin brown. **Similar species:** see Pelagic Cormorant. **Habitat:** rocky coasts, islands. **Distribution:** breeds on Pacific coast of north part of East Asia; believed to stay in nearby seas in non-breeding period.   KS

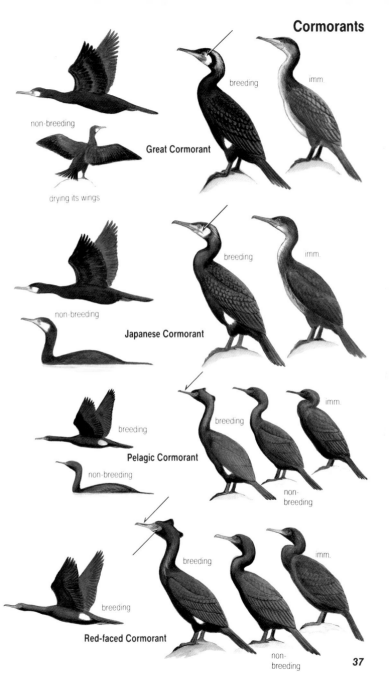

Cormorants

non-breeding

drying its wings

Great Cormorant

breeding

imm.

non-breeding

Japanese Cormorant

breeding

imm.

breeding

non-breeding

Pelagic Cormorant

breeding

imm.

non-breeding

breeding

breeding

Red-faced Cormorant

non-breeding

imm.

37

INDIAN DARTER [Oriental Darter] *Anhinga melanogaster* L 90cm. Distinguished from cormorants by longer, much more slender neck; pointed bill; longer fan-shaped tail. Head and neck brown; wings and body blackish. Whitish streaks on sides of neck and upperparts. In flight, shows peculiar kink in outstretched neck and long tail. Spears fish underwater with pointed bill; swims with body submerged and outstretched head and neck protruding. Occasionally seen in soaring flight. **Juvenile:** paler and browner. **Voice:** seldom heard except when nesting, loud disyllabic "chigi-chigi-chigi". **Similar species:** see Australian Darter. **Habitat:** lakes, reservoirs, occasionally flowing rivers, mangroves. **Distribution:** resident in South Asia and South-East Asia. BB

AUSTRALIAN DARTER *Anhinga novaehollandiae* L 90cm. Similar to Indian Darter, but shows pronounced sexual dimorphism. Shorter bill and tail, longer tarsus. **Male:** like Indian Darter. **Female:** brighter than male; chin, throat, breast, belly and undertail-coverts white to pale-buff. **Habitat:** lakes, reservoirs, and occasionally flowing rivers. **Distribution:** resident from east end of Indonesia to Australia. DMP

Flamingos Family *Phoenicopteridae* (World: 5 species; Asia: 2 species)
Large birds with extremely long, slender neck and legs. Large, lamellate sharply downcurved bill. Sexes similar, but female somewhat smaller and paler. In flight, extended neck and legs distinctive. Feeds actively in shallow water with bill immersed and pumps water through lamellae in bill to filter out algae and small crustaceans. Gregarious. BB

GREATER FLAMINGO *Phoenicopterus ruber* L 140cm. Rosy white with bright scarlet-and-black wings and large black tipped pink bill. In flight, long slender outstretched neck and legs, and scarlet-and-black underwing diagnostic. Highly gregarious. **Juvenile:** overall greyish-brown with brownish bill and dark slaty-brown legs. **Voice:** single hoarse brassy goose-like honk. Constant babbling while feeding. **Similar species:** see Lesser Flamingo. **Habitat:** brackish lakes and lagoons, salt pans, estuaries, tidal mudflats. **Distribution:** resident in South Asia. BB

LESSER FLAMINGO *Phoenicopterus minor* L 100cm. Smaller than Greater Flamingo. Deeper rose-pink plumage, and darker bill with crimson feathers around the base. Female has no crimson on back or breast. In flight, crimson-and-black underwing; comparatively thicker neck, shorter leg projection than Greater. Gregarious, large concentrations, sometimes with Greater. **Juvenile:** overall greyish-brown as in Greater with shorter, darker bill. **Habitat:** inland salt lakes, preferably heavily saturated brine, salt pans. **Distribution:** very localised in South Asia. BB

Darters, Flamingos

Indian Darter

juv.

Greater Flamingo

juv.

Australian Darter

♂

♀

juv.

Lesser Flamingo

juv.

39

Herons and Bitterns

Family *Ardeidae* (World: 60 species, Asia: 30 species) Middle to large wading birds. Flight direct with slow beating of broad wings, slender necks retracted in S-shape. Occasionally fly for short periods with neck extended. Sexes similar in most species.　　　　KS

GREY HERON *Ardea cinerea* L 94cm. Active at night as well as day. **Adult:** white crown; white neck with black lateral markings; sides of belly black. In flight, on upperwing grey wing-coverts contrast with black primaries, secondaries; white patches at primary-base conspicuous. Underwings blue-grey. At rest, black shoulder-patch stands out. For part of the breeding season iris, bill, legs become deep orange. **Juvenile:** head, neck greyer; body colour duller. **Voice:** deep "gwaa"; in flight high-pitched "frarnk". **Similar species:** Purple Heron is smaller; from flat crown to more slender bill is in straight line. See Imperial Heron. **Habitat:** marshes, rice-fields, rivers, lakes, mudflats. **Distribution:** breeds widely in Central, South, South-East and central part of East Asia; northern breeders move south in non-breeding period.　　　　KS

IMPERIAL HERON [White-bellied Heron] *Ardea imperialis* L 127cm. Large heron. Massive blackish bill. Similar appearance to Dusky-grey Heron but darker and with more dusky grey plumage. Both sides of wing dark-grey in flight. Legs dull grey. Iris yellow. **Habitat:** swamps, lakes. **Distribution:** resident in south-eastern foothills of the Himalayas, Bhutan, Assam and northwest Myanmar. Current status is little known.　　　　BB

PURPLE HERON *Ardea purpurea* L 79cm. Distinguished by slender neck, chestnut hindneck. **Adult:** crown dark; black markings running down chestnut neck. In flight, little contrast between dark-grey wing-coverts and black primaries, secondaries; chestnut patch at base of primaries; underwing very dark with coverts mostly chestnut. **Juvenile:** upperwing-coverts brownish. **Voice:** like Grey Heron but higher pitched. **Similar species:** see Grey and Goliath Herons. **Habitat:** marshes, rice-fields, lakes, mudflats, mangrove swamps. **Distribution:** breeds in Central, South and South-East Asia; northern breeders move to south in non-breeding period.　　　　KS

GOLIATH HERON *Ardea goliath* L 140cm. Similar to a 'gigantic' Purple Heron. Large black bill with paler lower mandible. **Adult:** crown and crest deep vinous-chestnut, neck rufous-cinnamon. Upperparts, wings and tail slaty-grey. **Juvenile:** head and neck duller and paler rufous. Upperparts grey with rufous edgings. Underparts white streaked with brown. **Voice:** loud deep barks; "Arrk" when disturbed. **Habitat:** rivers, lakes. **Distribuiton:** very localised in South Asia.　　　　BB

DUSKY-GREY HERON [Great-billed Heron] *Ardea sumatrana* L 115cm. Large, heavily built grey heron with long and stout bill. **Adult:** Head dark brown-grey to bronze-brown; neck brown-grey with long silver-grey plumes on lower foreneck; back brown; tail and wings dark brown-grey, slightly paler on underwing. Colour of bill and legs variable. In flight, uniform brown wings with head drawn back. In breeding plumage, silver-grey nuchal crest and long silver plumes on back. **Juvenile:** light rusty-brown lacking adult's whitish plumes. **Voice:** call consists of prolonged bouts of roaring; harsh croak in breeding season. **Habitat:** mangroves, estuaries, mudflats, coastal marshes. **Distribution:** resident in South-East Asia.　　DMP

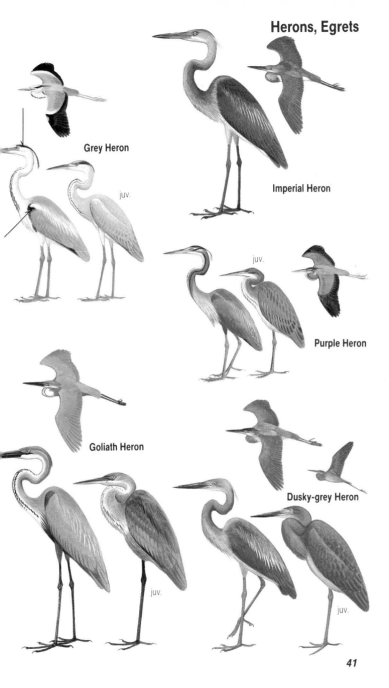

Herons, Egrets

Grey Heron

juv.

Imperial Heron

juv.

Purple Heron

Goliath Heron

Dusky-grey Heron

juv.

juv.

41

GREAT EGRET [Large Egret] *Egretta alba* L 94cm. Largest white egret. All-white body; fairly long bill, neck, legs. Gape extends well behind eye; blackish streak along gape. Tibia pale. Flies with slow beats of long wings. Northern race *alba* same size as Grey Heron; black feet have yellow soles. Southern race *modesta* smaller than Grey Heron; feet all-black. **Breeding:** bill black; lores yellow-green; plumes on lower back only. For a part of season tibia become dark pink. **Non-breeding:** bill, lores yellow; no plumes. **Voice:** "graa". **Similar species:** Intermediate Egret smaller with short bill, gape to below the eye but not beyond. Little Egret smaller with yellow feet; in breeding plumage has long slender crest, yellow lores. **Habitat:** marshes, rice-fields, rivers, lakes, mudflats. **Distribution:** breeds in Central, South, East and South-East Asia. Northern breeders move south in non-breeding period. KS

INTERMEDIATE EGRET [Smaller Egret, Plumed Egret] *Egretta intermedia* L 68.5cm. Bill shorter than Little Egret, head looks smaller, lores yellow. Gape extends to below eye, not beyond. Legs/feet black. **Breeding:** bill black; some have yellow at base. Plumes on upper breast, lower back. For part of season lores become yellow-green. **Non-breeding:** bill dull yellow with dark tip. Australian race *plumifera*, in east part of Indonesia, has red tibia; bill orange or red in breeding, orange-yellow in non-breeding. **Similar species:** Little Egret has black bill throughout year, yellow feet; in breeding plumage has long slender plumes on nape. Non-breeding Cattle Egret is smaller, bill yellow throughout year, base of lower mandible gives heavy-jowled look. See Great Egret. **Habitat:** marshes, rice-fields, grasslands. **Distribution:** breeds in Central, South, East and South-East Asia; northern breeders move south in non-breeding period. KS

PIED HERON *Egretta picata* L 50cm. A small slate-grey heron with dark crown and crest and long white neck. Upperwing and underwing slaty-black. **Breeding:** head and nuchal crest dark blue to slaty black; feathers of mantle form long dark lanceolate plumes of the lower foreneck overhang slaty-black breast. **Non-breeding:** nuchal plumes shorter. **Juvenile:** head, neck white, no nuchal crest; upperparts dark grey brown; breast white; vent and belly white and rest of underparts grey-brown; secondaries tipped white. Bill olive-brown; iris pale yellow. **Voice:** soft cooing at nest. **Similar species:** White-faced Egret is slightly larger with white face with grey body. **Habitat:** marshes, lakes, ponds with low vegetation, estuarine and flooded grasslands. **Distribution:** resident from eastern Indonesia to Australia. DMP

WHITE-FACED EGRET *Egretta novaehollandiae* L 67cm. A medium-sized blue-grey egret with white face and upper throat. In flight, dark flight feathers contrast with paler upperwing- and underwing-coverts. **Breeding:** long lanceolate pale brown plumes on nape, mantle and back; short lanceolate pinkish-brown plumes on lower foreneck and breast; chestnut wash on breast and belly. **Juvenile:** similar to adult, but grey plumes largely missing; underparts with browner tinge. **Voice:** flight call a guttural "graaw"; descending "gow-gow" on return to the nest and a high-pitched "wrank" of alarm. **Similar species:** see Reef Heron. **Habitat:** shallow water (fresh or marine), mudflats, grasslands, mangroves. **Distribution:** resident from eastern Indonesia to Australia. DMP

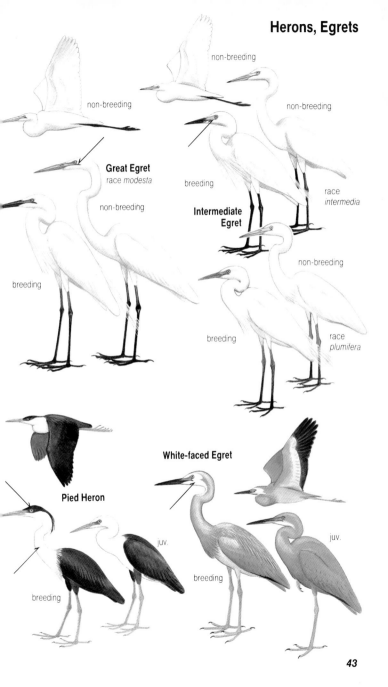

Herons, Egrets

non-breeding

non-breeding

non-breeding

non-breeding

Great Egret
race *modesta*

non-breeding

breeding

Intermediate Egret

race *intermedia*

non-breeding

breeding

breeding

race *plumifera*

White-faced Egret

Pied Heron

juv.

juv.

breeding

breeding

43

LITTLE EGRET *Egretta garzetta* L 60cm. Race *garzetta*, widely distributed across Asian continent, is all-white with long black bill, conspicuous yellow feet, usually extending onto lower legs. Lores yellow. **Breeding:** long slender crest on rear crown usually consisting of two plumes; also plumes on breast, lower back; tips of those on back curl upwards. For part of season lores become dark pink, feet red. **Non-breeding:** no plumes. **Juvenile:** upper mandible black, lower mandible pale; feet greenish. Philippine and Indonesian race *nigripes* has black feet, otherwise resembles race *garzetta*. Race *schistacea* of the west coast of India, has dark and white morphs; bill size, colour of bare skin highly variable. Dark morph has blue-grey body; white on throat; occasionally white patch on wings; greenish-yellow bill; olive-green legs; yellow feet. **Voice:** "graa". **Similar species:** see Great and Intermediate Egrets. White morph of Reef Heron has yellow bill, shorter legs. **Habitat:** marshes, rice-fields, rivers, lakes, mudflats, lotus-ponds, mangroves. **Distribution:** breeds in South, South-East and East Asia etc.; some move in non-breeding period.   KS

SWINHOE'S EGRET [Chinese Egret] *Egretta eulophotes* L 68cm. Neck and legs shorter and thicker than Little Egret. Bill becomes steadily narrower from base to tip. **Breeding:** bill orange-yellow; bare skin on lores blue; shaggy white crest; plumes on lower back. Legs black; feet bright-yellow, yellow not extending onto legs as in Little Egret. **Non-breeding:** no crest or plumes; lores greenish-grey, legs yellow-brown. Bill black with pale pinkish base to lower mandible. Legs pale-brown with yellowish tinge. **Similar species:** difficult to distinguish from non-breeding white morph of Reef Heron; but latter's bill is thick until near tip, then narrows sharply; in flight legs project less; less exposed skin on tibia; soles of toes yellowish. **Habitat:** marshes, rice-fields, rivers, mudflats, mangroves; mainly breeds on offshore rocky islands. **Distribution:** breeds in coastal East Asia (from Korean Peninsula to South China); moves to South-East Asia. Extremely low in numbers.   KS

REEF HERON [Pacific Reef-Egret] *Egretta sacra* L 62.5cm. Medium-sized; mainly inhabits sea-coasts; has white and dark morphs. Bill thick until near tip. Legs/feet greenish. Plumes on nape, foreneck and lower back in breeding plumage. In flight, legs project less from tail than other white egrets. **Dark morph:** dark slaty-grey overall; most have narrow white mark on throat. Bill yellow to blackish. **White morph:** white all over; some have dark marks on neck, back etc.; bill usually yellow. **Similar species:** see Little and Swinhoe's Egrets and Black Bittern. **Habitat:** rocky coasts, coral reefs, mangroves, mudflats, marshes. **Distribution:** breeds in South, South-East and East Asia; some seasonal movements.   KS

CATTLE EGRET *Bubulcus ibis* L 53cm. Shorter bill and neck than other white egrets. Bill, lores yellow; upper mandible slightly down-curved; base of lower mandible gives heavy-jowled look. When standing, looks hunch-backed. **Breeding:** conspicuous orange-yellow plumes on whole head, foreneck, back. For part of season lores, bill, legs become vermilion-red. **Non-breeding:** no plumes; body all-white though some have yellow tinge on crown. **Similar species:** see Intermediate, Little and Swinhoe's Egrets. **Habitat:** marshes, rice-fields, grasslands. Often follows grazing cattle and feeds on insects they disturb. **Distribution:** breeds from South Asia to East Asia; northern breeders move south in non-breeding period.   KS

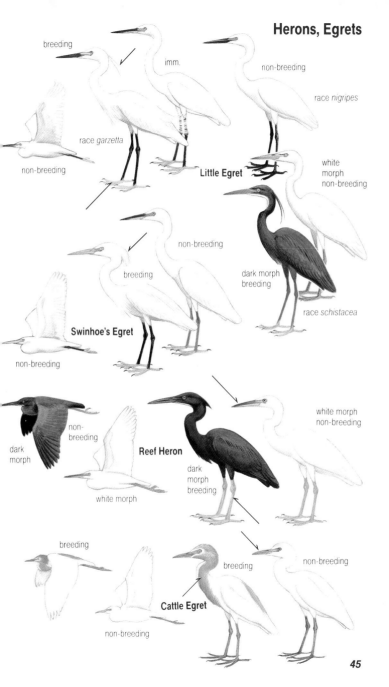

Herons, Egrets

breeding

imm.

non-breeding

race *nigripes*

race *garzetta*

non-breeding

Little Egret

white morph non-breeding

non-breeding

breeding

dark morph breeding

race *schistacea*

Swinhoe's Egret

non-breeding

white morph non-breeding

dark morph

non-breeding

Reef Heron

dark morph breeding

white morph

breeding

breeding

non-breeding

Cattle Egret

non-breeding

45

BLACK-CROWNED NIGHT HERON [Night Heron] *Nycticorax nycticorax* L 57.5cm. Mainly nocturnal, but also active in day-time. **Adult:** from crown to mantle black tinged with green. Wings grey. Two or three long white plumes on hindneck. In flight black back and uniform grey wings make conspicuous pattern. **Juvenile:** dark-brown body with buff/white spots on upperparts, buff/white streaks on underparts. Iris yellow; immature has red iris. **Voice:** "kwok" at night in flight. **Similar species:** Green-backed Heron is dark brown from mantle to wings, has slender bill, yellow lores and iris, calls "kuwee". **Habitat:** rivers, pools, lakes, marshes, mangroves. **Distribution:** breeds in South, East and South-East Asia; some northern breeders migrate south in non-breeding period. KS

NANKEEN NIGHT HERON *Nycticorax caledonicus* L 59cm. **Adult:** crown, nape black; upperparts dark-rufous; underparts white; foreneck, breast often have pale-chestnut wash, lores green. In breeding plumage, two or three long white plumes; for part of season lores become blue and legs bright pink. **Juvenile:** Very similar to juvenile Black-crowned Night Heron, but crown dark-brown and different wing-coverts pattern. **Similar species:** see Japanese and Malaysian Night Heron. **Habitat:** marshes, rocky coasts. **Distribution:** breeds on islands of South-East Asia, where most are sedentary. KS

MAGNIFICENT NIGHT HERON [White-eared Night Heron, Chinese Night Heron] *Gorsachius magnificus* L 54cm. Stout straight black bill with greenish base. Dark grey-brown upperparts, flight feathers slate-grey; black crown and crest, white stripe behind eye and black ear-coverts; throat white, separated from buffy-yellow to orange sides by blackish mesial streak. Female has shorter crest than male; duller head and neck, more mottled back and wings, and spotted with white on wing-coverts. **Voice:** not recorded. **Similar species:** see Japanese and Malaysian Night Herons and Black Bittern. **Habitat:** well watered forested areas. **Distribution:** endemic to a small area in south-eastern China. Current status is little known, but very rare. TM

JAPANESE NIGHT HERON *Gorsachius goisagi* L 49cm. Short thick bill. **Adult:** crown chestnut; lores yellowish. In flight, black primaries and secondaries have conspicuous tawny trailing edge. **Juvenile:** similar to adult, but crown blackish-brown; streaks and spots on neck; wing-coverts paler. **Similar species:** Malaysian Night Heron has black crown, more strongly mottled flanks, and white spots on tips of primaries. See Magnificent Night Heron. **Habitat:** breeds in mountain forest, feeds in marshes, streams in dense forests. **Distribution:** only known to breed in Japan; migrates to south part of East Asia in non-breeding period. KS

MALAYSIAN NIGHT HERON [Malay Bittern, Tiger Bittern] *Gorsachius melanolophus* L 47cm. Short thick bill. **Adult:** crown, hindneck black; lores blue-green; flanks and undertail-coverts mottled brown and white. In flight, tips of greater primary coverts and primaries are white. **Juvenile:** upperparts brown mottled with black; crown blackish barred with white; fine black barring on breast. **Similar species:** see Japanese, Nankeen and Magnificent Night Herons. **Habitat:** dense forest with marshes. **Distribution:** breeds in East Asia and South-East Asia; some migrate south in non-breeding period. KS

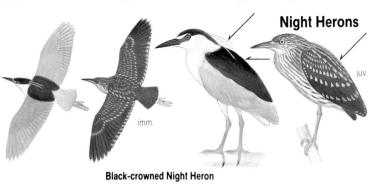

Night Herons

imm.

juv.

Black-crowned Night Heron

juv. moulting to adult

Nankeen Night Heron

Magnificent Night Heron

Japanese Night Heron

Malaysian Night Heron

juv.

47

GREEN-BACKED HERON [Little Heron, Little Green Heron] *Butorides striatus* L 52cm. Smaller than Black-crowned Night Heron. Mainly nocturnal, but also active during daytime. **Adult:** crown black. Back and wing-coverts dark brown with green gloss; wing-coverts have white to yellow feather edges. Bill long and slender; lores, legs/feet yellow. In flight, back and wings tinged with glossy dark-brown. **Juvenile:** body dark brown with buff spots on wing-coverts, buff streaks on underparts. **Voice:** piercing "kuwee" in flight. **Similar species:** Black Bittern has dark lores, legs/feet. See Black-crowned Night Heron. **Habitat:** rivers, lakes, marshes, rice-fields, mangroves. **Distribution:** breeds in South, East and South-East Asia; northern breeders move south in non-breeding period.   KS

INDIAN POND HERON [Pond Heron, Paddybird] *Ardeola grayii* L 46cm. Effectively camouflaged earth-brown at rest. Gregarious at roost. **Breeding:** head and neck buff with pale-yellow wash, crown browner; back rich maroon, breast brownish-buff. **Voice:** in a nesting colony, constantly utters conversational "wa-koo". **Similar species:** see Chinese Pond Heron and Javanese Pond Heron. Non-breeding adults and immatures of all three species difficult to distinguish from each other. **Habitat:** marshes, streams, rice-fields, ponds. **Distribution:** resident in South Asia and west part of South-East Asia.   BB

JAVANESE POND HERON [Javan Pond Heron] *Ardeola speciosa* L 45cm. In flight, white wings contrast with dark back and prominent white patches on flanks. **Breeding:** head, crest feathers and neck golden-yellow; mantle, back and scapulars blackish or purplish-bronze; ornamental breast plumes and a collar at base of neck cinnamon. **Voice:** a squawk when flying, creaky "krak" when disturbed. **Similar species:** see Indian Pond Heron and Chinese Pond Heron. **Habitat:** rice-fields, marshes, mangroves. **Distribution:** resident in South-East Asia.   DMP

CHINESE POND HERON *Ardeola bacchus* L 45cm. Conspicuous contrast in flight between white wings and colour of back. **Breeding:** head to neck reddish-brown; black back is distinctive; lores to base of bill slate-blue; at rest, white of wings not easily visible. **Non-breeding:** head to breast white with brown streaks; back dark-brown; wings white. **Similar species:** breeding Indian Pond Heron has buff head, neck with pale yellow wash; rich maroon mantle and scapulars. Breeding Javanese Pond Heron has pale golden-yellow head, neck; cinnamon breast. **Habitat:** rice-fields, marshes, grasslands. **Distribution:** breeds in East and South-East Asia, northern breeders migrate to South-East Asia in non-breeding period.   KS

EURASIAN BITTERN [Bittern] *Botaurus stellaris* L 70cm. Usually skulks in reed-beds, and often seen only when flushed. When alarmed, remains motionless for a time with bill pointing skywards, neck extended. Active by day and night. **Adult:** thick neck; black crown; narrow moustachial stripe; upperparts golden-brown with complex black markings; legs/feet greenish. **Juvenile:** like adult, but crown browner, whole body slightly paler and browner. **Voice:** breeding males make low, resonant booming: "upwoomp". **Similar species:** see juvenile Black-crowned Night Heron. **Habitat:** reed-beds, marshes. **Distribution:** breeds in a belt from central part of East Asia to Central Asia; stays in South and East Asia, and in part of South-East Asia in non-breeding period.   KS

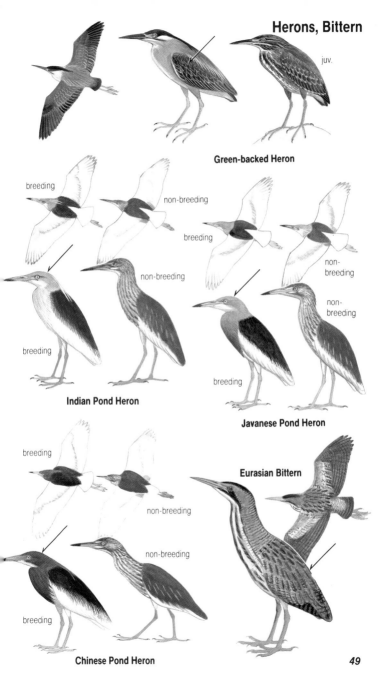

Herons, Bittern

juv.

Green-backed Heron

breeding

non-breeding

breeding

non-breeding

breeding

Indian Pond Heron

breeding

non-breeding

non-breeding

breeding

Javanese Pond Heron

breeding

non-breeding

non-breeding

breeding

Chinese Pond Heron

Eurasian Bittern

LITTLE BITTERN *Ixobrychus minutus* L 36cm. In flight, yellowish-buff shoulder patch contrasting with blackish wings. Largely crepuscular. **Male:** black crown, and black upperparts; sides of head and neck greyish pink or vinous. **Female:** black largely replaced by chestnut-brown; chestnut-brown shoulder patch. Underparts chiefly chestnut and rufous streaked with rufous buff. **Juvenile:** dark brown with rufous streaking. Underparts chiefly white and buff streaked with chestnut and buff. **Voice:** occasional frog-like "wuk". **Habitat:** marshes, reed-beds. **Distribution:** resident in South Asia and North-West China.   BB

CHINESE LITTLE BITTERN [Yellow Bitter] *Ixobrychus sinensis* L 37cm. In flight, contrast visible between yellow-brown wing-coverts, dark-brown back and black flight-feathers. **Male:** black crown; yellow-brown body. **Female:** crown reddish-brown with black stripe along it; brown streaks on underparts. **Juvenile:** heavily streaked above and below; underparts pale. **Voice:** "aw, aw" in breeding season. **Similar species:** at close range, pupil of Chinese Little Bittern appears simply circular; in Schrenck's and Cinnamon Bitterns, small black spot behind circular pupil appears joined onto it. Tibia of Chinese Little and Cinnamon Bitterns almost completely covered by feathers; tibia of Schrenck's Bittern show larger exposed part. See Little Bittern. **Habitat:** rice-fields, reed-beds, marshes. **Distribution:** breeds in East and South Asia; northern breeders move south in non-breeding period.   KS

SCHRENCK'S BITTERN *Ixobrychus eurhythmus* L 39cm. In flight, compared with Chinese Little Bittern, less strong contrast between yellowish-grey wing-coverts, deep chestnut back, slaty-grey flight feathers. **Male** from crown to back deep-chestnut; dark stripe down centre of foreneck **Female:** from crown to back deep chestnut; small white spots on upperparts. **Juvenile:** like female, but browner and more heavily streaked. **Voice** "baw, baw" in breeding season. **Similar species:** see Little and Chinese Little Bitterns. Female and juvenile Cinnamon Bittern have rufous flight-feathers. **Habitat:** rice-fields, reed-beds, grasslands. Prefers drier habitat than Chinese Little Bittern. **Distribution:** breeds in East and a part of North Asia; northern breeders migrate south in non-breeding period.   KS

CINNAMON BITTERN [Chestnut Bitter] *Ixobrychus cinnamomeus* L 40cm Distinguished from other bitterns by reddish-brown wings in flight. **Male** conspicuous uniform reddish-brown from head to back, tail. **Female** reddish-brown from head to back and tail; small white spots on back and wing-coverts. **Juvenile:** like female, but upperparts barred brownish. **Similar species:** see Chinese and Schrenck's Bitterns. **Habitat:** rice-fields, reed-beds, marshes. **Distribution:** breeds from Far East Russia, South-East Asia to South Asia.   KS

BLACK BITTERN *Ixobrychus flavicollis* L 58cm. In flight, upperparts appear coal-black. Dark legs/feet. Crepuscular. **Male:** crown and upperparts black; yellow-buff stripe on side of neck. **Female:** like male, but upperparts blackish-brown, underparts whitish. **Juvenile:** like female, upperparts dark brown with buff fringes. **Voice:** hoarse croak in flight **Habitat:** rice-fields, reed-beds, marshes, mangroves, fast streams. **Distribution:** breeds in East, South-East and South Asia; some northern breeders move south in non-breeding period.   KS

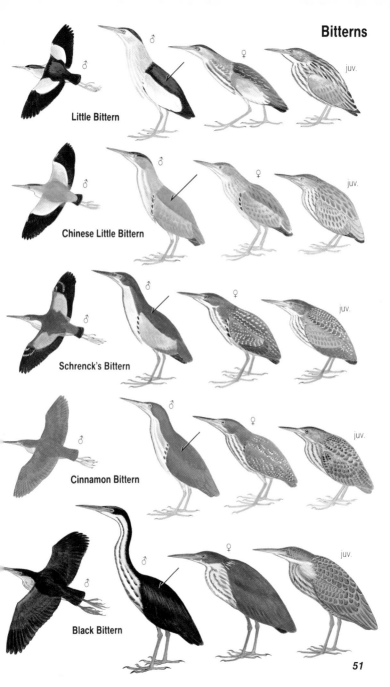

Bitterns

Little Bittern ♂ ♂ ♀ juv.

Chinese Little Bittern ♂ ♂ ♀ juv.

Schrenck's Bittern ♂ ♂ ♀ juv.

Cinnamon Bittern ♂ ♂ ♀ juv.

Black Bittern ♂ ♂ ♀ juv.

Storks

Family *Ciconiidae* (World: 19 species; Asia: 11 species) Large wading birds with long and powerful bills, broad wings, short tails and long necks. Sexes similar, but males are usually larger than females. Breeding and non-breeding plumage similar. Usually found in open shallow water or wetland areas, but some species prefer drier or forest regions. Feeding solitarily or in small groups on invertebrates and small vertebrates. **DMP**

MILKY STORK *Mycteria cinerea* L 92cm. A very large stork with white plumage and black wings. Bill long, slightly decurved and rounded at tip. Usually occurs singly or in small flocks not far from the coast. **Breeding:** facial skin red; bill bright-yellow; legs dark-red. **Non-breeding:** face pinkish-red; bill yellowish; legs grey. **Juvenile:** greyish-brown upperparts and white rump and uppertail-coverts. **Voice:** quiet except young birds' croak. **Similar species:** White and Oriental White Stork are larger and body entirely white. See Painted Stork. **Habitat:** marshes, muddy and flooded areas, coastal mudflats, mangroves, rice-fields. **Distribution:** resident in South-East Asia. **DMP**

PAINTED STORK *Mycteria leucocephala* L 93cm. Long, yellow, slightly decurved bill and pinkish head distinctive. White neck and mantle, wing coverts and breast closely barred blackish; greater coverts white producing white band across closed wing; scapulars rose-pink. Bare skin of face red in breeding season. **Juvenile:** head and neck dull brown; back pale-brown, rump and uppertail-coverts white; entire underwing blackish. **Voice:** silent except for the characteristic clattering of mandibles. **Similar species:** Milky Stork lacks blackish band on breast and blackish bars on wing coverts. **Habitat:** marshes, coastal mudflats, rice-fields. **Distribution:** resident in South Asia, South-East Asia and southern part of East Asia. **BB**

ASIAN OPEN-BILL STORK [Open-bill Stork, Asian Openbill] *Anastomus oscitans* L 81cm. Smaller than Painted Stork. Body white but usually appears quite dirty white; black scapulars, primaries, secondaries and tail. Bill dull-brown; legs dull-pink. Bill with arching mandibles diagnostic. **Non-breeding:** white upperparts replaced by dull smoky-grey. **Juvenile:** similar to non-breeding plumage, but darker smoky brown-grey with blackish-brown mantle. **Voice:** silent except for clattering of mandibles. **Similar species:** White Stork has bright red bill, and white tail. **Habitat:** rivers, lakes, marshes, rice-fields. **Distribution:** resident in South Asia and South-East Asia. **BB**

BLACK STORK *Ciconia nigra* L 99cm. Head, neck, upperparts, breast, tail and wings black with green/purple gloss. Belly, undertail-coverts and axillaries white. Breast feathers elongated, but less so than White Stork and Oriental White Stork. **Breeding:** bill, orbital ring and legs scarlet. **Non-breeding:** bill, orbital ring, legs dark-red. **Juvenile:** generally browner. Bill, legs olive-green; orbital ring grey-green. **Similar species:** Common, Hooded and Demoiselle Cranes lack white underparts. **Habitat:** breeds in virgin forest containing streams; lakes, marshes, rice-fields etc in non-breeding period. **Distribution:** breeds in Central Asia, south part of North Asia and north part of East Asia; moves to north part of South Asia, south part of East Asia in non-breeding period. **SU**

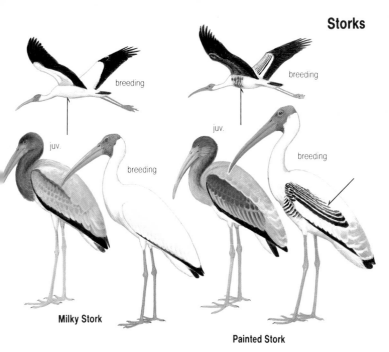

breeding

breeding

juv.

juv.

breeding

breeding

Milky Stork

Painted Stork

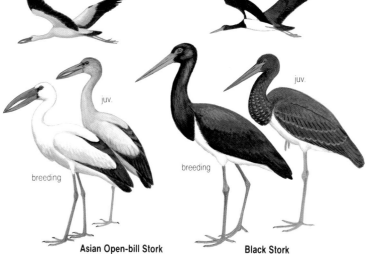

juv.

juv.

breeding

breeding

Asian Open-bill Stork

Black Stork

WOOLLY-NECKED STORK [White-necked Stork] *Ciconia episcopus* L 106cm. Conspicuous white neck and black crown. Undertail-coverts white. Rest of plumage including short tail black glossed with purple or greenish-blue. Bill black; legs red. Feeds on dry areas, seldom in water. Roosts in tall trees. **Juvenile:** glossy black replaced by dull dark-brown, but sometimes as in adult. **Voice:** silent except for clattering of mandibles with neck bent over backwards and crown resting between the shoulders. **Similar species:** see Storm's Stork. **Habitat:** drier areas than most storks, edges of lakes, dried rice-fields, agricultural lands well away from water. **Distribution:** resident in South Asia and South-East Asia. BB

STORM'S STORK *Ciconia stormi* L 85cm. Rare. Large, long, straight red bill with small knob at the base of culmen; yellow facial skin distinctive; black crown, iridescent black body, foreneck and wings contrast with white cheeks, throat, and nape. Three central tail feathers white. Legs red. **Similar species:** Woolly-necked Stork is bigger with white neck and black bill. **Voice:** "karau". **Habitat:** freshwater swamp forests. **Distribution:** resident in central part of South-East Asia. DMP

WHITE STORK *Ciconia ciconia* L 106cm. All white except for scapulars, primaries and secondaries which are black. Heavy pointed bill and legs bright red. Lores black; iris brown. Stalks for food on marshy grasslands or fallow fields. Migrates in large flocks. **Juvenile:** similar to adult, but black feathers tinged brown. **Voice:** poorly developed. Characteristic bill-clattering. **Similar species:** see Oriental White Stork. **Habitat:** lowland marshes, lakes. **Distribution:** breeds eastern part of Europe, moves to South Asia in non-breeding period. BB

ORIENTAL WHITE STORK *Ciconia boyciana* L 112cm. Bill is thick, long and blackish-grey. Body white; flight-feathers black. On upperwing outer webs of secondaries and inner primaries are irregularly whitish-grey. Orbital ring greyish-red; lores red. **Breeding:** legs orange; iris blue. **Non-breeding:** legs reddish-orange; iris yellow. **Voice:** clatters mandibles together to make castanet-like sound. **Similar species:** White Stork has red bill; lores black; iris brown. **Habitat:** lowland marshes, lakes; breeds in nearby woods. **Distribution:** breeds in south part of Far East Russia, north part of East Asia; moves to south part of East Asia in non-breeding period. SU

Storks

Woolly-necked Stork

Storm's Stork

White Stork

Oriental White Stork

non-breeding

BLACK-NECKED STORK *Ephippiorhynchus asiaticus* L 135cm. Huge black-and-white stork with massive black bill and long coral-red legs. In flight, large size, black neck and bill, white underparts including all flight feathers, and a broad black diagonal band across each wing diagnostic. Usually found wading in shallow water or soaring and circling. **Adult:** head, neck, wings and tail black, brilliantly glossed with green-blue, purple and bronze; back white; upper breast to undertail-coverts white. Sexes similar except for colour of iris; brown in male, bright lemon-yellow in female. **Juvenile:** glossy black replaced by dull-brown; white parts less pure and duskier. **Habitat:** marshes, rivers, lakes. **Distribution:** resident in South Asia and South-East Asia.   BB

LESSER ADJUTANT STORK [Lesser Adjutant] *Leptoptilos javanicus* L 110cm. Massive dirty yellowish wedge-shaped bill. Chiefly glossy metallic-black upperparts, white underparts, with sparse hair-like feathers on almost naked reddish-yellow head and neck; upper-and underwing black. **Juvenile:** upper plumage less glossy; head and neck more feathered. **Similar species:** see Greater Adjutant. **Habitat:** marshes, lakes, rice-fields, mangroves, mudflats. **Distribution:** resident in South Asia and South-East Asia, but not numerous.   BB

GREATER ADJUTANT STORK [Adjutant, Greater Adjutant] *Leptoptilos dubius* L 135cm. Black, grey and dirty-white with naked dull flesh and yellow head and neck, and a huge wedge-shaped bill. Large naked pinkish gular pouch hanging from base of neck. White ruff around base of neck; wings and tail blackish slightly glossed with green; innermost secondaries and greater wing-coverts silvery-grey forming a broad band on closed wing. **Juvenile:** scantily feathered on the naked parts; inner secondaries and coverts dark-brown. **Voice:** bill clattering. **Similar species:** Lesser Adjutant lacks a big gular pouch, white ruff around base of neck, broad grey bands on closed wings. **Habitat:** marshes, rice-fields, lakes, open forests; sometimes in dry areas. **Distribution:** resident in South Asia and South-East Asia, but not numerous, possibly endangered. Much rarer than Lesser Adjutant Stork.   BB

Storks

♀ ♂

juv.

Black-necked Stork

Lesser
Adjutant Stork

Greater
Adjutant Stork

Ibises and Spoonbills
Family *Threskiornithidae* (World: 31 species; Asia: 9 species) Medium to large in size. Sexes similar. Ibises have long bills curved downwards; Spoonbills have long bills spatulate at the tip. Catch small fish, snails, insects etc in shallow water. Flight direct with necks and legs extended; wing-beats shallower than egrets. Flocks fly in formation. Many species breed in colonies in woods or bamboo thickets, sometimes mixed with other species. SU

ORIENTAL IBIS [Black-headed Ibis, White Ibis] *Threskiornis melano-cephalus* L 68cm. Bare, black skin on head and upper neck. White body. Long, black bill curved downwards. Deep red patch of naked skin along inner leading edge of underwing; pinkish in non-breeding period. Black legs. **Breeding:** grey plumes on back. **Immature:** blackish-brown feathers grow on part of head; tips of some primaries black; bill shorter than adult's. **Similar species:** Australian White Ibis has tips of all primaries greenish-black; plumes in breeding plumage black. Japanese Crested Ibis has red face and legs. **Habitat:** breeds in woods near water; frequents rice-fields, mudflats etc. **Distribution:** breeds in South Asia, north part of South-East Asia, south part of East Asia; also breeds in North China. Northern breeders move to south in non-breeding period. SU

AUSTRALIAN WHITE IBIS *Threskiornis molucca* L 70cm. Adult: upper- and underparts white, tips of primaries and outer secondaries black; head and neck naked, black; rear of crown with transverse pinkish-red bands. Bright red patch of naked skin along inner leading edge of underwing. Bill black; legs reddish-brown. **Immature:** as adult, but duller with feathered blackish-brown head and nape, white streaks on throat; shorter bill. **Voice:** harsh croaks. **Similar species:** see Oriental Ibis. **Habitat:** shallow water in freshwater marshes, coastal mudflats. **Distribution:** resident from Indonesia to Australia. TM

BLACK IBIS [White-shouldered Ibis, Red-naped Ibis] *Pseudibis papillosa* L 68cm. Small dark ibis. Dark brown plumage with glossy-black wings and tail. South Asian race *papillosa* has a small but conspicuous white patch near shoulder of wing, and brick-red legs. A triangular patch of brilliant red warts covering top of naked black head. **Immature:** overall dull brown including feathered crown, head and throat. Race *davisoni* has naked black head with pale blue nape and neck collar; white patch on lesser wing-coverts conspicuous in flight, but not usually visible at rest. Legs red. **Habitat:** lakes, rivers, marshes, rice-fields. **Distribution:** resident in South Asia and north part of South-East Asia. BB

GIANT IBIS *Thaumatibis gigantea* L 104cm. Large ibis with a notably angular headshape. Upper- and underparts dull-brown glossed greenish; primaries black, silvery-grey wing-coverts; tail bluish-green. Bill pinkish; iris crimson; legs red. **Voice:** not recorded. **Similar species:** Black Ibis is smaller, and has white wing patch. **Habitat:** Solitary or in pairs in marshes, lowland plains. **Distribution:** very rare resident endemic to Thailand, Cambodia, Vietnam and Laos; possibly extinct. TM

Ibises

Oriental Ibis

imm.

Australian White Ibis

imm.

race *davisoni*

Black Ibis

race *papillosa*

imm.

Giant Ibis

imm.

59

JAPANESE CRESTED IBIS [Crested Ibis] *Nipponia nippon* L 76cm. Red face; white head with crest. Body white; crest, wings, tail with orange-red tinge; orange-red flight-feathers are best seen in flight. Long bill is black with red tip. Legs red, relatively short, do not extend beyond tail in flight. **Breeding:** head, back and upperwings become grey-black. **Voice:** a low-pitched "tha-aa", "gha-aa". **Habitat:** breeds in woods near rice-fields, marshes. **Distribution:** at present only confirmed as resident in small numbers in Shaanxi Province, China.   SU

GLOSSY IBIS *Plegadis falcinellus* L 52cm. Small dark ibis with feathered head and characteristic slender down-curved bill. **Breeding:** head, neck, chin, throat, lower back and rump rich dark-chestnut heavily glossed with green and purple; tail black glossed with green and purple; underparts including undertail-coverts and axillaries deep purple-brown. **Non-breeding:** as breeding, but head, throat and neck brown-black streaked white; underparts brown-black with chestnut tinge. **Immature:** similar to non-breeding. **Voice:** usually silent. **Similar species:** Black Ibis has naked black head and small white patches on wings. **Habitat:** marshes, lakes. **Distribution:** resident or visitor in South and South-East Asia.   BB

WHITE SPOONBILL [Spoonbill] *Platalea leucorodia* L 86cm. Long bill with flat, spatulate tip. Long neck, legs. Bill is black, except central area of tip which is yellow. Black line of bare skin from base of bill to eyes. Legs black. When feeding, sweeps bill from side to side in shallow water, opening and closing it. **Breeding:** white body; long, orange-yellow crest. Orange-yellow band on lower neck/upper breast; orange-red patch on throat. Tip of bill becomes deeper yellow. **Non-breeding:** no orange-red on breast or throat. Yellow on bill duller. **Immature:** tips of flight-feathers black; bill is all yellowish-pink. **Similar species:** Black-faced Spoonbill is smaller, has wider area of black skin on face, and all-black bill. **Habitat:** shallow areas of lakes, marshes, pools, rivers. Likes large reed-beds etc for breeding. **Distribution:** breeds in Central Asia; moves to south part of East Asia in non-breeding period. Resident in South Asia.   SU

BLACK-FACED SPOONBILL *Platalea minor* L 73cm. Bill all-black; legs black. Wedge of black, bare skin from base of bill to eyes. Male has yellow crescent marking below eye, size and shape of which can vary. **Breeding:** white body; long, orange-yellow crest. Orange-yellow band on lower neck/ upper breast. **Non-breeding:** crest shorter; no orange-yellow on breast. **Immature:** tips of flight-feathers black; bill is all dark grey-pink. **Habitat:** nests on coastal cliffs etc; frequents rice-fields, marshes etc. **Distribution:** breeds in part of D.P.R.Korea and possibly North-East China; moves to south part of East Asia, mainly Taiwan in non-breeding period.   SU

ROYAL SPOONBILL *Platalea regia* L 80cm. **Breeding:** red skin on fore-crown and yellow wattles above and below eye; very long white plumes on rear of head; dull cream breast band. Bill and legs black. Non-breeding and immature plumage appear identical to Black-faced Spoonbill in equivalent plumages, and they cannot be safely separated outside the breeding season, except on range. **Voice:** quiet grunts and groans at nest. **Habitat:** rice-fields, marshes, mudbanks, mangroves. **Distribution:** rare visitor to Indonesia from Australia.   DMP

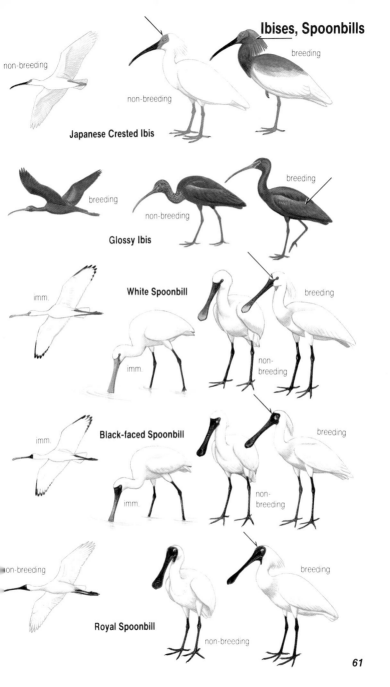

Ibises, Spoonbills

non-breeding

breeding

non-breeding

Japanese Crested Ibis

breeding

non-breeding

breeding

Glossy Ibis

imm.

White Spoonbill

imm.

breeding

non-breeding

imm.

Black-faced Spoonbill

imm.

breeding

non-breeding

non-breeding

breeding

Royal Spoonbill

non-breeding

Ducks, Geese and Swans
Family *Anatidae* (World: 149 species; Asia: 62 species except Sea Ducks) Small- to large-sized waterbirds with rather short legs, narrow pointed wings. DMP

Whistling Ducks
Medium-sized ducks with long necks, elongated bodies and broad rounded wings. When flying, wings produce a whirring sound. Sexes are similar and both sexes have whistling calls. DMP

SPOTTED WHISTLING DUCK *Dendrocygna guttata* L 45cm. Dark-brown stripe extends from crown to nape, blackish eye-stripe. Face, throat and sides of upper neck greyish-brown, clearly distinct from dark brown lower neck; upperparts and tail dark brown; breast, flanks reddish-brown spotted with white; belly whitish-grey; undertail-coverts barred black and white. **Juvenile:** duller; sides of breast more streaked with white than adult. **Voice:** a harsh low call. **Habitat:** vegetated lagoons, rivers etc. **Distribution:** resident from eastern Indonesia to Australia. DMP

FULVOUS WHISTLING DUCK [Large Whistling Teal, Fulvous Treeduck] *Dendrocygna bicolor* L 50cm. Crown rusty-brown continuing into dark stripe on nape. Front and sides of neck buffish. Mantle, back and wings dark-brown fringed with buff; breast and underparts fulvous and elongated flank feathers creamy buff, similar to Wandering Whistling Duck; rump buffy-white, undertail-coverts creamy white and tail blackish. **Juvenile:** duller, uppertail-coverts less conspicuous. **Voice:** double noted whistle "tsii-ee, tsoo-ee"; higher pitched in female. **Similar species:** see Indian Whistling Duck. **Habitat:** rice-fields, marshes, shallow lakes. **Distribution:** resident in South Asia. DMP

WANDERING WHISTLING DUCK *Dendrocygna arcuata* L 57cm. Reddish-brown with black crown and nape. Face and rest of head light-brown becoming paler on chin and throat; mantle and scapulars dark-brown tipped with golden-brown; upper- and underwing dark-brown; breast and underparts light rufous with occasional black spots on breast; buff flank plumes elongated broadly streaked with white, black and chestnut; under-tail-coverts and outer uppertail-coverts creamy white; tail, rump and central uppertail-coverts blackish. **Juvenile:** duller. **Voice:** a shrill, twittering whistle. **Similar species:** see Indian Whistling Duck. **Habitat:** lakes, marshes. **Distribution:** resident in South-East Asia. DMP

INDIAN WHISTLING DUCK [Lesser Whistling Teal, Lesser Tree Duck] *Dendrocygna javanica* L 40cm. Forehead, crown and nape dusky grey-brown. Supercilium, face, neck and breast are greyish-buff. Dark-grey back with rufous barring. Flanks, belly tawny-rufous, with creamy streaks on upper flanks. Undertail-coverts and vent whitish. Rump black; uppertail-coverts rich chestnut; tail dark-brown. Upperwing; flight feathers black, coverts dark chestnut; underwing blackish. **Voice:** "whi-whee". **Similar species:** Fulvous Whistling Duck is larger, with buffy-white uppertail-coverts, all dark-brown wings, and narrow whitish lines on neck. Wandering Whistling Duck also large, has dark crown extending below eyes, black spots on breast, and whitish uppertail-coverts. **Habitat:** shallow pools, marshes. **Distribution:** resident in South and South-East Asia; also breeds in south part of East Asia. SU

Whistling Ducks

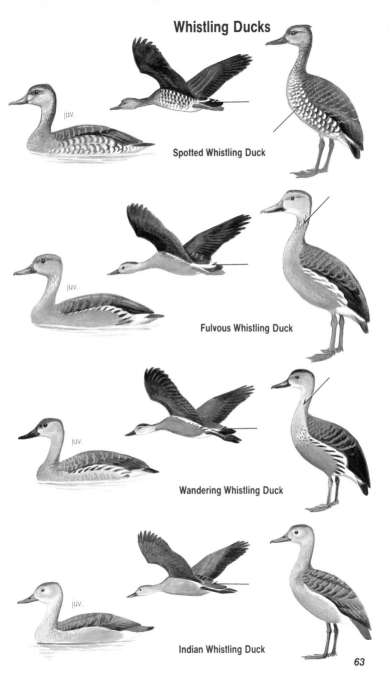

juv.

Spotted Whistling Duck

juv.

Fulvous Whistling Duck

juv.

Wandering Whistling Duck

juv.

Indian Whistling Duck

Swans

Extremely large water-birds, with heavy bodies and long necks. Adults are all-white; immatures grey. Sexes similar. To help gain momentum for take-off, use long, striding kicks on water or ground. Fly with necks extended and powerful wingbeats. Flocks fly in formation. Feed on plant material by dabbling on surface of water, immersing head and neck, and up-ending. Spend non-breeding period in flocks based on family units, on lakes, marshes, estuaries, large rivers etc. **SU**

MUTE SWAN *Cygnus olor* L 152cm. Largest of 3 Asian species. Swims with neck slightly curved in S-shape, bill slanting slightly down; sometimes with wings arched upwards. Tail relatively long. Bill orange-red with black knob at base; basal triangle and edges of bill black. In early spring, male's knob larger than female's. Legs black. **Juvenile:** generally grey; bill pinkish-grey; basal knob still small. **Similar species:** Whooper Swan has yellow and black bill, no basal knob. Tundra Swan smaller with yellow and black bill, no knob. **Habitat:** lowland lakes, marshes, reservoirs, pools, rivers, ponds in parks; sometimes frequents brackish coastal areas. **Distribution:** localised breeding in Central Asia, north east of East Asia; moves to East Asia in non-breeding period. Introduced birds are often seen in parks and lakes. **SU**

WHOOPER SWAN *Cygnus cygnus* L 140cm. Adult all-white, but some are stained rusty on face and neck. Long, straight neck; swims with bill horizontal, neck vertical. Short tail. Bill black with yellow base, which extends more than halfway down the bill and ends in a point. Legs black. **Juvenile:** generally brown-grey; bill dirty-pink at base with black tip. **Voice:** loud, trumpeting "whoop, whoop". **Similar species:** Tundra Swan smaller, with rounder head, different bill-pattern. **Habitat:** breeds on open, shallow lakes and marshes; otherwise on lakes, marshes, rivers, estuaries. **Distribution:** breeds across North Asia; moves to East Asia in non-breeding period. **SU**

TUNDRA SWAN [Whistling Swan] *Cygnus columbianus* L 120cm. Adult all-white, but some are stained rusty on face and neck. Rounder head and shorter, thicker neck than Whooper Swan. Swims with bill horizontal, neck vertical. Short tail. Black legs. Bill of race *jankowskii,* which breeds in Asia, is black with rounded, yellow base; some have black on top of bill up to forehead, leaving rounded, yellow sides. North American race *columbianus,* rare non-breeding visitor to East Asia, has bill mainly black with small yellow spot in front of the eye. **Juvenile:** generally brown-grey; bill dirty pinkish-yellow with black tip. **Voice:** like Whooper Swan's but softer and lower. **Similar species:** Snow Goose is smaller with black wing-tips, reddish-pink bill and legs. See Whooper Swan. **Habitat:** breeds in marshes on tundra; otherwise on lakes, marshes, rivers, estuaries. **Distribution:** breeds in polar region; moves to East Asia in non-breeding period. **SU**

Swans

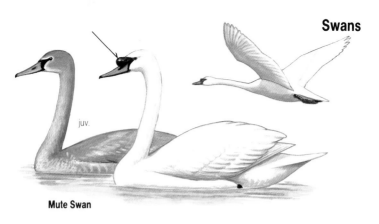

Mute Swan

Whooper Swan

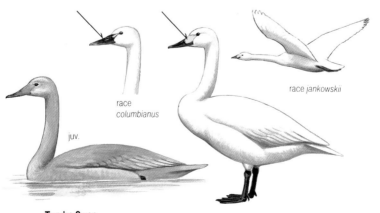

race
columbianus

race *jankowskii*

Tundra Swan

65

Geese
Heavy-set bodies, long necks, short legs. Sexes similar. SU

SWAN GOOSE *Anser cygnoides* L 87cm. Large body with long bill and neck. Sharp contrast between dark-brown crown, hindneck, and light-brown throat, sides of head and foreneck. Body grey-brown, paler than other *Anser* species. Black bill; adult has white line at base. Legs orange **Voice:** "gua-hwang, gu-hwang". **Similar species:** Bean Goose has uniform dark-brown head and neck; black bill with orange band on tip. White-fronted Goose is smaller with brown head and neck, and in adult black patches on belly. **Habitat:** breeds by lakes, marshes; otherwise on lakes marshes, grasslands. **Distribution:** breeds in North-East China; moves to East China in non-breeding period. SU

BEAN GOOSE *Anser fabalis* L 85cm. Body blackish-brown with particularly dark head, and long bill and neck. Bill black with orange near tip Legs orange. Contrast between head and paler breast. Race *middendorffi* is the largest race of this species, has particularly long body and bill. Race *serrirostris* has short body, neck and particularly short thick bill. **Juvenile** like adult, but less dark; more scaling on upperparts and flanks. **Voice:** "gaahang-gahang". **Similar species:** White-fronted Goose is a little smaller and paler; adult has white patch at base of bill, black patches on belly **Habitat:** breeds in marshes of tundra and taiga; otherwise on open farmlands, lakes, marshes. **Distribution:** breeds in North Asia; moves to East Asia in non-breeding period. SU

WHITE-FRONTED GOOSE [Greater White-fronted Goose] *Anser albifrons* L 72cm. Chunky body with relatively short bill and neck. White surround to base of bill, and black patches on belly distinctive. Bill fleshy-pink with whitish nail. Legs orange. **Juvenile:** no white on face or black on belly. Bill blackish with dark nail. **Voice:** "kwahang-kwahang". **Similar species:** Lesser White-Fronted Goose is smaller, has rounder head and bright-yellow eye-ring, faster walk and feeding action. **Habitat:** breeds by lakes, marshes on tundra; otherwise on farmlands, grasslands. **Distribution:** breeds in north part of North Asia; moves to central/south part of East Asia, and South Asia in non-breeding period. SU

LESSER WHITE-FRONTED GOOSE *Anser erythropus* L 58cm. Smaller than White-fronted Goose. Bill is short, bright-pink with white nail; white patch at base of bill extends to crown; head rounded. Black patches on belly. Bright-yellow eye ring. Legs orange. **Juvenile:** no white at base of bill, or black patches on belly. **Voice:** a high-pitched "kioo-yoo-yoo" **Similar species:** see White-fronted Goose. **Habitat:** little known in breeding season; in non-breeding period often mixed in flocks of other species **Distribution:** breeds in north part of North Asia; moves to East Asia. SU

GREYLAG GOOSE *Anser anser* L 84cm. Whole body is uniform greyish-brown. Bill bright-pink with white nail; adult has white line at base of bill Legs pink. In flight upperwing-coverts pale, leading edge whitish; underwing-coverts pale-grey. **Juvenile:** like adult, but has stripes on upperparts no dark spots on belly. **Voice:** "aahng-ung-ung". **Habitat:** breeds by lakes marshes in grasslands; otherwise on open farmlands, grasslands with lakes, marshes nearby. **Distribution:** breeds in Central Asia; moves to South Asia, south part of East Asia in non-breeding period. SU

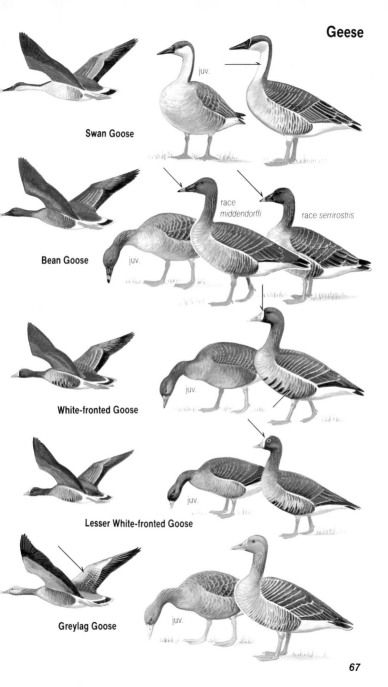

Geese

Swan Goose

juv.

Bean Goose

juv.

race *middendorffi*

race *serrirostris*

White-fronted Goose

juv.

Lesser White-fronted Goose

juv.

Greylag Goose

juv.

BAR-HEADED GOOSE *Anser indicus* L 74cm. Two black bars on the back of white head; neck black with a white stripe down each side. Body grey; rear flanks blackish. Bill, legs yellow-orange. At rest, wings extend beyond tail. In flight, wing-coverts and belly grey, flight-feathers black. **Juvenile:** crown, nape and lores dark grey; no bars. **Voice:** like other geese but slightly lower and more nasal. **Similar species:** juvenile Snow Goose has whiter underparts, blackish bill and legs. **Habitat:** breeds on saline and fresh water lakes; otherwise on marshes, rivers. **Distribution:** breeds in uplands of Central Asia; mainly moves to India in non-breeding period. SU

SNOW GOOSE *Anser caerulescens* L 67cm. All-white except black primaries. Head and neck sometimes stained rusty. Bill, legs reddish-pink; bill short and thick. **Juvenile:** grey with blackish bill, legs. **Voice:** like other geese. **Similar species:** Swans larger with all-white wings. **Habitat:** breeds on low tundra; otherwise in coastal areas. **Distribution:** breeds in North America and far east part of North Asia; rare visitor to East Asia. SU

EMPEROR GOOSE *Anser canagicus* L 67cm. Short, pink bill. Head and nape white, often stained rusty. Body blue-grey with black and white scaling. Thick short neck. Tail white. **Juvenile:** grey with blackish bill; legs dull olive-brown. **Voice:** like other geese except a distinctive "kla-ha, kla-ha". **Habitat:** breeds on coastal tundra; otherwise on mudflats and rocky coasts. **Distribution:** breeds in far east part of North Asia and Alaska; rare visitor to north part of East Asia. SU

CANADA GOOSE *Branta canadensis* L 67cm. Head and neck black; white cheeks and throat form chinstrap; clear white collar round lower neck, but some races lack white collar. Upperparts dark brown with pale barring; rump, tail black; uppertail-coverts white. Breast, belly are grey-brown; vent and undertail-coverts white. Bill, legs black. **Juvenile:** very like adult, but barring on upperparts less distinct. **Voice:** "ah-honk" **Habitat:** breeds near lowland lakes, marshes; otherwise on rice-fields etc. **Distribution:** breeds in the Aleutians and North America; rare visitor to north part of East Asia. SU

BRENT GOOSE *Branta bernicla* L 61cm. Head, neck, breast black; upperparts slaty-brown; large patch of white streaked with black on throat and sides of neck. Belly black; flanks, vent, upper- and undertail-coverts white. Bill, legs black. Wing-coverts slaty-brown, flight-feathers black. **Juvenile:** generally duller; pale barring on upperparts. White throat-patch begins to develop during first winter. **Voice:** in flocks, calls "ruk-ruk-gruk". **Similar species:** Canada Goose has black head and neck, white cheeks and throat. **Habitat:** breeds on lakes, marshes in coastal tundra; otherwise on mudflats, coastal grasslands. **Distribution:** breeds in east part of North Asia and Alaska; rare visitor to north part of East Asia in non-breeding period. SU

RED-BREASTED GOOSE *Branta ruficollis* L 61cm. **Adult:** crown, nape, sides of neck and back black. Sides of head boldly patterned black, white and chestnut. Chin, throat and breast bright chestnut; bright chestnut breast separated from black nape and belly by white stripes. **Juvenile:** browner and duller with chestnut areas paler and more cinnamon. **Habitat:** breeds on tundra, otherwise in open steppe and lowland hills. **Distribution:** breeds in south west part of Russia and surrounding areas; rare visitor to South Asia. BB

Geese

Bar-headed Goose

juv.

Snow Goose

juv.

Emperor Goose

juv.

Canada Goose

Brent Goose

juv.

Red-breasted Goose

juv.

Shelducks

Large ducks. Both sexes have similar plumage. Habits similar to Geese. Build nests in holes in trees and embankments.　　SU

RUDDY SHELDUCK *Tadorna ferruginea* L 64cm. Body rusty-orange. Head paler; whitish around face in female. Tail, uppertail-coverts, and lower half of rump, black. Wings above and below have black primaries, green-glossed secondaries and white coverts. Bill, legs black. **Breeding:** male has black collar, female lacks collar. **Non-breeding:** collar is indistinct or absent in male. **Habitat:** breeds near rivers, saline lakes in open grasslands and uplands; otherwise on rivers, lakes, marshes inland. **Distribution:** breeds in Central Asia; moves to South Asia, north part of South-East Asia, south part of East Asia in non-breeding period.　　SU

COMMON SHELDUCK *Tadorna tadorna* L 63cm. White body; greenish-black head and neck; black scapulars; chestnut band round breast and back; black stripe down centre of belly. White tail with black tip; flight-feathers black, wing-coverts white; tertials chestnut. Bill red, legs orange-red. **Male:** red knob at base of bill in breeding plumage. **Female:** generally duller; body-band and belly-stripe narrower; base of bill white. **Immature:** even duller than female; some have no belly-stripe. Secondaries and some primaries have white tips. **Similar species:** male Mallard has dark-chestnut breast, olive bill. Male Northern Shoveler has chestnut flanks. Male Goosander has all-white underparts, thin bill. **Habitat:** mudflats, saline inland lakes, brackish lakes. **Distribution:** breeds in Central Asia; moves to South Asia and south part of East Asia in non-breeding period.　　SU

RADJAH SHELDUCK *Tadorna radjah* L 53cm. A distinctive white and black shelduck with flesh-coloured bill. Head, neck, breast, belly and lesser coverts white; greenish-black mantle, narrow breast band, back, rump and tail. Bill slightly broader and more upturned than Common Shelduck. Iris white to pale yellow; legs pink. Sexes similar but breast band of female is narrower. In flight, black primaries contrast with glossy-green speculum on white secondaries; underside of primaries contrast with distinctively white coverts and secondaries. **Voice:** male whistle, female harsh rattling note. **Habitat:** mangroves, marshes, mudbanks of rivers; shallow brackish water near coast. **Distribution:** resident from east part of Indonesia to Australia.　　DMP

CRESTED SHELDUCK *Tadorna cristata* L 64cm. **Male:** crown glossy black with short crest; face and neck pale grey; chin black; upperparts reddish-brown; breast black; flanks and belly slaty-grey. Tail black; flight-feathers black, wing-coverts white. Bill, legs orange-yellow. **Female:** body browner; neck, chin and area surrounding eye white. **Habitat:** understood to breed in mountainous areas; otherwise in estuaries, sheltered bays. **Distribution:** last observed in 1971 in north east of D.P.R. Korea; now possibly extinct. Past records limited to south part of Far East Russia, Korean Peninsula and Japan.　　SU

Shelducks

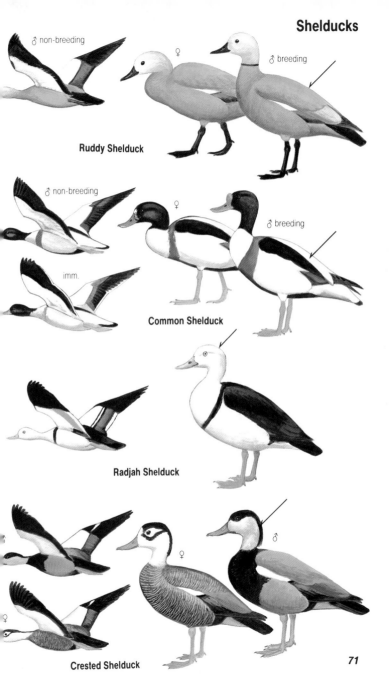

♂ non-breeding

♀   ♂ breeding

Ruddy Shelduck

♂ non-breeding

imm.

♀   ♂ breeding

Common Shelduck

Radjah Shelduck

♀   ♂

Crested Shelduck

71

Marsh Ducks

Generally found in shallow water where they feed either by dabbling noisily on the surface or by immersing heads and necks and up-ending. Rarely dive. Take off directly from the surface. SU

WHITE-WINGED WOOD DUCK *Cairina scutulata* L 70cm. Head and neck white heavily spotted with black; back, rump, uppertail-coverts, tail and upper breast black with glossy-green; primaries dark-brown; underparts dark-brown. Bill orange-yellow with black tip; iris orange-brown; legs orange-yellow. In flight, white wing linings contrast with blackish flight-feathers. Sexes similar but female smaller and duller. Sumatran population shows entirely white head, neck and breast, and this type is also recorded in Assam. **Voice:** flight calls, whistles and grunts. **Habitat:** dense tropical rainforest with swamps, sluggish streams or weedy ponds; sometimes on rice-fields but rarely seen on open water. **Distribution:** rare and very localised resident in east part of South Asia and South-East Asia. DMP

COMB DUCK *Sarkidiornis melanotos* L 76cm. Upperparts black glossed with blue-green and purple; rump paler. Head and neck white speckled with black. Black half-collar down side of white breast. Centre of belly white, flanks whitish with pale-grey. **Male:** fleshy knob on base of bill at forehead, becoming greatly swollen in breeding season. No eclipse plumage. **Female:** like male, but without knob on bill; smaller, and duller, especially on flanks. **Voice:** usually silent. **Habitat:** lakes and marshes in sparsely wooded open country. **Distribution:** resident from South Asia to west part of South-East Asia. BB

GREEN PYGMY GOOSE *Nettapus pulchellus* L 30cm. In flight, entire wings look dark with conspicuous white speculum. **Male:** head, neck, nape, mantle and wings glossy dark-green; lores and cheeks white; upper breast, rump, uppertail-coverts and flanks vermiculated dark-brown and white. **Female:** crown and nape dark-brown; rest of head, neck and upper breast narrowly barred dark-brown and white. **Male eclipse:** head and chin white freckled with dark-green, foreneck mottled grey, white and green. **Voice:** shrill whistle and high-pitched whistling "whit". **Similar species:** Cotton Teal has white sides of head and neck and grey-washed flanks. **Habitat:** freshwater with aquatic vegetation in lowland. **Distribution:** rare visitor to east part of Indonesia from Australia. DMP

COTTON TEAL [Quacky Duck, Cotton Pygmy Goose] *Nettapus coromandelianus* L 33cm. **Male:** crown blackish-brown, white head, neck and underparts; a greenish-black band running from low behind neck around middle of breast; back glossy greenish-black. Iris red. In flight, dark wings have broad white band across primaries and white trailing edge to secondaries. **Female:** black eye-stripe; face and neck barred brown; back duller; foreneck and breast white barred with brown. In flight, dark wings with white trailing edge to secondaries. Iris brown. **Male eclipse:** like female, but wing pattern same as breeding male. **Voice:** male rattling cackle, female squeaky quack. **Similar species:** see Green Pygmy Goose. **Habitat:** like Green Pygmy Goose. **Distribution:** resident in South and South-East Asia, population in southern East Asia moves to south in non-breeding period. DMP

Marsh Ducks

White-winged Wood Duck

♀

white type

♂

Comb Duck

♂

♀

♂

Green Pygmy Goose

♂

♀

♂

Cotton Teal

♂

♀

♂

♀

73

MANDARIN DUCK *Aix galericulata* L 45cm. Often perches in trees; nests in treeholes. Relatively large head, short neck. In flight, both sexes have white trailing edges to wings, egg-shaped white patch on belly; tail looks long. **Male:** crest on rear crown. Inner webs of tertials are broad and project upwards like sails. Bill red with white tip; legs orange. **Female:** generally grey-brown. White spectacles around eyes; white throat and base of bill. Bill brown to pink. **Male eclipse:** like female but bill red. **Voice:** calls "wrrick". **Similar species:** female Wigeon is browner with no white spectacles or trailing edges of wings. **Habitat:** breeds by fast mountain streams and forest lakes/marshes; otherwise in flocks on fairly secluded lowland lakes, marshes. **Distribution:** resident in East Asia; northern breeders move south in non-breeding period.   SU

EUROPEAN WIGEON [Wigeon, Eurasian Wigeon] *Anas penelope* L 48cm. Medium-sized with short neck, small bill. **Male:** head and neck chestnut; crown and forehead cream-yellow. Body grey; breast tinged light-brown. Undertail-coverts black. Wing-coverts conspicuous white; speculum green. **Female:** deeper brown than other species. Head pinkish-brown with black spots. Wing-coverts grey-brown; white bar in front of green speculum; axillaries grey. **Male eclipse:** like female but wing-coverts white. **Voice:** male calls loudly "pi-wheeoon". **Similar species:** male American Wigeon has whitish crown and forehead, glossy green stripe behind eye. Female is whiter overall with more distinct black spots on head, blackish surround to eye. White axillaries and central underwing-coverts; European Wigeon's are greyish. Tertials edged white; European Wigeon's are normally buffer and narrower, but white from September to December, so care required. **Habitat:** breeds by small lakes, marshes in open country; otherwise on lakes, marshes, rivers, sheltered bays. **Distribution:** breeds across North Asia; moves to East Asia, north part of South Asia, north part of South-East Asia in non-breeding period.   SU

AMERICAN WIGEON *Anas americana* L 48cm. **Male:** grey head with whitish crown and forehead, and glossy green stripe behind eye. Breast and flanks pinkish-brown. Undertail-coverts black. Wing-coverts conspicuous white; speculum green. **Female:** generally brown; upperparts have greyish tinge, contrasting with underparts. Greater coverts paler than European Wigeon. Tertials have broad, white edges. **Male eclipse:** like female but wing-coverts white. **Voice:** "wheeoo-wheeoo-wheeoo" less loud than European Wigeon. **Similar species:** see European Wigeon; hybrids are often found, so care required. **Habitat:** like European Wigeon. **Distribution:** breeds in North America; rare visitor to East Asia.   SU

FALCATED TEAL *Anas falcata* L 48cm. In flight both sexes have conspicuous dark green speculum behind pale bar. Bill black; legs grey-brown. **Male:** head is glossy green and reddish-purple with maned crest; white spot on forehead. Throat white; black collar. Body grey with narrow black crescents on breast; cream-yellow patches on both sides of vent; tertials are long and falcated. **Female:** brown overall; uniform colour on unmarked head. **Male eclipse:** like female but upperparts darker. **Similar species:** male Northern Shoveller has white breast, chestnut flanks. **Habitat:** breeds by lowland lakes, marshes; otherwise on lakes, marshes, rivers, sheltered bays. **Distribution:** endemic to East Asia and Far East Russia. Breeds in the north; moves to the south in non-breeding period.   SU

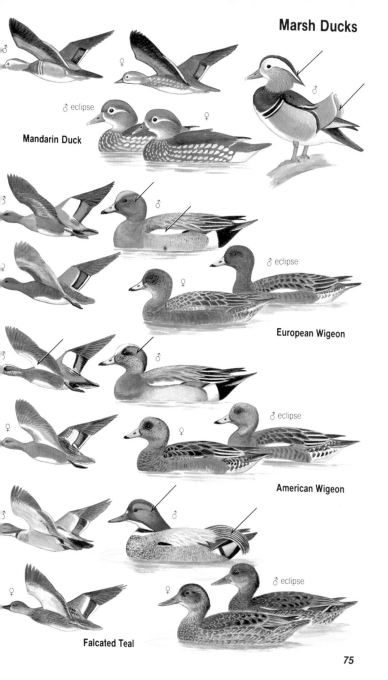

Marsh Ducks

♂ ♀

♂ eclipse ♀

Mandarin Duck

♂

♂

♂

♀

♂ eclipse

♀

European Wigeon

♂

♂

♀

♀

♂ eclipse

American Wigeon

♂

♂

♀

♀

♂ eclipse

Falcated Teal

75

BAIKAL TEAL *Anas formosa* L 40cm. In flight both sexes have white trailing edges to wings, white belly. Bill dark-grey; legs yellowish-grey. **Male:** head has distinctive pattern of cream and metallic green, and vertical stripe on sides of breast and vent are distinctive at a distance. **Female:** Small white oval patch at base of bill; white extends in crescent shape from throat to below the eyes. **Male eclipse:** like female but facial pattern less distinct; sometimes has long, cream-bordered scapulars. **Voice:** "wot-wot-wot". **Similar species:** female Mandarin Duck has white trailing edges to wings, but is greyer with white speculums; legs orange. See female of Green-winged Teal and Garganey. **Habitat:** breeds by marshes in tundra; otherwise on lakes, marshes, rivers. **Distribution:** breeds in tundra of North Asia; moves to north part of East Asia in non-breeding period. SU

GREEN-WINGED TEAL [Common Teal] *Anas crecca* L 37cm. Both sexes have black bill, legs. **Male:** head has a distinct yellow line surrounding green part. Body grey with white horizontal scapular line. On each side of vent, cream yellow patches bordered with black. In flight has green speculum with white greater-coverts, whitish trailing edge. The North American race, *carolinensis*, a rare visitor to East Asia has vertical white line on side of breast but no white scapular line, with indistinct buff line on head. **Female:** two white bars on upperwing are narrow. **Male eclipse:** like female but duller and darker; eye-stripes indistinct. **Voice:** male's call is flute-like "preep" or "krit" female's is loud quack. **Similar species:** male Baikal Teal has distinctive facial pattern, vertical white stripe on side of breast. Female has small white oval patch at base of bill, white throat extending in crescent shape to below eye. Both sexes have white trailing edge to wings. Male Garganey looks whiter overall, has conspicuous white supercilium, blue-grey median wing-coverts. Female has distinct white supercilium and line from lower lores; small pale oval patch at base of bill. **Habitat:** lakes, marshes, rivers, pools. **Distribution:** breeds across North Asia; moves to South Asia, East Asia, north part of South-East Asia in non-breeding period. SU

GREY TEAL *Anas gibberifrons* L 40cm. Crown and nape blackish-brown, speckled with light-brown; throat and chin plain greyish-white; rest of body greyish with brownish edging to feathers on back and dark blotches on underparts. In flight, conspicuous white patch and glossy green speculum. Sexes similar but female smaller and duller. Race *gibberifrons* (not illustrated) darker than race *gracilis,* and has prominent forehead bulge. Race *albogularis* is endemic to Andaman Islands. **Voice:** male whistling and grunts, female decrescendo calls. **Habitat:** freshwater, brackish marshes. **Distribution:** resident in the Andamans and Indonesia. DMP

GARGANEY *Anas querquedula* L 38cm. In flight has conspicuous white bars on each side of speculum; white belly. Bill dark-grey, almost black in male; legs grey. **Male:** black crown; conspicuous white supercilium extends to nape; head otherwise purple-brown. Wing-coverts blue-grey. **Female:** distinct black eyestripe. Small pale oval patch at base of bill. Wing-coverts grey-brown. **Male eclipse:** like female but wing-coverts blue-grey. **Voice:** male gives rattling call "rrrrp"; female quacks. **Habitat:** lakes, marshes, rivers. **Distribution:** breeds in south part of North Asia and north part of Central Asia; moves to South Asia, central and north part of South-East Asia in non-breeding period. SU

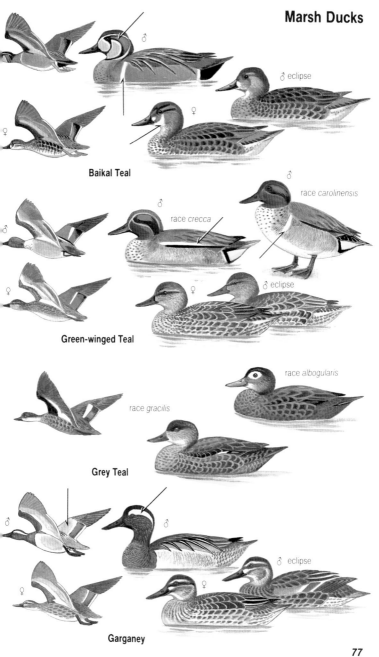

Marsh Ducks

Baikal Teal

♂
♂ eclipse
♀
♀

Green-winged Teal

race *crecca*
race *carolinensis*
♂
♀
♂ eclipse
♂
♂

Grey Teal

race *gracilis*
race *albogularis*

Garganey

♂
♀
♂
♂ eclipse
♀

MALLARD *Anas platyrhynchos* L 59cm. Large bulky duck with longish bill, head, neck. Both sexes in flight show blue speculum with white bars in front and behind; both have orange-red legs. **Male:** head black with metallic-green gloss; white collar; breast dark chestnut. Body greyish-white; uppertail- and undertail-coverts black; tail white with black central tail-feathers curled upwards. Bill yellow to olive. **Female:** brown with dark brown markings; whitish tail; black bill with orange patches on sides. **Male eclipse:** like female, but darker, and more uniform above; bill yellow to olive. **Voice:** male has soft quack; female calls "QUACK-QUACK-quack-quack", descending towards the end. **Similar species:** Spotbill Duck is brown with pale face, and white tertials. Male Falcated Teal has grey-looking body, white throat, black collar. Male Northern Shoveller has white breast, chestnut flanks, large bill. **Habitat:** all kinds of lowland still water from shallow lakes, marshes to sheltered bays. **Distribution:** breeds widely from Central Asia to north part of East Asia; moves to South Asia, north part of South-East Asia, and East Asia in non-breeding period. SU

SPOTBILL DUCK [Spot-billed Duck] *Anas poecilorhyncha* L 60cm. Body brown with dark-brown markings; face pale; bill black with yellow tip; tertials white; legs orange-red. In flight, conspicuous black and white pattern on underwing. South Asian race *poecilorhyncha* has whitish throat, breast; green speculum; male has red patch on forehead. East Asian race *zonorhyncha* has two black lines on face and dark-blue speculum; sexes similar but can be distinguished by colour of uppertail- and undertail-coverts. Race *haringtoni,* which inhabits the intervening regions, closely resembles *poecilorhyncha*. **Voice:** "quack-quack". **Similar species:** female Mallard has black bill with orange sides, white bars in front of and behind speculum, whitish tail. Female Gadwall is slightly smaller, has white secondaries, yellow legs. Female Northern Shoveller has large bill, blue-grey wing-coverts with reddish tinge. **Habitat:** shallow lakes, marshes, pools. **Distribution:** resident in South Asia, north part of South-East Asia, south part of East Asia; north China breeders migrate south in non-breeding period. SU

PACIFIC BLACK DUCK *Anas superciliosa* L 55cm. Large blackish duck with distinctive off-white supercilium and black eye stripe. Crown black; cheek and throat pale-yellow; rest of body feathers dark-brown with light-brown edgings; wings dark-brown with glossy-green speculum and white patch on underwing-coverts. Bill greyish-black; iris brown; legs yellowish-brown. Sexes similar, but female duller. **Voice:** male "raab-raab-raab", female deep descending "kwark-kwark". **Similar species:** Spotbill Duck *race zonorhyncha* has dark-blue speculum, legs orange-red, and browner. Race *haringtoni* brighter, and legs orange-red. **Habitat:** ponds, lakes, marshes, on shore and sometimes seen in mountainous streams up to 3000m. **Distribution:** resident from Indonesia to Australia. DMP

PHILIPPINE DUCK *Anas luzonica* L 50cm. Crown, nape and eye stripe dark-brown. Remainder of head and neck yellowish-brown; most of body greyish-brown; upperparts slightly darker; wings brown with iridescent green superculum. Bill greyish-blue; iris brown; legs brownish-black. Sexes similar. **Voice:** "quack-quack". **Similar species:** see Mallard, Spotbill Duck. **Habitat:** rivers, lakes, tidal creeks, small ponds. **Distribution:** endemic to the Philippines. DMP

Marsh Ducks

♂
♀
♂ eclipse

♂
♀
Mallard

race poecilorhyncha
♂
♀
♂

race zonorhyncha
♂
♀
♂
Spotbill Duck

Pacific Black Duck

Philippine Duck

NORTHERN PINTAIL [Pintail, Common Pintail] *Anas acuta* L 75cm (male), 53cm (female). Slender body with long neck and bill. Male's long black tail distinctive; female's tail also longer than other species. Both sexes have grey underwings. **Male:** head and hindneck chocolate-brown; back and flanks grey; scapulars black broadly edged grey; foreneck, breast and underparts white; narrow white stripe from breast up side of head. Upper-tail- and undertail-coverts black; sides of vent cream-yellow. In flight, green speculum with buff bar in front, white bar behind. Bill black with dark blue-grey sides; legs lead-grey. **Female:** brown with dark brown markings; bill black with grey sides. In flight, brown speculum with white bar behind. **Male eclipse:** like female, but bill colour differs. **Voice:** weak "proop-proop" or "whee". **Similar species:** female Falcated Teal has black bill. Female Mallard has black bill with orange sides. **Habitat:** breeds by open lakes etc; otherwise on lakes, marshes, rivers. **Distribution:** breeds widely in North Asia; moves to South Asia, north part of South-East Asia, south and central parts of East Asia in non-breeding period.   SU

GADWALL *Anas strepera* L 50cm. Plumage dull, rather uniformly-coloured. **Male:** head and neck grey-brown, darker at rear; body dark-grey; small black crescents on breast; rump, uppertail- and undertail-coverts black; belly white; bill black. Median coverts reddish-brown; greater coverts black; central secondaries white and visible at rest. **Female:** brown with dark brown markings; bill black with well-defined orange-yellow sides. **Male eclipse:** like female, including bill, but darker. **Similar species:** female Mallard larger with blue secondaries, orange legs. Spotbill Duck larger with paler face, black belly, black bill with yellow tip, orange-red legs. **Habitat:** open lakes, marshes, rivers in lowlands. **Distribution:** breeds from Central Asia to north part of East Asia; moves to north part of South Asia, and East Asia in non-breeding period.   SU

NORTHERN SHOVELER [Shoveler] *Anas clypeata* L 50cm. Heavy-looking with huge conspicuous spatulate black bill. **Male:** head black with green gloss; breast, sides of vent and scapulars white; iris yellow; flanks and belly chestnut; uppertail- and undertail-coverts black; tail white. Wing-coverts blue-grey; secondaries green. **Female:** brown with dark brown markings; whitish tail; iris black; upperwing duller than male. **Male eclipse:** like female, but head blackish, iris yellow. **Similar species:** male Mallard has dark-chestnut breast, grey flanks. Shelduck larger with chestnut breast, black belly-stripe, red bill. **Habitat:** lowland still water, lakes, rivers. **Distribution:** breeds in North Asia; moves to South Asia, northern South-East Asia, and East Asia in non-breeding period.   SU

MARBLED TEAL *Marmaronetta angustirostris* L 40cm. Pale grey head and neck with brown markings and dark-brown patch around eye extending towards nape, and with short crest. Body creamy-white and greyish-brown, spotted and mottled creating a marbled effect; wings brown with pale secondaries; belly and undertail-coverts whitish and tail light-brown. Bill greyish-black; iris brown; legs olive-brown. Sexes similar but female has shorter crest and paler eye stripe. **Juvenile:** duller, less spotted flanks, paler nape. **Voice:** male gives a wheezing squeak, female a feeble quack. **Similar species:** see Green-winged Teal and Garganey. **Habitat:** freshwater lakes and ponds, brackish pools, marshes. **Distribution:** resident in west part of South Asia.   DMP

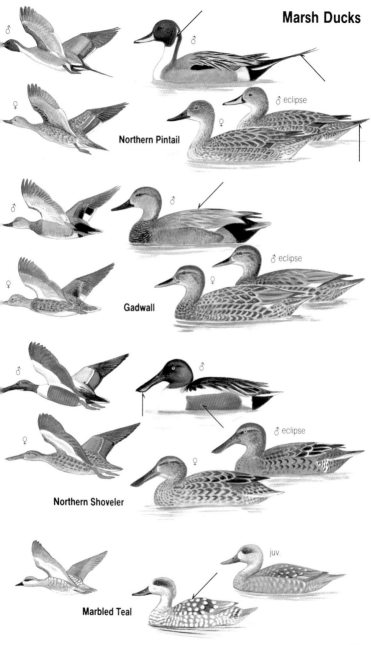

Marsh Ducks

♂

♀

Northern Pintail

♂

♀   ♂ eclipse

♂

♀

Gadwall

♂

♀   ♂ eclipse

♂

♀

Northern Shoveler

♂

♀   ♂ eclipse

juv.

Marbled Teal

Diving Ducks

Diving and swimming underwater to feed on small aquatic animals and plants, Flight is attained by running for take-off. Generally form huge flocks in non-breeding period. **SU**

PINK-HEADED DUCK *Rhodonessa caryophyllacea* L 60cm. **Male:** brownish-black upper- and underparts. Tufted head, nape and bill bright-pink. **Female:** overall blackish-brown. Head merely suffused with pink, and not sharply demarcated as in male. **Habitat:** marshes, and pools among elephant grass jungle. **Distribution:** Formerly recorded in India, current status is little known; possibly extinct. **BB**

RED-CRESTED POCHARD *Netta rufina* L 50cm. Large duck with round head, longish neck. In flight, both sexes show conspicuous large white band on upperwing, white underwing. **Male:** head golden-chestnut; neck, underparts, uppertail- and undertail-coverts black; tail grey-brown; flanks white; back grey-brown; iris, bill and legs red; white shoulder-line. **Female:** brown with dark brown cap, hindneck; cheeks and throat pale; underparts grey-brown with some barring; iris brown; bill dark with pink edges and band near tip. **Male eclipse:** like female, but mottled whitish on breast, and with red iris, bill, legs. **Similar species:** male Pochard smaller with blackish bill and legs, and grey wing-stripe. Female Pochard is browner overall with different facial-pattern. **Habitat:** lakes, marshes, inlets. **Distribution:** breeds in west part of Central Asia; moves to north parts of South and South-East Asia in non-breeding period. **SU**

CANVASBACK *Aythya valisineria* L 55cm. Large duck with long bill; profile shows smooth slope from peaked crown to tip of bill. In flight, wings of both sexes whitish above and below, but female's darker. **Male:** head and neck reddish-brown; forehead and throat blackish; breast, upper-tail- and undertail-coverts black; body whitish-grey above and below; iris red; bill black; legs grey. **Female:** from head to neck and breast brown; pale on face and around eyes; iris brown; upperparts brownish-grey; underparts grey; rump and tail dark-brown. **Male eclipse:** like female, but browner overall. **Similar species:** both sexes similar to Common Pochard, but latter's body and bill smaller; shape of head differs; male is browner; wing-stripe grey. **Habitat:** lakes, marshes, inlets, bays. **Distribution:** breeds in North America; rare visitor to East Asia. **SU**

COMMON POCHARD *Aythya ferina* L 45cm. Both sexes have grey wing-stripe; female's upperwing-coverts browner than male's. **Male:** head and neck reddish-brown; breast, uppertail- and undertail-coverts black; body grey; iris red; bill black with pale-grey band near tip. **Female:** head and neck brown; pale yellowish-brown lines round and behind eyes; iris brown; body grey-brown; rump, uppertail- and undertail-coverts and tail dark grey-brown. **Male elcipse:** like normal male plumage, but duller. **Similar species:** both sexes similar to Redhead, but latter has rounder head, steeper forehead, smooth crown; male has yellow iris, tricoloured bill; female's plumage is more uniform, warm-brown in colour; in flight, some secondaries pale, wings otherwise dark. **Habitat:** lakes, marshes, rivers, pools. **Distribution:** breeds in west part of Central Asia; moves to north part of South-East Asia, and East Asia in non-breeding period. **SU**

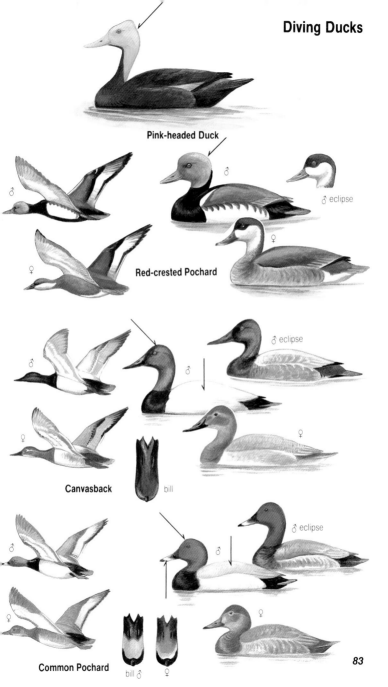

Diving Ducks

Pink-headed Duck

♂
♀
♂
♂ eclipse
♀

Red-crested Pochard

♂
♀
♂
♂ eclipse
♀

Canvasback

bill

♂
♀
♂
♂ eclipse
♀

Common Pochard

bill ♂   ♀

REDHEAD *Aythya americana* L 49cm. Round head, steep forehead, smooth crown. In flight, both sexes show conspicuous pale-grey secondaries. **Male:** head and neck reddish-brown; breast and upper mantle black; uppertail- and undertail-coverts, rump, tail blackish; body grey; bill grey with black tip and narrow white band in middle; iris yellow. **Female:** brown with dark brown crown and back, pale chin and throat, pale lines round and behind eyes; iris dark brown; uppertail- and undertail-coverts often whitish. **Male eclipse:** browner and duller; iris yellow. **Similar species:** see Common Pochard. **Habitat:** brackish lakes, marshes, inlets, bays. **Distribution:** breeds in North America; rare visitor to East Asia.   SU

RING-NECKED DUCK *Aythya collaris* L 40cm. In flight, both sexes show dark grey wing-bar. **Male:** head black with purple gloss; rear crown looks swollen. Upperparts black; underparts white; flanks pale grey with faint vermiculation; distinct white vertical bar between flanks and breast; blue-grey bill with broad white band and black tip; iris yellow. **Female:** dark brown from head to back; white spectacles round eyes; base of bill and throat pale; iris dark. **Male eclipse:** like female, but no white spectacles; blackish head, breast. **Similar species:** male Tufted Duck has long crest, different bill-pattern, white flanks; female has different face-pattern, yellow iris, white wing-bar. Male Greater Scaup has grey back; female has clear white patch at base of bill, iris yellow, white wing-bar. **Habitat:** lakes, marshes, brackish inlets, bays. **Distribution:** breeds in North America; rare visitor to East Asia.   SU

BAER'S POCHARD *Aythya baeri* L 45cm. Round head; relatively long bill with black oval nail lengthwise. In flight, both sexes show distinct white wing-bar. Belly white extending onto fore flanks. **Male:** head black with greenish gloss; small white spot on chin; breast dark reddish-brown; flanks brown; upperparts dark brown; undertail-coverts white; iris white. **Female:** head, breast, upperparts dark-brown; pale-brown oval patch at base of bill; flanks brown; belly white; iris brown. **Male eclipse:** like female, but iris white. **Similar species:** Ferruginous Duck somewhat smaller; bill looks smaller; flanks all reddish-brown, never have white extending onto them from belly. See Tufted Duck. **Habitat:** shallow lakes, marshes, sometimes inlets, bays. **Distribution:** breeds in south-east North Asia, north-east China; moves to East China, south of Yangtze River and northern South-East Asia and a small number are regularly found in east part of South Asia in non-breeding period.   SU

FERRUGINOUS DUCK [White-eyed Pochard] *Aythya nyroca* L 41cm. In flight, both sexes show distinct white wing-bar. **Male:** dark-chestnut from head to breast; small white spot on chin; back, uppertail-coverts, tail dark brown; flanks reddish-brown; belly white; sides of vental regions blackish, contrasting with white undertail-coverts; iris white. **Female:** like male, but duller, brown all over; iris brown. **Male eclipse:** like female, but iris white. **Similar species:** see Baer's Pochard. **Habitat:** mainly breeds by shallow lowland lakes; otherwise on lakes, marshes, slow rivers, sometimes inlets and bays. **Distribution:** breeds from west part of Central Asia westwards; moves to north part of South Asia in non-breeding period.   SU

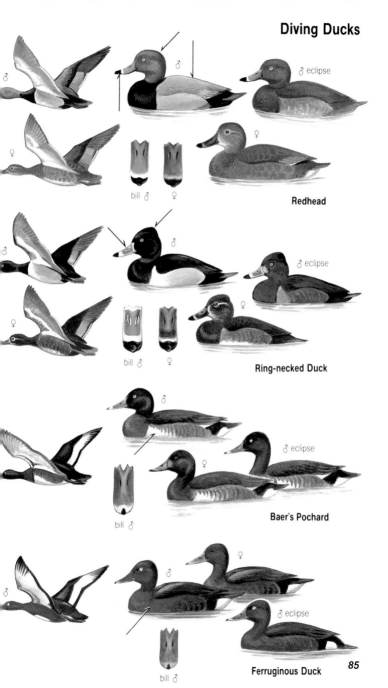

Diving Ducks

♂

♀

♂

bill ♂ ♀

♂ eclipse

♀

Redhead

♂

♀

♂

bill ♂ ♀

♂ eclipse

♀

Ring-necked Duck

♂

bill ♂

♀

♂ eclipse

Baer's Pochard

♂

♂

♀

bill ♂

♂ eclipse

Ferruginous Duck

85

AUSTRALIAN WHITE-EYED DUCK *Aythya australis* L 50cm. Medium-sized chocolate-brown duck. Upperwings brown with white band across base of primaries and secondaries; underwing whitish; belly and undertail-coverts white. Bill greyish-black with broad pale blue band near tip; legs grey. **Male:** distinctive white eye. **Female:** duller with brown iris and narrower band on bill. **Voice:** male soft whistle, female gruff croak. **Habitat:** deep freshwater lakes, marshes, fast-flowing water. **Distribution:** rare visitor to eastern part of Indonesia from Australia. DMP

TUFTED DUCK *Aythya fuligula* L 40cm. Rounded head; on rear crown male has drooping crest, female short one; neck looks short; iris yellow. Both sexes have black upperwings with broad white wing-bar; underwings whitish. **Male:** head black with purple gloss; belly, flanks white; otherwise black; bill blue-grey with black tip and usually narrow white line just behind tip. **Female:** dark-brown overall, mixed with cinnamon on mantle and breast; belly white; flanks variably mottled pale; often white patch at base of bill; some have white undertail-coverts; bill darker than male. **Male eclipse:** darker than female when with white mottling on flanks. **Similar species:** male Greater Scaup has green gloss on head, no crest, light grey back. Female is a little larger, has larger white patch at base of bill, no crest. Male Baer's Pochard had green gloss on head, reddish-brown breast, browner body, white iris. Female is browner overall, has pale oval patch at base of bill, brown iris. **Habitat:** lakes, marshes, pools, rivers. **Distribution:** breeds widely in North Asia; moves to north parts of South and South-East Asia, and East Asia in non-breeding period. SU

GREATER SCAUP [Scaup Duck] *Aythya marila* L 45cm. Broad-bodied with large bill; steep forehead, peak of head in front of eyes, head sloping smoothly down at back; iris yellow. Both sexes have black upperwings, broad white wing-bar; underwings whitish. **Male:** head black with greenish gloss; breast black; back looks pale grey; flanks, belly white; bill blue-grey with small black triangular nail at tip. **Female:** head dark-brown with large white patch at base of bill. Ear-coverts white in summer; some birds retain trace of this in winter. Breast, back brown; flanks yellow-brown mixed with white; belly white; bill darker than male. **Male eclipse:** browner overall than normal male; belly and flanks grey-brown; touch of white at base of bill. **Similar species:** Lesser Scaup smaller with different head-shape (peak at rear of eyes), smaller rectangular nail on bill, white on upperwing limited to secondaries; male has blacker back. See Tufted Duck. **Habitat:** sheltered bays, estuaries, inlets. **Distribution:** breeds in North Asia; moves to East Asia in non-breeding period. SU

LESSER SCAUP *Aythya affinis* L 42cm. Distinctive head-shape with high rear-crown; iris yellow. Both sexes have black upperwings, white second-aries; whitish underwings. **Male:** head black with purple gloss; breast, uppertail- and undertail-coverts and tail black; flanks whitish; back looks pale grey; bill blue-grey with small black rectangular nail at tip. **Female:** head dark brown, white at base of bill; breast and back dark brown; flanks brown; bill darker than male. **Male eclipse:** browner overall than normal male; pale patch at base of bill. **Similar species:** see Greater Scaup. **Habitat:** lakes, marshes, rivers. **Distribution:** breeds in North America; rare visitor to East Asia. SU

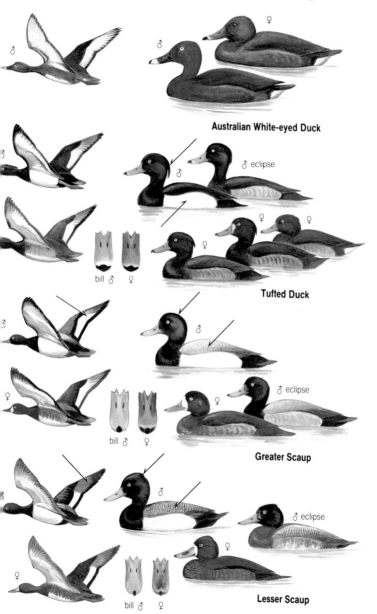

Australian White-eyed Duck

Tufted Duck

Greater Scaup

Lesser Scaup

bill ♂ ♀

BUFFLEHEAD *Bucephala albeola* L 35.5cm. **Male:** head black with greenish and purple gloss; large white patch starting just below eyes and extending round hindcrown. In flight, shows black primaries and leading edges, white scapulars, wing-coverts and secondaries. **Female:** head and upperparts greyish-brown; white patch just behind eye; underparts whitish grey-brown; in flight, only secondaries and a part of greater coverts are white. **Male eclipse:** like female, but larger white patch on head, and more white on wings. **Similar species:** male Common Goldeneye larger, with white patch near base of bill; female has no white patch on head, does have white collar. Female Smew has white cheeks. **Habitat:** lakes/marshes near seas, estuaries. **Distribution:** Breeds in North America; rare visitor to eastern North Asia and northern East Asia.
SU

COMMON GOLDENEYE *Bucephala clangula* L 45cm. **Male:** head triangular, black with greenish gloss; white patch near base of bill; outer scapulars predominantly white with black edges; short black bill. In flight, shows black primaries, forewings; white wing-coverts and secondaries. **Female:** head greyish-brown; white collar; body grey; bill black with yellow band at tip. In flight, shows black primaries, white secondaries and coverts, and dark line between greater coverts and forewing. **Male eclipse:** like female, but head darker with washed-white patch; back, flanks browner. **Similar species:** see Bufflehead. **Habitat:** sheltered bays, rivers, lakes, marshes. **Distribution:** breeds in North Asia; moves to East Asia in non-breeding period.
SU

WHITE-HEADED DUCK [White-headed Stiff-tailed Duck] *Oxyura leucocephala* L 45cm. Stiff-tailed duck with swollen base of bill. **Male:** white head with black crown, nape and collar; upperparts greyish-chestnut, uppertail-coverts greyish-brown. Bill bright-blue; legs dark-grey. **Female:** crown, nape and sides of head stripe dark-brown, cheek and throat buff. Bill bluish-grey; legs black. **Male eclipse:** like normal adult male, but less chestnut on body and greyish bill. **Immatuare male:** whole head black with bright-blue bill. **Juvenile:** similar to female but duller; juvenile male has dirty white face. **Voice:** male utters rattling and high pitched piping call, female gives a quiet "gek". **Habitat:** brackish or freshwater marshes with dense vegetation. **Distribution:** rare visitor to South Asia from West Asia.
DMP

LONG-TAILED DUCK [Old Squaw] *Clangula hyemalis* L 60cm (male), 38cm (female). Rounded head with short bill. Wings black. Male has long pointed tail. Moult sequence differs from other ducks; two main plumages described here. **Winter male:** white from head to neck; pale greyish-brown around eye; blackish-brown cheeks. Breast, most upperparts and tail black; scapulars, white. Bill black with fleshy-pink band; legs bluish-grey. **Winter female:** crown, cheeks blackish-brown. Face and upperpart of neck white; breast, upperparts, tail black. Bill, legs grey. **Summer male:** white surround to eye; head, neck, breast, upperparts blackish-brown. Scapulars have black centres and tawny-buff fringes. **Summer female:** head and neck largely dusky, with narrow whitish area around eye, sides of head and neck. **Voice:** distinctive; "owa-owaa". **Habitat:** breeds by freshwater lakes in tundra; otherwise on bays, coasts. **Distribution:** breeds in North Asia; moves to east part of North Asia and north part of East Asia in non-breeding period.
SU

Diving Ducks

♂

♂

♀

♂ eclipse

Bufflehead

♂

♂ eclipse

♀

Common Goldeneye

♀

♂ eclipse   ♂ imm.   ♀

♂   juv.

White-headed Duck

♂ winter

♂ summer

♀ summer

♂ winter

♀ winter

Long-tailed Duck

♀ winter

Mergansers

Diving ducks feeding mainly on fish. Bills slender with hooked tips and serrated edges.

SU

SMEW *Mergus albellus* L 42cm. Has smaller bill, smaller crest than other mergansers. Bill, legs blue-grey. **Male:** looks almost all-white, but in flight shows black primaries and back. **Female:** slightly smaller than male; body grey; distinguished by chestnut cap and white cheeks. **Male eclipse:** like female, but slightly bigger, cap redder, no black on lores, back blacker in flight. **Similar species:** non-breeding Slavonian Grebe has black cap, lower forehead; profile shows smooth curve joining cap and straight bill. See Bufflehead. **Habitat:** breeds close to rivers in lowland forests; otherwise on lakes, rivers etc. **Distribution:** breeds in east part of North Asia; moves to East Asia in non-breeding period.

SU

RED-BREASTED MERGANSER *Mergus serrator* L 55cm. Has long thin bill, thin neck and divided shaggy crest. Bill, legs red. **Male:** head greenish-black; breast chestnut with black spots; white collar. In flight, black primaries, two black bars on upperwing. **Female:** pale chestnut from head to neck; ill-defined white throat. In flight, primaries blackish, lesser coverts grey. **Male eclipse:** like female, but back and scapulars blacker; in flight same wing-pattern as normal adult male. **Similar species:** male Goosander has no crest, white breast and flanks; female is larger with thicker bill and neck, brighter chestnut head, which is sharply demarcated from white on neck. Male Chinese Merganser has larger crest, white breast; female has longer crest, thicker bill and neck, whitish breast; both sexes have distinct scaling on flanks. **Habitat:** breeds by rivers etc in forest zones; otherwise on seas, lakes etc. **Distribution:** breeds in east part of North Asia; moves to East Asia in non-breeding period.

SU

CHINESE MERGANSER [Scaly-sided Merganser] *Mergus squamatus* L 57cm. Both sexes in flight show black primaries, two black bars on upperwing. Scaling on flanks. Rump and vent grey with scaling in male, fine markings in female. Bill thick and red with yellow tip; legs red. **Male:** head greenish-black with long shaggy crest. **Female:** head rufous, crest shorter than male. **Immature male:** like female, but some black marks on head, and lesser coverts grey. **Similar species:** see Red-breasted Merganser. **Habitat:** breeds by rivers in forest zones; otherwise on rivers and lakes. **Distribution:** breeds from north-east China to part of southern Far East Russia; recorded in non-breeding period from Japan, Taiwan, Yangtze River basin, Korean Peninsula and Thailand.

SU

GOOSANDER [Common Merganser] *Mergus merganser* L 65cm. Largest merganser. Both sexes have grey rump, red bill with black nail and red legs. **Male:** head greenish-black with no crest; body white except black back and scapulars. In flight shows black primaries, white wing-coverts and secondaries. **Female:** head rufous with short crest; throat and breast white, sharply demarcated from rufous head. In flight, primaries black, wing-coverts grey, secondaries white. **Male eclipse:** like female, but crest even shorter, usually has white line from lores to bill. **Similar species:** see Red-breasted Merganser. **Habitat:** breeds by rivers etc in forest zones; otherwise, on rivers, lakes. **Distribution:** breeds in North Asia; moves to East Asia, north part of South Asia in non-breeding period.

SU

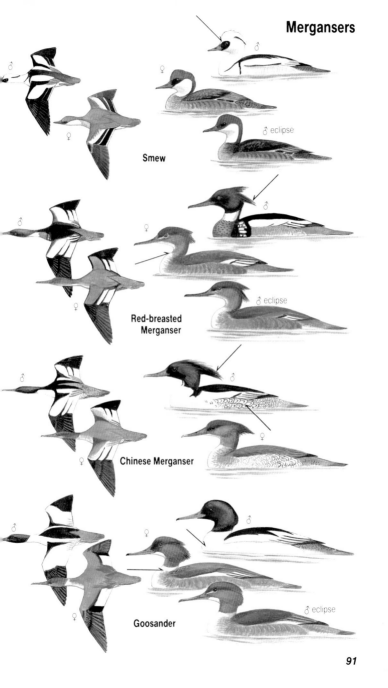

Mergansers

Smew

♂

♀

♂ eclipse

Red-breasted
Merganser

♂

♀

♂ eclipse

Chinese Merganser

♂

♀

Goosander

♀

♂

♂ eclipse

91

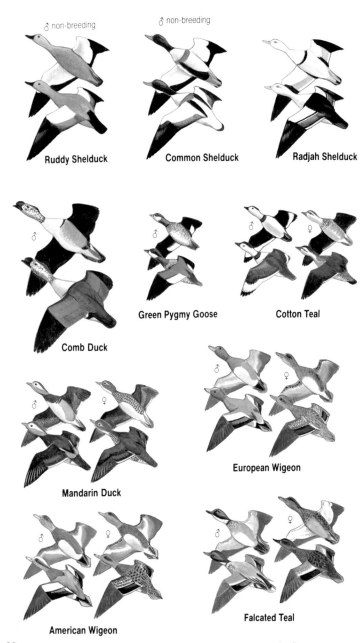

♂ non-breeding

♂ non-breeding

Ruddy Shelduck

Common Shelduck

Radjah Shelduck

♂

♂

♂

♀

Comb Duck

Green Pygmy Goose

Cotton Teal

♂

♀

Mandarin Duck

♂

♀

European Wigeon

♂

♀

American Wigeon

♂

♀

Falcated Teal

Ducks in Flight

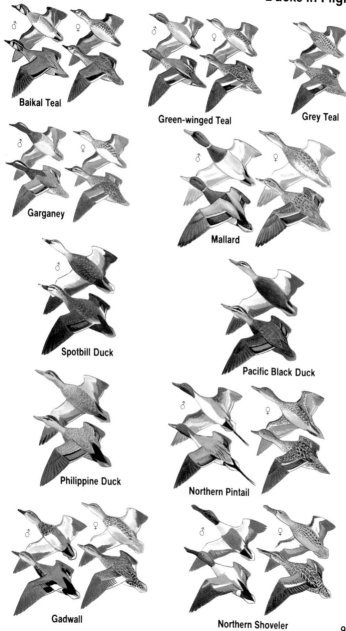

Baikal Teal

Green-winged Teal

Grey Teal

Garganey

Mallard

Spotbill Duck

Pacific Black Duck

Philippine Duck

Northern Pintail

Gadwall

Northern Shoveler

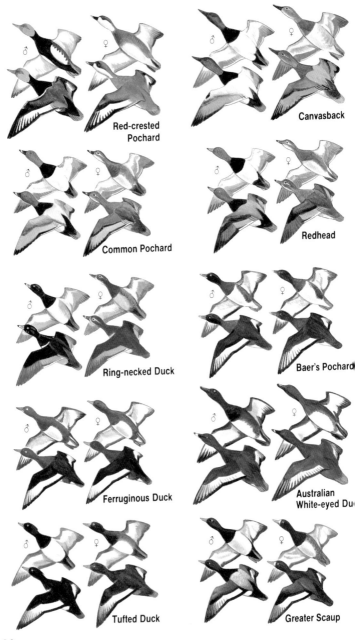

Red-crested Pochard

Canvasback

Common Pochard

Redhead

Ring-necked Duck

Baer's Pochard

Ferruginous Duck

Australian White-eyed Duck

Tufted Duck

Greater Scaup

Ducks in Flight

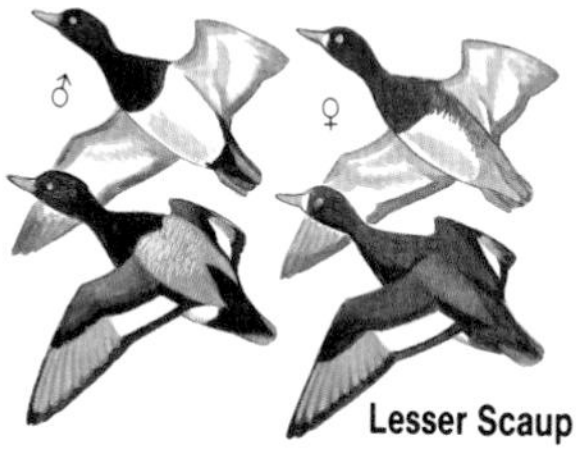

Lesser Scaup

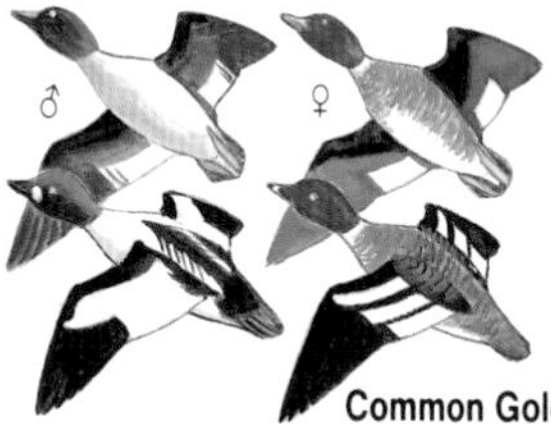

Common Goldeneye

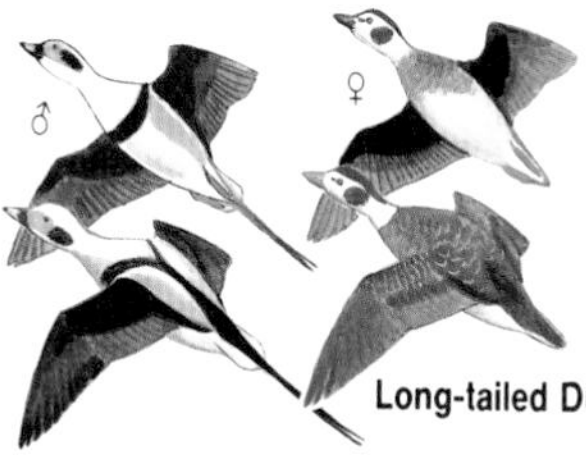

Long-tailed Duck

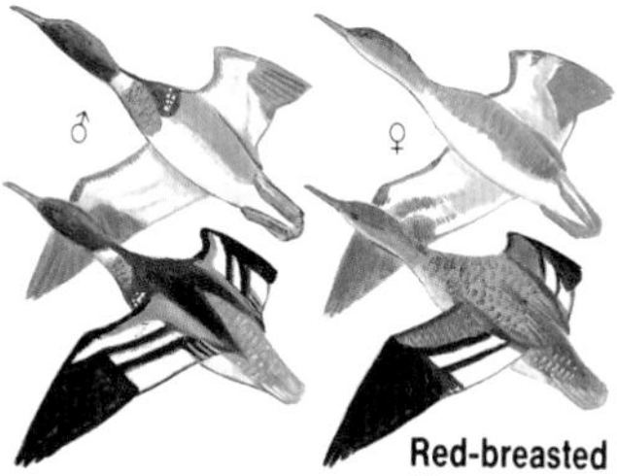

Red-breasted Merganser

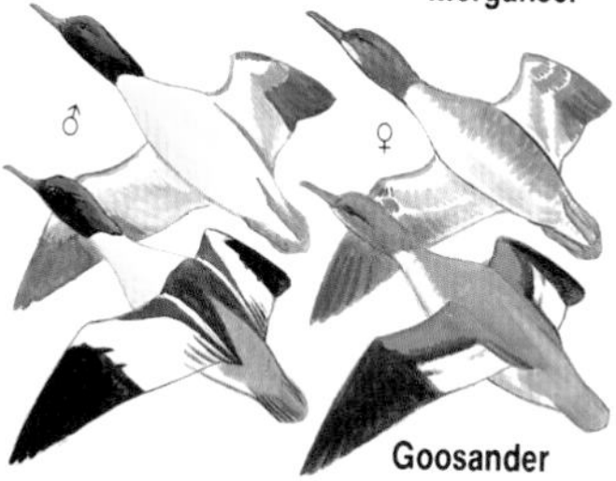

Goosander

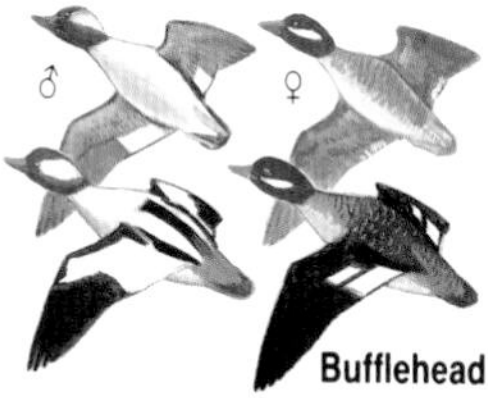

Bufflehead

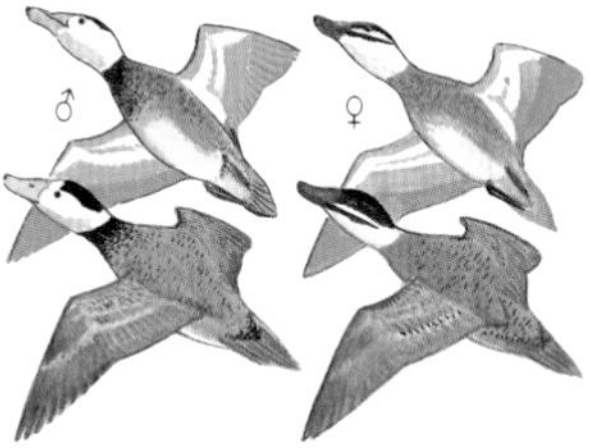

White-headed Duck

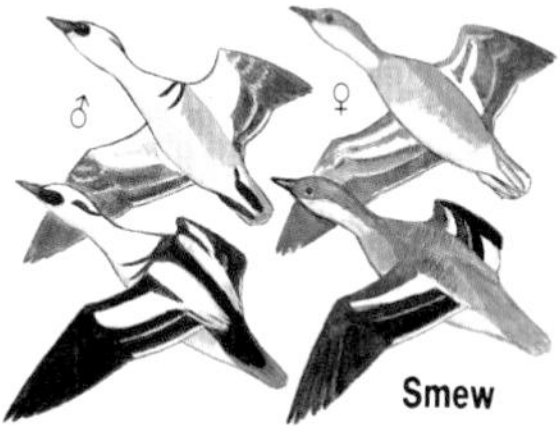

Smew

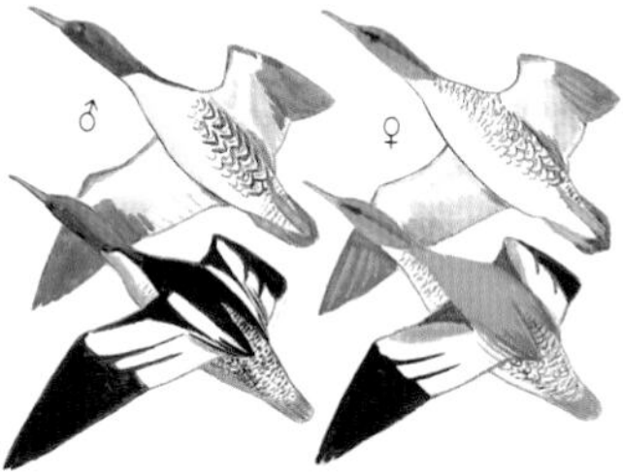

Chinese Merganser

Cranes

Family *Gruidae* (World: 15 species; Asia: 9 species) Large birds with long bills, necks, legs. Sexes similar, but females slightly smaller. SU

COMMON CRANE *Grus grus* L 114cm. Grey-brown overall. Red skin exposed on crown. White stripe from behind eye down side of neck contrasts with black stripe from throat down foreneck. Bill greenish-yellow; legs black. In flight sharp contrast between black flight-feathers and grey wing-coverts. **Immature:** grey overall with black on lores, throat. **Voice:** piercing "kurr" or "krrooah". **Similar species:** Demoiselle Crane smaller; black on neck extends to breast. Hooded Crane has all-white neck; wings all slaty-black. Grey Heron is more delicate overall, flies with neck retracted, has brownish legs. See Japanese White-naped Crane. **Habitat:** breeds in marshes of taiga; otherwise on grasslands, farmlands, lakes and rivers. **Distribution:** breeds in North Asia; moves to South Asia, central and south parts of East Asia in non-breeding period. SU

BLACK-NECKED CRANE *Grus nigricollis* L 139cm. Tall crane with black head and neck. Lores and entire crown naked and dull red; small patch of white feathers below and behind eye. In flight, primaries, secondaries and tail black. **Immature:** buff/brownish head and neck, otherwise plumage slightly paler than that of adult, smaller than adult. **Voice:** loud and trumpet-like, resemble those of other cranes. **Habitat:** open grasslands, rice-fields, marshes, lakes. **Distribution:** endemic to Tibetan Plateau. BB

HOODED CRANE *Grus monacha* L 97cm. Head and neck white, except red skin exposed on crown and black skin on forehead, lores. Bill greenish-yellow; legs blackish-brown. Wings slaty-black with dark flight-feathers. **Immature:** like adult, but body blacker, head stained rusty, black mark around eye. **Voice:** adult calls "kurrk" or "kurr"; immature "piii". **Similar species:** see Common Crane. **Habitat:** breeds in marshes of taiga; otherwise on grasslands, farmlands etc. **Distribution:** breeds in north-east China, Far East Russia; moves to east China, south Japan and Korean Peninsula in non-breeding period. SU

SANDHILL CRANE *Grus canadensis* L 95cm. Red skin exposed on crown, forehead, lores. Throat, cheeks dirty white. Primaries blackish. Bill, legs black. **Immature:** brown head, neck; grey body has feathers tipped brownish. **Voice:** "kurrk" or "kurr". **Habitat:** breeds by lakes, marshes in tundra; otherwise on farmlands, grasslands. **Distribution:** breeds in north-east North Asia and North America; rare visitor to central part of East Asia. SU

MANCHURIAN CRANE [Red-crowned Crane] *Grus japonensis* L 140cm. Red skin exposed on crown, black on forehead, lores. Throat, neck black; white from behind eyes to back of head. Wings white with black secondaries, tertials. At rest, long tertials cover white tail-feathers. Bill greenish-yellow; legs black. **Immature:** like adult, but primaries and greater primary coverts have dark-brown tips. **Voice:** piercing "kurrk". **Similar species:** Great White Crane has white head, red face; black primaries, white secondaries; legs fleshy-pink. **Habitat:** breeds in open marshes; otherwise on farmlands, grasslands. **Distribution:** breeds in north-east China, south part of Far East Russia; moves to Korean Peninsula, east China in non-breeding period. Resident in Hokkaido (Japan). SU

Cranes

Common Crane

imm.

Black-necked Crane

Hooded Crane

imm.

Sandhill Crane

imm.

Manchurian Crane

imm.

imm.

JAPANESE WHITE-NAPED CRANE [White-naped Crane] *Grus vipio* L 127cm.
Body dark-grey; long, narrow tongues of dark-grey extend from breast
halfway up sides of neck. Red skin exposed from forehead to around eyes;
rest of head, throat, hindneck, upper foreneck white. Wing-coverts blue-
grey, flight-feathers black; tertials long, white. Bill greenish-yellow; legs
pink. **Immature:** head partly brown; brownish streaks on upperparts. **Voice:**
"kruuu"; immature "piii". **Similar species:** Common Crane has red crown,
black stripe on neck, black legs. Demoiselle Crane is small with black
foreneck. **Habitat:** breeds in marshes; otherwise on farmlands, grasslands.
Distribution: breeds in north-east China, east Mongolia, south part of Far
East Russia; moves to Japan, east China, Korean Peninsula in non-
breeding period.   SU

SARUS CRANE *Grus antigone* L 152cm. Large grey crane. Grey with
naked red head and upper neck; primaries black, secondaries grey and
tertials grey with broad white tips. **Immature:** brownish-grey overall; head
and neck covered with short rusty buff cinnamon-brown feathers. Race
antigone, western population, has white neck-collar, race *sharpii*, eastern
population, lacks white neck-collar and darker than *antigone*. **Voice:** loud
sonorous far-carrying trumpeting, usually as a duet by paired birds.
Habitat: marshes, ponds, lakes, rice-fields. **Distribution:** race *antigone*
resident in South Asia, race *sharpii* very localised in South-East Asia and
Australia.   BB

GREAT WHITE CRANE [Siberian Crane] *Grus leucogeranus* L 135cm.
Almost all-white. Red bare skin on forehead, forecrown and around eye.
Primaries and primary coverts black; but not visible when bird is at rest, so
it looks all-white. Bill is long, thick, dark-pink; legs fleshy-pink. **Immature:**
head, neck, wing-coverts, tertials are yellowish-brown. **Similar species:**
White Stork and Oriental White Stork have all flight-feathers black; at rest
this makes rear part of body look black. See Manchurian Crane. **Habitat:**
breeds in low tundra in the Arctic; shallow marshes in non-breeding
period. **Distribution:** breeds in part of North Asia; moves mainly to Lake
Poyang (China). Non-breeding population at Bharatpur, India, breeds far
west of North Asia.   SU

DEMOISELLE CRANE *Anthropoides virgo* L 95cm. Small, graceful crane.
Ash-grey crown and body. Face to neck black; long black plumes hang
down from foreneck. White drooping tufts from behind eye. Primaries,
primary coverts, secondaries black; tertials grey with black tips. At rest
elongated tertials cover blue-grey tail. Bill olive-grey with pink tip. Legs
grey-black. **Immature:** like adult, but colours of head/neck duller; tertials
and neck plumes shorter; body has brown tinge. **Voice:** "krruorr". **Habitat:**
breeds in dry grasslands up to 3000m; otherwise on farmlands, reservoirs,
lakes, rivers. **Distribution:** breeds in Central Asia; moves mainly to South
Asia in non-breeding period.   SU

Cranes

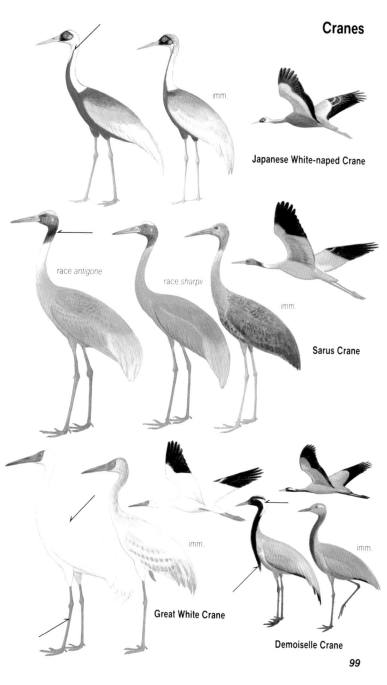

imm.

Japanese White-naped Crane

race antigone

race sharpii

imm.

Sarus Crane

imm.

Great White Crane

imm.

Demoiselle Crane

99

Rails and Coots

Family *Rallidae* (World: 124 species; Asia: 34 species) Small to large-sized crepuscular or diurnal marsh birds. Walk, run and swim well but fly very poorly with legs dangling, although some species are long distance migrants. Long legs with very strong toes, and in some species toes webbed partially. Wings short and rounded. Cock short tail upwards. Sexes similar in most species.   DMP

CHESTNUT-BELLIED RAIL *Eulabeornis castaneoventris* L 51cm. Large rail with head and nape grey; mantle and back olive; wings, tail and underparts chestnut. Bill greenish-yellow with greyish-white tip; iris red; legs yellowish-green. **Voice:** loud resonant trumpeting. **Similar species:** Bare-eyed Rail is smaller, head is chestnut. **Habitat:** thick mangrove forest. **Distribution:** endemic to Aru Islands, Indonesia.   DMP

BARE-EYED RAIL *Eulabeornis plumbeiventris* L 32cm. Medium size forest rail with pinkish patch of bare skin around eyes. Head, upper breast and back chestnut; throat pale-chestnut; wings olive-green; breast and belly dull-grey; flanks blackish; rump and tail black. Bill yellowish-green; iris brown; legs pinkish-red. **Similar species:** Red-necked Crake is smaller, darker on mantle and barred on flanks. **Habitat:** primary forest floor; marshes, wet grassy areas near lowland rivers or lakes. **Distribution:** endemic to Maluk Islands, Indonesia.   DMP

BALD-FACED RAIL *Eulabeornis rosenbergii* L 30cm. Medium-sized rail with bald cobalt-blue face. Head, neck and belly greyish-black; wings, mantle and back purplish-chestnut; rump and tail black. Bill pale cobalt-blue; iris brownish-red; legs brownish-grey. **Habitat:** primary forest, rice-fields. **Distribution:** endemic to Sulawesi Island, Indonesia.   DMP

PLATEN'S RAIL *Rallus plateni* L ?cm. Rare and little known rail. Upper-parts olive-brown with dull bluish-grey on scapulars and mantle; mid crown and nape dark-brown; lower nape and rump chestnut; chin and throat white; face, foreneck and breast grey; flanks barred black-and-white; belly dusky barred white; tail dull. Bill brownish- and yellowish-green; iris brown legs black. **Habitat:** dense lianas and bamboos; secondary growth on edge of forest. **Distribution:** endemic to Sulawesi Island, Indonesia.   DMP

WALLACE'S RAIL *Rallus wallacii* L ?cm. Dark flightless rail. Head and neck dark bluish-grey; back and rump dark brown; wings brownish-grey with blackish primaries; tail blackish-brown; underparts brighter than upperparts. Bill and iris bright red. **Habitat:** marshes. **Distribution:** endemic to Halmahera Island, Indonesia.   DMP

BUFF-BANDED RAIL *Rallus philippensis* L 30cm. Medium-sized. Head brown with pale grey supercilium; throat and foreneck greyish-white; back and wings streaked black and reddish-brown with mottled white; breast band buff; underparts barred black-and-white; tail browish-black with yellowish margins and white spots. Bill reddish-brown; iris red; legs olive-brown. **Voice:** creaking "swit-swit" and squeak "krek-krek-krek". **Similar species:** Blue-breasted Banded Rail is smaller and lacks supercilium and buff breast band. **Habitat:** rice-fields, mangroves, marshes; grassy uplands. **Distribution:** resident in South-East Asia.   DMP

Chestnut-bellied Rail

Bare-eyed Rail

Bald-faced Rail

Platen's Rail

Wallace's Rail

Buff-banded Rail

BLUE-BREASTED BANDED RAIL [Slaty-breasted Rail] *Rallus striatus* L 27cm. Long bill, chestnut crown and nape. Fine white barring on entire upperparts, not distinct on nape; breast slate-grey; chin white; flanks and undertail-coverts with black-and-white bars. Bill black, lower mandible reddish; iris red; legs grey. **Voice:** sharp though not loud whistled note or short jerking screams. **Habitat:** mangroves, marshes, swamps, rice-fields. **Distribution:** resident in South Asia and South-East Asia.   BB

BARRED RAIL *Rallus torquatus* L 30cm. Bill long. Plain olive-brown upperparts and black underparts with white barring; broad chestnut breast band; black underwing; chin grey-black; black eye-stripe; white stripe from base of bill to sides of neck. Bill blackish; iris red; legs blackish. Indonesian races differs from nominate Philippines's race in having pale breast-band or lacking breast-band. **Voice:** "t'kling-t'kling" accompanied by dull thudding sounds. **Habitat:** swampy reed-beds, edge of lakes, marshes, river banks. **Distribution:** resident in the Philippines and east part of Indonesia.   BB

SLATE-BREASTED RAIL *Rallus pectoralis* L 22cm. Small rail with long pink bill. Crown, nape chestnut. Back heavily streaked blackish-brown; lores blackish; chin washed-white; sides of head, neck and breast slate-grey; wings barred with black-and-white. Iris dark brown; legs pinkish-red. **Habitat:** reed-beds, marshes, mangroves; prefers coastal regions. **Distribution:** resident in east part of Indonesia.   SU

WATER RAIL *Rallus aquaticus* L 29cm. Medium rail with comparatively long bill. Laterally compressed silhouette. Combination of olive-brown back with bold black streaking, greyish face and breast, and black-and-white banded lower underparts diagnostic. Undertail-coverts white, boldly barred black. Pattern on belly indistinct in young birds. Legs yellowish-brown; iris dark-red. Most active at dawn and dusk. **Breeding:** bill almost all-red. **Non-breeding:** only lower mandible red. **Voice:** a variety of grunts and squeals; a sharp "kik" often heard when feeding. **Habitat:** marshy ground with fairly tall, dense vegetational cover; reed-beds, disused rice-fields, overgrown ditches. **Distribution:** breeds in North and Central Asia; moves to East Asia and north part of South-East Asia in non-breeding period.   AH

OKINAWA RAIL *Rallus okinawae* L 30cm. Underparts black, finely banded with white. Face and throat black except for broad white stripe which runs from below eye down upper neck but is broken by a narrow black line just below ear-coverts. Back plain dark-brown. Undertail-coverts white. Bill thick, bright-red with yellowish tip; iris red; strong legs coral-red. **Similar species:** none within range. **Habitat:** undergrowth in decidious evergreen forest; roosts in trees. **Distribution:** endemic to north part of Okinawa Island (Ryukyu Islands), Japan.   AH

Rails

Blue-breasted
Banded Rail

Barred Rail

Slate-breasted
Rail

Water Rail

Okinawa Rail

RED-NECKED CRAKE *Rallina tricolor* L 28cm. Head, neck and upper breast reddish-brown; throat buff; upper- and underparts dark olive-brown to slate-grey; lower flanks, vent and undertail-coverts buff with dull rufous cross bars. In flight, white wing-bars on upper wings. Bill yellowish-green; legs dull green. **Habitat:** rain forest and riverine shrub forest. **Distribution:** resident from east part of Indonesia to Australia. TAM

ANDAMAN BANDED CRAKE *Rallina canningi* L 34cm. Upperparts and breast deep glossy ruddy-chestnut. Underparts and undertail-coverts dark-grey with chestnut tinge, narrowly banded with dirty-white. Bill pale-green with whitish tip; legs olive-green. **Similar species:** Banded Crake has darker back and whitish throat. **Habitat:** swamp forest. **Distribution:** endemic to Andaman Islands. BB

RED-LEGGED CRAKE [Red-legged Banded Crake, Malayan Banded Crake] *Rallina fasciata* L 24cm. Head, neck, nape, breast reddish-brown; chin white; upperparts brownish-chestnut, white barring on primaries and outer secondaries; broad black-and-white bands on underparts and undertail-coverts conspicuous. Bill short and brown; legs red. **Similar species:** see Banded, Band-bellied and Ruddy-breasted Crake. **Habitat:** open marshes. **Distribution:** resident in South Asia and South-East Asia. SU

BANDED CRAKE [Slaty-legged Crake, Philippine Banded Crake] *Rallina eurizonoides* L 26cm. Head and breast chestnut, white throat; rest of underparts barred black-and-white. Upperparts uniform dark-brown; shows white on wing in flight, but none at rest. Iris red; legs dark greenish-grey. **Juvenile:** head and breast olive-brown; iris dull brown. **Similar species:** Red-legged Crake has coral-red legs, white bars on wing. Ruddy-breasted Crake has red legs, and chestnut on underparts extending to lower belly. Band-bellied Crake has red legs, broader bands on underparts. **Voice:** "kek-kek, kek-kek" or "phat, phat, phat". **Habitat:** moist floor of dense forest and secondary growth. **Distribution:** breeds from South to South-East Asia, in south part of East Asia; South-East Asian population migrates south to the Sundas. AH

BAND-BELLIED CRAKE [Chestnut-breasted Crake] *Rallina paykullii* L 22cm. Crown and nape ashy-brown; pale chestnut-rufous sides of head; upperparts olive-brown; wings with white barring on coverts; throat white, breast chestnut, belly, flanks, vent and undertail-coverts blackish with fine bars. Bill greenish; iris and eye-ring red; legs red. **Similar species:** Red-legged Crake is more reddish-brown on upperparts with black-and-white barring on flight-feathers. Banded Crake lacks white barring on wing coverts and has grey-green legs. See Ruddy-breasted Crake. **Habitat:** damp scrub, rice-fields, wet grasslands. **Distribution:** resident in South-East Asia and south part of East Asia. TM

YELLOW RAIL *Coturnicops noveboracensis* L 12.5cm. Tiny crake. Upperparts chestnut with bold dark-brown stripes and fine white bars. Head, neck and sides of breast yellowish-brown barred with white. Secondaries white, conspicuous in flight. Throat, centre of breast and belly white. **Habitat:** wet marshes and rice-fields. **Distribution:** reported breeding in south-east part of North Asia, north east of China; moves to central part of East Asia in non-breeding period. AH

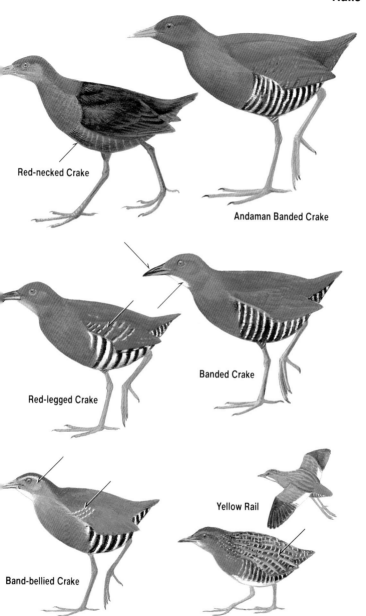

Red-necked Crake

Andaman Banded Crake

Red-legged Crake

Banded Crake

Band-bellied Crake

Yellow Rail

CORN CRAKE *Crex crex* L 25cm. Upperparts yellowish-buff, feathers streaked with dark brown; supercilium grey-blue, ear-coverts buff; chin and throat white; breast pale ashy-grey; flanks and undertail-coverts barred with reddish-brown. Bill pale brown, darker at tip; legs pale flesh. Chestnut wingcoverts conspicuous in flight. **Voice:** loud rasping disyllabic "arp-arp" or "crake-crake" persistently repeated usually in late evening and at night. **Habitat:** agricultural fields, edges of marshes. **Distribution:** breeds in west part of Central Asia; rare visitor to South Asia. BB

WHITE-BROWED RAIL *Porzana cinerea* L 17cm. Small rail with conspicuous white supercilium and line below eye contrasting with black eye-stripe; upperparts brown with blackish streaks, wings grey-brown; head, neck and breast grey; belly white, flanks buffy-brown, undertail-coverts sandy-buff. Bill green with red base; iris red; legs olive-green. **Voice:** high-pitched nasal "cutchi-cutchi-cutchi". **Habitat:** rice-fields, dense marshes. **Distribution:** resident in east part of South-East Asia. TM

SOOTY CRAKE *Porzana tabuensis* L 19cm. Head, neck and underparts slate-grey; upperparts dark olive-brown; faint white bars and spots on undertail-coverts. Bill blackish; iris and legs red. **Habitat:** mangroves, marshes. **Distribution:** rare visitor to east part of Indonesia from New Guinea. TM

LITTLE CRAKE *Porzana parva* L 20cm. **Male:** head, neck, supercilium dark ashy-grey; crown, nape dark-brown; upperparts olive-brown; upper back, scapulars and innermost secondaries broadly streaked with black; breast ashy-grey; flanks, belly, vent ashy-grey with fine whitish bars. **Female:** pale grey head and underparts browner than male. **Similar species:** see Baillon's Crake. **Habitat:** reed-beds, marshes. **Distribution:** breeds locally in Central Asia; moves to South Asia in non-breeding period. BB

BAILLON'S CRAKE *Porzana pusilla* L 19.5cm. Small crake with chestnut-brown upperparts, clear blue-grey underparts. Broad chestnut-brown eye-stripe. Mantle boldly streaked with black-and-white. Flanks and belly to undertail-coverts finely barred dark-brown and white. Bill short, all greenish-yellow; iris red; legs vary from green to pale pinkish-brown. **Juvenile:** whiter underneath with less barring; back browner. **Similar species:** Little Crake is lighter in colour, has less white streaking, and red base to bill. **Habitat:** rice-fields, marshes, edges of ponds and ditches in flat terrain. **Distribution:** breeds in temperate Asia from Europe to East Asia; moves to South and South-East Asia in non-breeding period. AH

SPOTTED CRAKE *Porzana porzana* L 23cm. Head and neck bluish-grey, speckled with white; bluish-grey supercilium contrasts with brown crown and dark-brown eye-stripe; upperparts olive-brown with broad black streaks and small white spots; wing-coverts olive-brown with small white spots; breast bluish-grey; flanks and vent strongly barred with black-and-white. Bill yellow, red spot at base; legs olive-green. **Similar species:** Little Crake and Baillon's Crake are smaller and lack white spots. **Habitat:** reed-beds, marshes. **Distribution:** breeds in Central Asia; moves to South Asia in non-breeding period. BB

Rails

Corn Crake

White-browed Rail

Sooty Crake

Little Crake

Baillon's Crake

Spotted Crake

RUDDY-BREASTED CRAKE [Ruddy Crake] *Porzana fusca* L 22.5cm. Medium-sized crake with chestnut head and underparts. Crown, hindneck and upperparts, including wings and tail, are plain, dark greyish-brown. Lower belly behind legs to undertail is black with narrow white barring. Bill black with grey base; iris bright red; legs red. **Voice:** song is a series of loud metallic staccato "kyot-kyot-kyot-kyot" uttered at night especially at dusk; also a short "ket". **Similar species:** Red-legged and Band-bellied Crakes have white wing-markings and extensive black-and-white bands on underparts. Banded Rail is larger with greyish-green legs. **Habitat:** marshes, rice-fields, along streams in forest and secondary growth. **Distribution:** resident in South-East Asia and East Asia; northern breeders migrate south in non-breeding period.   AH

RUFOUS-TAILED MOORHEN *Amaurornis olivaceus* L ? cm. A very shy and secretive rail. Head, back, wings and rump dark olive-brown; tail rufous and marked with olive-brown; underparts grey; flanks bright-brown; undertail-coverts buffish. Bill greenish-yellow; iris reddish-brown; legs greenish-yellow. **Similar species:** Purple Swamphen and Dusky Moorhen are bigger and have red bills and red legs. **Habitat:** freshwater marshes, fields, lakes, swamp forests. **Distribution:** resident in the Philippines and east part of Indonesia.   DMP

SULAWESI WATER HEN *Amaurornis isabellinus* L ? cm. Upperparts olive-brown tinged with grey; face and throat pinkish-fawn with more rufous on sides of neck; underparts vinous-chestnut. Bill light green; iris red; legs brownish-green. **Habitat:** edges of rice-fields or maize fields, grassy low scrub such as long grass along rivers from sea level to 800m. **Distribution:** endemic to Sulawesi Island, Indonesia.   DMP

BROWN CRAKE *Amaurornis akool* L 28cm. Supercilium indistinct with ashy-grey sides of head and neck; upperparts, wings and tail dark olive-brown; chin and centre of throat whitish, rest of underparts ashy-grey tinged brown. Bill pale green with bluish tip; legs fleshy-brown to deep reddish-purple. **Habitat:** swampy reed-beds, *Pandanus* swamps and banks of watercourses. **Distribution:** resident in South Asia and north part of South-East Asia.   BB

ELWES' CRAKE [Black-tailed Crake] *Amaurornis bicolor* L 22cm. Head and neck dark ashy-grey; upperparts rufous-brown; chin whitish; underparts dark ashy-grey; tail black. **Habitat:** rice-fields, marshes. **Distribution:** resident from north part of South Asia, north part of South-East Asia to south part of East Asia.   BB

WHITE-BREASTED WATER HEN *Amaurornis phoenicurus* L 32.5cm. Adult unmistakable with dark slate-grey back, white face and underparts, reddish vent and undertail-coverts. Bill greenish-yellow with red base; iris red; legs yellowish-green. Young birds are generally less distinctly marked. **Voice:** calls "kwak" or "kwok". **Habitat:** any wet place including marshes, ditches, edges of ponds, rice-fields; also sugar-cane fields, grasslands. **Distribution:** resident in South-East Asia and south part of East Asia including the Ryukyus, Japan.   AH

Rails

Rufous-tailed Moorhen

Ruddy-breasted Crake

Sulawesi Water Hen

Brown Crake

Elwes' Crake

White-breasted Water Hen

WATER COCK   *Gallicrex cinerea* L 40cm. **Male:** in breeding plumage, unmistakable with slaty-black body, bright yellow bill, bright red legs. In non-breeding plumage, legs olive-green and this may persist until July. Red frontal shield extending onto crown to form short crest. Non-breeding plumage like female. **Female:** tawny-buff overall; dark-brown feather centres on upperparts including crown give scalloped appearance; bill dull yellow; legs greenish-yellow. **Voice:** song is a series of booming "gok-gok-gok-gok-gok"'s accelerating in tempo. **Similar species:** Moorhen is much smaller, has white line on flank and white on undertail. **Habitat:** wet grasslands, rice-fields, irrigated sugar-cane fields; edges of ponds and ditches with vegetational cover. **Distribution:** resident in South, South-East and East Asia; northern breeders move to south.   AH

DUSKY MOORHEN   *Gallinula tenebrosa* L 31cm. Head, upperparts and tail dusky olive-brown; underparts dark-grey with lighter colour on throat; undertail-coverts white. Bill red with yellow tip; frontal shield red; iris dark-brown; legs red. **Voice:** harsh grating note "krik"; a piercing scream by female. **Similar species:** Black Coot has white bill and shield. Purple Swamphen is bigger and distinctly bluish. See Moorhen. **Habitat:** marshes, margins of ponds and streams in lowlands. **Distribution:** resident from east part of Indonesia to Australia.   DMP

MOORHEN   [Common Moorhen] *Gallinula chloropus* L 32.5cm. Wholly dark, with brownish tinge on upperparts, greyish tinge on underparts; white line along flanks diagnostic. Sides of undertail-coverts white. Anterior third of bill yellow; the rest and frontal shield red. Iris red; legs greenish with red tibia. **Immature:** like adult, but lacks red frontal shield. **Juvenile:** brown with lighter flank-lines. **Voice:** abrupt "krr't". **Similar species:** Dusky Moorhen lacks white flank-line; back lacks brownish tinge. **Habitat:** all kinds of marshy places with vegetational cover. **Distribution:** resident in Asia.   AH

PURPLE SWAMPHEN   [Purple Moorhen, Purple Gallinule] *Porphyrio porphyrio* L 43cm. Purplish-blue overall with long red legs and enormous toes. Head often paler, occasionally slightly whitish. Red frontal shield on forehead and short red bill. White undertail-coverts conspicuous. Legs pale dingy-red to dull-red. **Juvenile:** paler with duller frontal shield and bill; legs pale orange-brown. **Voice:** various hooting, craking, clucking and hoarse ripping notes. **Habitat:** dense reed-beds around large marshes and lakes. **Distribution:** resident in South and South-East Asia.   BB

BLACK COOT   [Coot, Common Coot] *Fulica atra* L 39cm. Large and fat with hunched appearance. White frontal shield diagnostic. Wholly dark except for narrow white trailing edge to secondaries (visible in flight). Bill white; iris red; legs dark greyish-green; long toes lobed. **Juvenile and immature:** brown to dark-brown with pale throat, breast, sides of neck and face markings. **Voice:** loud, high pitched, repeated "kyow". **Similar species:** none. White frontal shield diagnostic. **Habitat:** open inland waters such as lakes, reservoirs, ponds. **Distribution:** breeds in temperate Asia; moves to East Asia, South Asia and north part of South-East Asia in non-breeding period.   AH

Rails, Coots

♂ non-breeding

♂ breeding

♀

Water Cock

Dusky Moorhen

Purple Swamphen

juv.

Moorhen

juv.

Black Coot

Finfoot
Family *Heliornithidae* (World: 3 species; Asia: 1 species) Relatively large aquatic birds with long neck and heavy bill, swims partly submerged and dives well. Usually found near or in dense vegetation along rivers and in mangroves, singly or in small family groups. **TM**

MASKED FINFOOT *Heliopais personata* L 53cm. Both sexes with olive-brown upperparts and pale white underparts, a heavy pointed yellow bill and green legs. **Male:** black forehead, chin and throat separated from grey nape by narrow white stripe. Breeding male has a small knob above base of bill. **Female:** like male, but white chin and throat separated from greyish-brown nape by black-and-white stripe. **Juvenile:** like female, but lacks black on crown. **Voice:** utters a bubbling call, which is seldom heard. **Habitat:** dense jungle rivers, marshes, mangroves. **Distribution:** Little known; lowland resident in east part of South Asia, and South-East Asia. **TM**

Jacanas
Family *Jacanidae* (World: 8 species; Asia: 3 species) Small to medium-sized wading birds with wing spur, short and rounded wings, and short tail. Huge feet with very long toes and claws enable them to walk on floating vegetation. Sexes similar but female bigger than male. Found around freshwater lakes, ponds, lowland swamps. **DMP**

COMB-CRESTED JACANA *Irediparra gallinacea* L 23cm. Conspicuous pinkish-red comb on black crown. **Adult:** face and sides of neck white, lower neck cream-yellow; nape, breast, flanks, main flight feathers and tail black; back and upperwing-coverts brown; a black line from eye to base of lower bill; belly white. Bill greenish-yellow with black tip; iris yellow; legs bluish-black. In flight, wings lack white markings. **Juvenile:** head and rear crown rufous; breast white with blackish-rufous band down from black nape. **Voice:** soft squeaks, loud and shrill repeated rattling or piping notes. **Habitat:** marshes, lakes or ponds with rich aquatic weeds. **Distribution:** east part of South-East Asia. **DMP**

PHEASANT-TAILED JACANA *Hydrophasianus chirurgus* L 55cm (including tail). White-winged jacana with strikingly long black tail in breeding plumage. Wings white above and below, except black outer primaries. Bill, legs, feet bluish-grey; iris dark. **Breeding:** black line separates yellow hindneck from white foreneck and face; rear crown black. Underparts black from breast downwards. **Non-breeding:** tail much shorter. Underparts white with dark breast-band. Dark eye-stripe joins dark line down side of neck; yellow of hindneck duller. Upperwing-coverts brownish. **Voice:** nasal "tew" and "tewn"; high-pitched "miew-miew", audible from far off. **Habitat:** marshes, small lakes, ponds with dense vegetation. **Distribution:** resident in South and South-East Asia; northern breeders move south in non-breeding period. **AH**

BRONZE-WINGED JACANA *Metopidius indicus* L 25cm. Small chestnut-red shield, stout bill and a bold white supercilium. **Adult:** head, neck and underparts black with dark glossy green sheen; back and wings olive-bronze; tail chestnut. Bill greenish-yellow with red spot at base; iris brown; legs dull green. In flight, no white marking on wings. **Juvenile:** crown rufous-brown; short white supercilium; neck and breast rufous; underparts white. **Habitat:** marshes, ponds in lowland. **Distribution:** resident in South and South-East Asia. **DMP**

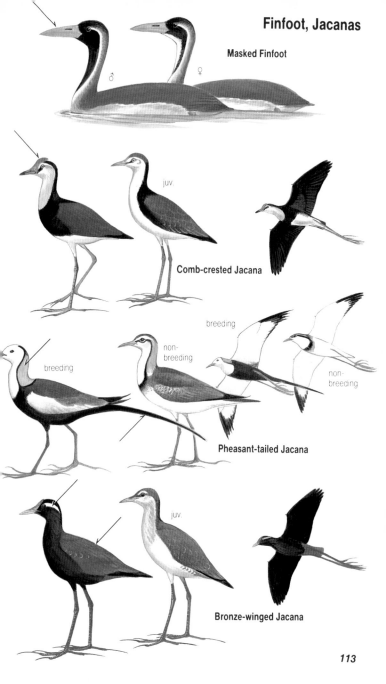

Finfoot, Jacanas

Masked Finfoot

♂ ♀

Comb-crested Jacana

juv.

breeding

non-breeding

Pheasant-tailed Jacana

breeding

non-breeding

Bronze-winged Jacana

juv.

Painted Snipe

Family *Rostratulidae* (World: 2 species; Asia: 1 species) Shows extensive sexual dimorphism. Polyandrous; male attends to nest and rears young. **AH**

PAINTED SNIPE [Greater Painted Snipe] *Rostratula benghalensis* L 23.5cm. Bill greyish-horn, tinged red in breeding female; iris dark-red; legs brownish-yellow. Flight weak with dangling legs. **Female:** dark-chestnut breast and neck; dark head with white around and behind eye. Conspicuous white line on side of breast joins yellowish scapular V-line. **Male:** markings on head more obscure, yellowish; area around eye yellowish-white. **Voice:** breeding female calls long drawn-out "koh-koh-koh" at night; otherwise usually silent. **Habitat:** wet places with short vegetational cover. **Distribution:** resident in South and South-East Asia; East Asian population moves south in non-breeding period. **AH**

Crab Plover

Family *Dromadidae* (World: 1 species; Asia: 1 species)

CRAB PLOVER *Dromas ardeola* L 38cm. Has heavy, pointed black bill, long pale grey legs. **Adult:** pied plumage. Black mantle, inner scapulars and flight feathers. Small blackish marks on lores, behind eye and rear crown; but absent in some places. Legs project well beyond tail in flight. Sexes similar; no seasonal variation in plumage. **Juvenile:** like adult, but dark grey (not black) back with black streaks on rear crown. **Voice:** harsh usually repeated rapidly, uttered often in non-breeding period. **Habitat:** coastal mudflats, reefs. **Distribution:** breeds around Arabian Peninsula; moves to South Asia and rare visitor to west part of South-East Asia. **TM**

Oystercatchers

Family *Haematopodidae* (World: 11 species; Asia: 2 species) Sexes similar, but female has longer and thinner bill. Mainly coastal, living on rocky shores feeding largely on bivalve molluscs. **AH**

PALAEARCTIC OYSTERCATCHER [Oystercatcher, Common Oystercatcher] *Haematopus ostralegus* L 45cm. White wing-bar conspicuous in flight; white extending onto inner primaries and part of median coverts, is visible on closed wings. Also conspicuous white rump and lower back. First-year birds have more pointed bills; adults' are blunt-ended. Bill red; iris, orbital ring red; legs pinkish. Bare parts duller in non-breeding period. **Similar species:** Pied Oystercatcher has shorter wing-bar restricted to greater coverts only; underwing has dark flight-feathers. **Voice:** high, clear "kleet" or "kleep". **Habitat:** breeds in open river-valleys and grasslands near lake-shores; outside breeding season, rocky or sandy coasts, estuaries, mudflats. **Distribution:** breeds in Central and East Asia; otherwise on coasts of South and South-East Asia. **AH**

PIED OYSTERCATCHER *Haematopus longirostris* L 45cm. **Adult:** head, throat, mantle, and tail black, rest white. Wings black but greater-coverts white, resulting in white wing-bar; underwing-coverts white. Long straight bill red; iris and orbital ring red. **Juvenile:** like adult but brownish with duller soft part colours. **Voice:** a piping "kleep" often uttered, a "pick-pick" when disturbed. **Habitat:** estuaries, beaches, and farmlands. **Distribution:** resident from Indonesia (Aru Islands) to Australia. **TM**

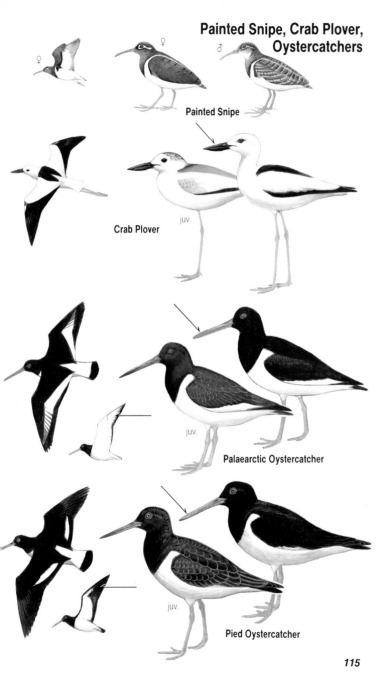

Painted Snipe, Crab Plover,
Oystercatchers

Painted Snipe

Crab Plover

juv.

Palaearctic Oystercatcher

juv.

Pied Oystercatcher

juv.

Ibis Bill
Family *Ibidorhynchidae* (World: 1 species; Asia: 1 species)

IBIS BILL *Ibidorhyncha struthersii* L 41cm. **Adult:** black facial mask, throat and breast band; upperparts largely ashy grey-brown; tail ashy-grey with narrow wavy blackish cross-bars; underparts white; white patch at base of primaries in flight; underwing white. Red bill long and down-curved; legs red. **Juvenile:** like adult, but plumage less distinct and duller, black areas fringed white. **Voice:** loud ringing single note or whistle quickly repeated, "tu-tu-tu", similar to Greenshank. **Habitat:** confined to shingle banks and sides of mountain rivers. Not found on coasts. **Distribution:** north part of South Asia. Altitudinal migrant. BB

Stilts and Avocet
Family *Recurvirostridae* (World: 12 species; Asia: 3 species) Extremely long legs and bill, upturned in avocets. Pied plumage in both groups. Seasonal plumage difference not extensive. Forages wading in shallow water. Sexes similar. AH

BLACK-WINGED STILT *Himantopus himantopus* L 32cm. Distinctive large black-and-white wader with long bill and extremely long legs. Bill black; iris red; legs pink. **Adult:** entirely white plumage except black back, black wings above and below, very pale-grey tail. Crown to hindneck varies in amount of dusky-black. Male's head tends to be whiter than female. Mantle, scapulars and tertials black in male, brownish in female. Some birds, greyish becomes more extensive on crown and nape in non-breeding plumage. **Juvenile:** back brown with pale fringes to feathers, giving scaly appearance. **Similar species:** see Australian Stilt. **Voice:** commonest calls are loud "keek" and "kee'it"; also continuous "kikikikiki". **Habitat:** open inland marshes, rice-fields, coastal and estuarine mudflats. **Distribution:** breeds from Central Asia to South and continental South-East Asia; northern breeders migrate south. AH

AUSTRALIAN STILT *Himantopus leucocephalus* L 37cm. Closely resembles Black-winged Stilt, but slightly larger with somewhat broader wings. **Adult:** white crown; a ridge of raised black feathers runs down whole length of hindneck. Black on hindneck often joins black collar on upper breast; collar sometimes broken, sometimes almost complete. **Immature:** like juvenile Black-winged Stilt. **Voice:** like Black-winged, but softer and more nasal. **Habitat:** open marshes, coastal mudflats. **Distribution:** Australasian species resident in Borneo, the Philippines and Java. AH

PIED AVOCET [Avocet] *Recurvirostra avosetta* L 43cm. Large white wader with distinctive upturned bill. Bill black; iris dark-red; legs blue-grey. **Adult:** unmistakable black-and-white pattern. Upperwing white except black outer primaries and primary-coverts, and black bars across coverts and scapulars. Underwing white with black outer primaries. **Juvenile:** dusky-brown replaces black; white on mantle, wings is mottled with pale brown and buff. **Voice:** clear soft "kluit". **Similar species:** Crab Plover lacks black on head, has different upperwing pattern, entirely white underwing, and thick heavy bill. **Habitat:** breeds in open saline marshes; otherwise on coastal and estuarine sandflats and mudflats. **Distribution:** breeds in temperate Central Asia east to outer Mongolia; moves to west part of South Asia, South-East Asia in non-breeding period. AH

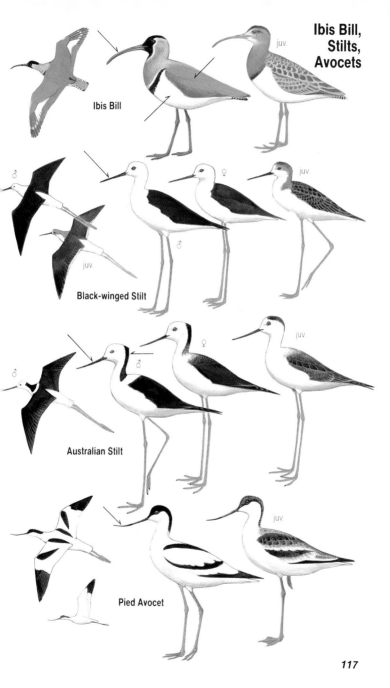

Ibis Bill,
Stilts,
Avocets

Ibis Bill

juv.

Black-winged Stilt

♂ ♀ juv.

Australian Stilt

♂ ♀ juv.

Pied Avocet

juv.

117

Stone-Curlews
Family *Burhinidae* (World: 9 species; Asia: 3 species)
Large, long-legged plover-like shorebirds with large yellow eyes. Sexes similar. Mostly nocturnal. Not all species are particularly associated with water, generally found in dry areas. Largely crepuscular and nocturnal, inactive during daytime. Pairs or small parties, occasionally large gatherings. Feed on small vertebrates, insects and other invertebrates.   SU

STONE-CURLEW *Burhinus oedicnemus* L 41cm. Dark-streaked sandy brown bird with large head, long bare yellowish 'thick-kneed' legs and huge yellow eyes. At rest, a narrow whitish bar and broad grey panel on closed wings, and in flight, two narrow white bars and a conspicuous grey patch in brown wings. Flight strong. **Juvenile:** paler than adult; more marked with buff; streaks on underparts narrower; white wing markings less distinct. **Voice:** call a distinct "cur-lee" rather similar to that of Western Curlew – hence the name 'Stone-Curlew'. **Similar species:** see Great Stone Plover. **Habitat:** open country; sometimes rivers and sandbanks. **Distribution:** resident in South Asia and west part of South-East Asia.   BB

GREAT STONE PLOVER   [Great Thick-knee] *Esacus recurvirostris* L 50cm. Upperparts more or less uniformly greyish-sandy; underparts buffish-white. Distinctly upturned massive black and yellow bill; huge yellowish eyes, with conspicuous white spectacle around them and blackish bands above and below. Blackish band near shoulder of closed wing. In flight, peculiar arched profile of back and a round white patch at base of black primaries. **Voice:** loud harsh single note. Wild wailing cries "kree-kree-kree, kre-kre-kre-kre". **Similar species:** Stone-Curlew is smaller, has straight bill and looks having longer legs. See Great Australian Stone Plover. **Habitat:** usually found on rivers or by inland lakes. Very unusual in coastal areas. **Distribution:** resident in South Asia and to Myanmar.   BB

GREAT AUSTRALIAN STONE PLOVER   [Great Stone Plover, Great Thick-knee] *Esacus magnirostris* L 53cm. Similar but larger than Great Stone Plover. Distinguished from it by comparatively heavy and straighter bill, and conspicuous white supercilium over eye but lacking white surround to eye. **Voice:** "eerie" double syllable; mournful "wee-loo" harsh in tone. **Similar species:** see Great Stone Plover. **Habitat:** strictly coastal. Keeping to reefs and sandy beaches in pairs or small parties. **Distribution:** resident in Andamans to South-East Asia.   BB

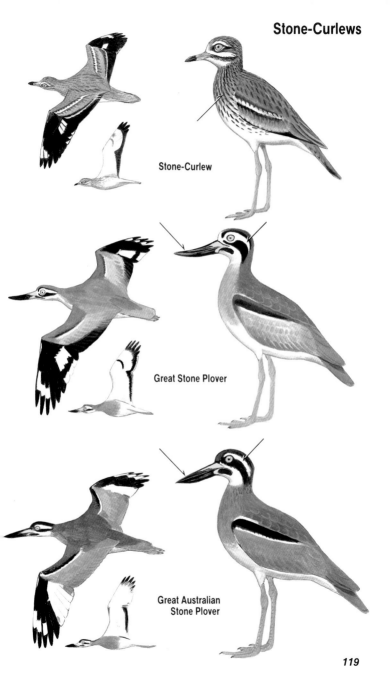

Stone-Curlews

Stone-Curlew

Great Stone Plover

Great Australian
Stone Plover

119

Pratincoles

Glareolidae in part (World: 18 species; Asia: 4 species)
Small to medium-sized migratory shorebirds with large gapes, short and slightly decurved bills, long pointed wings. Moving around open country near large rivers or marshes in large flocks. Feed mainly on insects by hawking in the air. Sexes similar. DMP

AUSTRALIAN PRATINCOLE *Stiltia isabella* L 23cm. Long legs; wings project well beyond squared tail at rest. In flight, underwing black, rump white, tail black with white sides and tip, legs protrude beyond tail. **Breeding:** head, upperparts and wings sandy-brown; chin and throat white; primaries black; breast pale orange-buff with chestnut band on flanks and belly; undertail-coverts white. **Non-breeding:** slightly duller; small black streaks on ear-coverts and around throat; chestnut patch on flanks and belly reduced in size. **Voice:** "wee teet". **Similar species:** Eastern Collared Pratincole is darker, fatter and has shorter legs and forked tail. **Habitat:** open grassy plains. **Distribution:** east part of Indonesia in their non-breeding period. DMP

PRATINCOLE [Collared Pratincole] *Glareola pratincola* L 25cm. Red gape and black bill; long wings project beyond tail at rest; tail forked. In flight, chestnut underwing with pale trailing edge to secondaries, and white rump. **Breeding:** upperparts pale brown with darker brown primaries; throat buff bordered with black outline; breast and flanks yellowish olive-brown; belly and vent white. **Non-breeding:** feathers of head and breast edged tawny and throat spotted and streaked. **Juvenile:** like non-breeding, but paler and throat lacks any outline. **Voice:** sharp chattering "kikki-kirrik". **Similar species:** separated from Eastern Collared Prationcole by paler mantle and pale tips to secondaries. Wing projection beyond tail longer than shown by Eastern. **Habitat:** open habitat near lagoons estuaries, river deltas. **Distribution:** breeds in west part of South Asia. DMP

EASTERN COLLARED PRATINCOLE [Large Indian Pratincole, Oriental Pratincole] *Glareola maldivarum* L 26.5cm. Superficially resembles a large swallow with long pointed wings and deeply forked tail. Flight erratic and tern-like. Underwing-coverts and axillaries deep chestnut-red. **Breeding:** creamy throat outlined with black; base of lower mandible conspicuous red; underparts warm mid-brown, ocherous on belly. **Non-breeding:** generally duller with black gorget replaced by dark brown streaks. **Juvenile:** pale buff fringes and dark subterminal lines on feathers. **Voice:** "krit-krit-krit". **Similar species:** see Pratincole. **Habitat:** breeds on pebbly river-beds and wasteland; otherwise on open habitat. **Distribution:** breeds from East Asia south to South-East and South Asia; non-breeders migrate South. AH

LITTLE PRATINCOLE [Small Pratincole] *Glareola lactea* L 17cm. Crown pale grey; mantle pale sandy-grey; throat pink-buff; breast buffish-grey; belly white. In flight, pale-grey mantle and upperwing-coverts contrast with white base of secondaries and black primaries; square cut white tail broadly tipped with black; white underparts, black wing linings contrast with white base of secondaries. Rather crepuscular. **Voice:** "tuck-tuck-tuck"; "tiririt, tiririt, tiririt", when disturbed. **Habitat:** more partial to water than its larger relatives. Rivers, marshes. **Distribution:** resident in South Asia and west part of South-East Asia. BB

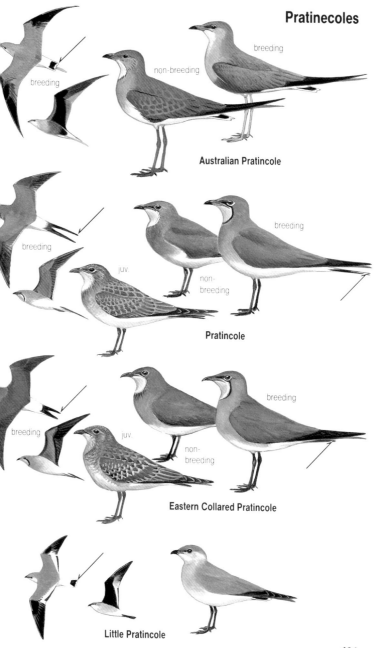

Pratincoles

breeding

non-breeding

breeding

Australian Pratincole

breeding

juv.

non-breeding

breeding

Pratincole

breeding

juv.

non-breeding

breeding

Eastern Collared Pratincole

Little Pratincole

Plovers
Family *Charadriidae* (World: 66 species; Asia: 22 species) Walk and run on comparatively long legs. Sexes similar. Diurnal and nocturnal. Mostly gregarious in non-breeding period. **AH**

NORTHERN LAPWING [Lapwing] *Vanellus vanellus* L 31.5cm. Crested appearance and fluttering flight on broad-tipped wings distinctive. Crest longer in older birds; underparts mostly white with black breast band; ventral area conspicuously orange-yellow. Black on the throat of adult male is lost in non-breeding plumage, when the face attains yellowish tinge. Uppertail-coverts and underwing-linings white. First-year birds are browner overall, with dusky breast band. **Voice:** has mewing call similar to those of kittens. **Habitat:** breeds in short grass damp meadows and pastures; otherwise on wet open land. **Distribution:** breeds in northern temperate zone throughout Asia; moves to East Asia and west part of South Asia in non-breeding period. **AH**

RIVER LAPWING [Spur-winged Lapwing] *Vanellus duvaucelii* L 31cm. Uppertail-coverts white, contrasting with largely black tail; breast grey-brown; centre of belly black, rest of underparts white. In flight, black flight-feathers contrast with a broad white wing-bar. **Voice:** "did, did, did" ending with "did-did-do-weet, did-did-do-weet". **Habitat:** usually seen near rivers. **Distribution:** resident in east part of South Asia, and west part of South-East Asia. **BB**

YELLOW-WATTLED LAPWING *Vanellus malabaricus* L 27cm. Bright-yellow wattle in front of eyes; white stripe between black cap and brown sides of head; black line along lower edge of brown breast; belly white. In flight, white wing-bar contrasting with brown mantle and black primaries and secondaries conspicuous. **Juvenile:** pale brown narrowly barred with dark brown; chin whitish. **Voice:** "ti-ee, ti-ee" punctuated with high-pitched "twit-twit-twit". **Habitat:** prefers drier habitat than most lapwings. **Distribution:** resident in South Asia. **BB**

SOCIABLE PLOVER [Sociable Lapwing] *Vanellus gregarius* L 29cm. In flight, black primaries contrast with white secondaries and brown mantle producing very distinctive pattern; white rump contrasts with black band on white tail. **Breeding:** crown and eye-stripe black; forehead and super-cilium white; mantle and upperparts grey-brown. **Non-breeding:** crown brown; forehead and supercilium buffish-white; eye-stripe brown; upperparts ashy-grey. **Juvenile:** like non-breeding, but upperparts fringed with light-brown and breast heavily streaked. **Voice:** "krech-krech-krech". **Habitat:** grasslands and farmlands. **Distribution:** breeds in north part of West Asia; moves to west part of South Asia in non-breeding period. **BB**

WHITE-TAILED PLOVER [White-tailed Lapwing] *Vanellus leucurus* L 28cm. Legs long and yellow. In flight, rump, uppertail-coverts and tail white; bold black-and-white pattern on wings. **Juvenile:** much darker than adult. **Voice:** silent in winter, "chee-viz" or "pi-wick". **Similar species:** very like Yellow-wattled Lapwing, but lacks black cap and yellow wattles, and unlike the lapwing, always near water. **Habitat:** prefers shallow margins of lakes. **Distribution:** breeds in north part of West Asia; moves to west part of South Asia in non-breeding period. **BB**

Plovers

non-breeding

non-breeding

non-breeding

juv.

Northern Lapwing

River Lapwing

breeding

Yellow-wattled Lapwing

juv.

juv.

breeding

non-breeding

Sociable Plover

breeding

juv.

White-tailed Plover

GREY-HEADED LAPWING *Vanellus cinereus* L 35.5cm. A large and slender lapwing with long neck. Combination of grey head and neck, dark-grey breast band, greyish-brown upperparts and white underparts is unique within the region; very small yellow wattle in front of eyes. Secondaries and greater coverts strikingly white in flight; outer wings black. Underwing white except for black primaries; tail white with black subterminal band. Rather long bill yellow tipped black; iris red; legs yellow. **Juvenile:** lacks breast band and head more brownish. **Voice:** sharp and loud "kirrit-kirrit". **Similar species:** White-tailed Plover in flight lacks dark breast band and black in tail, also shows more black on outer wings as part of secondaries are black. **Habitat:** rice-fields, wet grass meadows, wide river-beds. **Distribution:** breeds in east part of East Asia; moves to north part of South-East Asia in non-breeding period. Isolated population in central Japan mostly sedentary.   AH

RED-WATTLED LAPWING *Vanellus indicus* L 33cm. Crown, nape, chin, throat and breast black; crimson-fleshy wattle in front of eyes; rest of upperparts bronze-brown; underparts white. In flight, broad white wing-bar and rump with black band on white tail. Legs greenish-yellow to bright yellow. **Juvenile:** duller; chin and throat almost white; white fine spots on crown. Race *indicus,* western population, has broad white bands from behind eyes running down sides of neck to meet white underparts. Race *atronuchalis,* eastern population, has only white ear-coverts, a complete black head and narrow white collar. **Voice:** loud, penetrating "did-ye-do-it". **Habitat:** marshes, ditches, open country, farmlands. **Distribution:** resident in South Asia and west part of South-East Asia.   BB

JAVANESE WATTLED LAPWING *Vanellus macropterus* L 28cm. Long legs and large creamy-white wattle in front of eyes. Head and neck black with blackish-grey collar; mantle and coverts brown; uppertail-coverts white; primaries and secondaries black, contrasting with mantle in flight; breast and flanks brown with black belly; undertail-coverts and vent white; tail banded with black-and-white. Bill black with pinkish gape; iris brown; legs yellow. **Habitat:** open wetland areas. **Distribution:** endemic to north part of Java Island, Indonesia; rare and possibly extinct.   DMP

MASKED PLOVER *Vanellus miles* L 37cm. A distinctive plover with large yellow facial wattle in front of eyes hanging downward below bill and extending backward to terminate above and behind eyes. Head and nape white; crown black; upperparts greyish-brown; yellow wingspur with brown tip; underparts white; tail white with broad black band. Bill yellow with brown tip; iris yellow; legs purplish-red. In flight, greyish-brown back contrasts with white rump; primaries and secondaries black. Female has shorter wingspur than male. **Voice:** loud and harsh "keer-kick-ki-ki-ki". **Habitat:** pasture, mudflats, margins of marshes and rivers. **Distribution:** resident in east part of Indonesia and Australia.   DMP

Plovers

juv.

Grey-headed Lapwing

juv.

race *atronuchalis*

race *indicus*

Red-wattled Lapwing

Masked Plover

Javanese Wattled Lapwing

125

PACIFIC GOLDEN PLOVER [Lesser Golden Plover, Asiatic Golden Plover] *Pluvialis fulva* L 24cm. In flight shows no wing-bar; underwing including axillaries grey. Bill and legs dark brown. **Breeding:** underparts black; vent mottled with yellow and white. White line from sides of neck may be diffuse along flanks but always present. **Non-breeding:** pale-brown underparts and yellowish mottled greyish-brown upperparts. Thin but distinct pale-yellow supercilium. Autumn birds show varying amount of black on underparts. **Juvenile:** feathers on upperparts with extensive ochreous-yellow. **Voice:** disyllabic "kee-bit" and sharp "chu-wit". **Habitat:** estuarine and coastal mudflats, inland rice-fields, and moist grasslands. **Distribution:** breeds in far North Asia; moves to South and South-East Asia, Australasia and Pacific islands in non-breeding period. AH

GREY PLOVER [Black-bellied Plover] *Pluvialis squatarola* L 29.5cm. Larger and more robust than Pacific Golden Plover. In flight shows a white wing-bar, white rump, white underwings and black axillaries. Black on bend of wing conspicuous. Bill and legs black. **Breeding:** upperparts grey mottled white; face and underparts black; forecrown white; white line similar to Pacific Golden's, but broader at sides of neck terminating on flanks; ventral area all-white. **Non-breeding:** underparts dirty-white with extensive pale-grey markings on breast; white edgings to feathers on upperparts less marked. **Voice:** clear whistling "tlee-ee". **Habitat:** coastal and estuarine mudflats and sandflats. **Distribution:** breeds in far North Asia; moves to East, South and South-East Asia in non-breeding period. AH

RED-CAPPED DOTTEREL *Charadrius ruficapillus* L 15cm. In flight shows a narrow white wing-bar and white sides to tail. **Male:** white forehead and supercilium bordered by a black frontal bar; black eye-stripe, lores and line around ear-coverts to breast patches. Crown and nape rich-chestnut in breeding plumage. Mantle pale brown and underparts white. **Female:** lacks almost all black on head. No black on nape of either sex. **Juvenile:** like female, but mottled above, forehead greyish. **Voice:** brisk "tik" uttered singly or repeated accelerating into a hard trill. **Similar species:** Kentish Plover has a distinct white collar. **Habitat:** sandy and shelly shores. **Distribution:** resident from Indonesia to Australia. TM

MALAYSIAN SAND PLOVER [Malaysian Plover] *Charadrius peronii* L 15cm. Similar to Red-capped Dotterel and Kentish Plover. Distinguished from Red-capped Dotterel by white collar; lores pale-brown; legs paler. Separated from Kentish Plover by black hindneck collar and more extensive black breast band in male; rufous breast-band or patches in female and juvenile. **Voice:** a soft "chit". **Habitat:** sandy coastal beaches; rarely on mudflats or inland. **Distribution:** resident in South-East Asia. TM

DOTTEREL *Eudromias morinellus* L 21cm. Bill dark grey; legs yellowish. **Breeding:** unmistakable; broad white supercilium, white throat, grey brown breast bordered from orange upper belly by a white band, and dark lower belly. Female is brighter coloured than male. **Non-breeding:** mostly brown with yellow tinge, but the pattern of breeding plumage still discernable; broad pale supercilium meeting on nape and pale breast band diagnostic. **Habitat:** breeds on arctic and inland tundra. Dry, sandy areas in non-breeding period. **Distribution:** breeds in North and north Central Asia; otherwise moves to North Africa to west part of South Asia. AH

Plovers

non-breeding

juv.

breeding

juv.

Pacific Golden Plover

juv.

non-breeding

breeding

juv.

Grey Plover

non-breeding

♀ breeding ♂ breeding

juv.

non-breeding

Red-capped Dotterel

♂

♂

juv.

♀

Malaysian Sand Plover

non-breeding

♀ breeding

juv.

Dotterel

127

RINGED PLOVER [Common Ringed Plover] *Charadrius hiaticula* L 19cm. Medium-sized, compact plover with conspicuous white wing-bar. **Breeding:** broad black breast band somewhat thinner in the middle, broad white forehead bordered by wide black frontal bar from dark sandy-brown crown. Yellow bill tipped black; legs bright orange yellow. **Non-breeding:** Generally duller with black replaced by dark-brown; breast band thinner, may be broken in the middle. Bill may become all black; legs dull orange-yellow. **Juvenile:** like non-breeding adults, but paler overall with pale feather fringes. **Voice:** soft-disyllabic "too-it". **Similar species:** Little Ringed Plover lacks wing-bar, and has yellow eye ring. **Habitat:** wet paddies and meadows near coast. **Distribution:** breeds far North Asia; moves to west part of South Asia in non-breeding period.   AH

LONG-BILLED RINGED PLOVER [Long-billed Plover] *Charadrius placidus* L 20.5cm. Medium-sized, slender shaped plover with long legs. Facial markings mostly dark-brown throughout year, showing less contrast than Little Ringed or Ringed Plovers, only the frontal bar being near-black. Breast-band black but thin. Shows white but inconspicuous wing-bar in flight. Non-breeding birds and juvenile duller overall. Bill long, slender and black, legs pale-yellow or flesh. **Voice:** slightly up-ending, clear "pe-wee". **Habitat:** stony river beds and pebbly beaches of inland waters. **Distribution:** breeds in East Asia north to Amur River; moves to south part of East and north part of South-East Asia in non-breeding period.   AH

LITTLE RINGED PLOVER *Charadrius dubius* L 16cm. Compact small plover with conspicuous yellow eye ring and long pinkish legs. Lacks wing-bar, wings look uniformly dark. Bill black; eyes comparatively large, iris black. **Breeding:** single breast band may be very broad in some individuals in breeding season. **Non-breeding:** black replaced by brown, becoming non-descript; breast band may be broken in the middle reduced to large dark smudges on sides of breast. **Juvenile:** yellow tinge to face and throat. **Voice:** clear descending "pee-oo". **Similar species:** Kentish Plover in non-breeding plumage has only very small smudges on sides of breast. Ringed Plover is larger, shorter legged, with different facial pattern and a wing-bar. Long-billed Plover is larger and with a wing-bar. **Habitat:** breeds on stony river beds, shingly shores and reclamations; otherwise mudflats and sandflats. **Distribution:** breeds in the region except in the far north, desert regions and some part of South-East Asia; northern population migrates to South and South-East Asia in non-breeding period.   AH

KENTISH PLOVER [Snowy Plover] *Charadrius alexandrinus* L 17.5cm. Small plover with sandy-brown upperparts and short black or dark legs. **Male:** crown and hindneck chestnut-brown contrasting with white forehead and black frontal bar; eye-stripe black. Broken breast band small and black, never joins. Non-breeding plumage like female. **Female:** crown greyish-brown, darker fore; diffuse eye-stripe brown. Smudges at sides of breast same colour as back. **Juvenile:** like non-breeding, but upperparts paler with pale feather fringes. Overall impression is of pale sandy-brown bird. **Voice:** soft "prrr-prrr" and "prwit" calls. **Similar species:** see Malaysian Sand Plover. **Habitat:** sandy beachs by sea and inland water, along large rivers, coastal mudflats. **Distribution:** breeds throughout temperate and tropical Asia; northern breeders moves south in non-breeding period.   AH

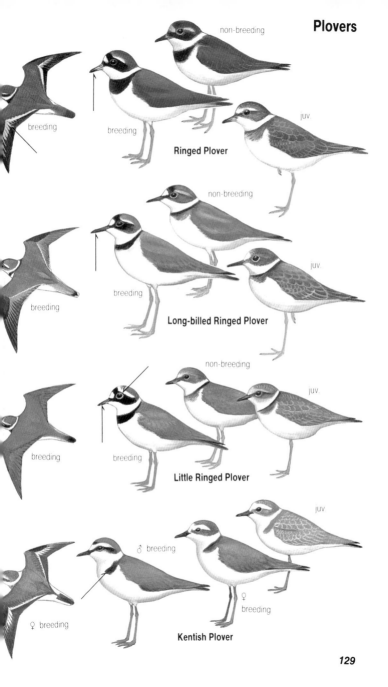

Plovers

non-breeding

breeding

breeding

Ringed Plover

juv.

non-breeding

breeding

breeding

Long-billed Ringed Plover

juv.

non-breeding

breeding

breeding

Little Ringed Plover

juv.

♂ breeding

non-breeding

♀ breeding

♀ breeding

Kentish Plover

juv.

LESSER SAND PLOVER [Mongolian Plover] *Charadrius mongolus* L 19.5cm
Legs dark brown or dark grey. **Breeding:** lores, areas around eye and
frontal bar black; sides of neck and broad breast-band rusty-red contrasting with white throat; often sharp demarcation between white on throat
and breast-band, with darker line in male. Female usually has black of
male replaced by dark-brown or rusty-red. **Non-breeding:** upperparts
sandy-brown; underparts white with dusky patches on sides of breast
forming incomplete breast-band. No traces of red or black. Race *mongolus*
has obscure sandy-brown facial markings tinged yellowish and pale-buff
supercilium. Race *atrifrons* has distinct dark-brown and white facial
pattern. **Juvenile:** like non-breeding adult, but brown is tinged buffish, and
feathers fringed with buff. **Voice:** normal call is short and hard "krri-krii".
Similar species: see Great Sand Plover. **Habitat:** breeds above tree-line in
Himalayas, and coastal sands in Siberia; otherwise coastal and estuarine
wetlands. **Distribution:** breeds discontinuously from Himalayas through
Tibet (up to 5,500 meters), east part of North Asia; moves to coasts of
South and South-East Asia and Australia in non-breeding period.   AF

GREAT SAND PLOVER [Large Sand Plover, Greater Sand-Plover]
Charadrius leschenaultii L 21.5cm. Very similar to Lesser Sand Plover, but
larger; has broader, more angular head and longer thicker bill; legs longer
toes project well beyond tail in flight; legs usually distinctly pale-brown or
greenish. Both species show white wing-bar in flight, but Great averages
more white. **Breeding:** black and rusty areas tend to be narrower than
Lesser's. **Voice:** trilling "krri-krri" or "trri-trri" similar to Lesser. **Habitat**
breeds near water at much lower altitude than Lesser, otherwise coastal
and estuarine sandflats, mudflats. **Distribution:** breeds in Central Asia
moves to coasts of South and South-East Asia in non-breeding period. AF

CASPIAN PLOVER *Charadrius asiaticus* L 19cm. Very similar to Eastern
Sand Plover, but Eastern is larger, longer-necked, lacks clear white wing
bar, and whole underwing brownish. **Breeding:** crown, nape and ear
coverts brown; chestnut breast-band with black lower border with white
underparts. **Non-breeding:** long and broad supercilium buff. **Habitat:** prefers
dry area. **Distribution:** breeds in east part of West Asia; moves mainly to
Africa and rare visitor to South Asia in non-breeding period.   SL

EASTERN SAND PLOVER [Oriental Plover] *Charadrius veredus* L 22.5cm
Large plover with very narrow white wing-bar, dark underwing. Wings
long, project well beyond tail at rest. **Breeding:** distinguished by combination of pale head with dusky crown and black eye, broad chestnut breast
band bordered by black, and white underparts distinctive. **Non-breeding**
may look uniform brown at a distance. Lores and faint supercilium off
white. **Juvenile:** like non-breeding adult, but with pale buff fringes to feathers
of upperparts; breast buff. **Voice:** flight-call a sharp whistling "chip-chip-
chip". **Similar species:** see Caspian Plover. **Habitat:** breeds on arid inland
steppes, muddy or stony flats in deserts; otherwise on dry grasslands
thinly vegetated plains. **Distribution:** breeds in Mongolia and north
eastern China; moves to Indonesia and northern Australia in non-breeding
period.   AF

Plovers

non-breeding

♂ breeding

race *atrifrons*

♂ breeding

juv.

race *mongolus*

Lesser Sand Plover

non-breeding

non-breeding

breeding

juv.

Great Sand Plover

non-breeding

non-breeding

♂ breeding

juv.

Caspian Plover

♀ breeding

non-breeding

♀ breeding

juv.

♂ breeding

Eastern Sand Plover

non-breeding

131

Sandpipers

Family *Scolopacidae* (World: 86 species; Asia: 60 species) Size, bill-length and -shape vary; animal food caught vary according to length and shape of each species' bill. SU

BLACK-TAILED GODWIT *Limosa limosa* L 39cm. Long, almost straight bill; long legs. Bill black at tip, flesh-pink at base. Legs dark-grey, project beyond tail in flight. From bill to crown gently sloping. Rump, uppertail-coverts, base of tail white; rest of tail black. Upperwing has bold white wing-bar at base of flight-feathers. **Breeding:** chestnut paler on female. Black bars on sides of breast and down to flanks. **Non-breeding:** from head to upperparts is uniform grey-brown with pale fringes. From neck to breast pale grey-brown. **Juvenile:** like non-breeding, but from head to upperparts has yellowish-brown tinge; scapulars, coverts are brown with pale fringes and blackish subterminal band. **Voice:** "kek-kek-kek". **Similar species:** see Bar-tailed Godwit. **Habitat:** breeds in grasslands near lakes and marshes or wet grasslands; in non-breeding period prefers mudflats, flooded inland grasslands. **Distribution:** breeds in North Asia, east part of East Asia; moves to South and South-East Asia. SU

BAR-TAILED GODWIT *Limosa lapponica* L 41cm. Long bill, slightly upturned; legs relatively short. Bill black at tip, flesh-pink at base. Legs dark-grey; only part of toes projects beyond tail in flight. Steep forehead. Lower back, rump, uppertail-coverts, tail are white with blackish-brown barring, so look whitish. No white bar on upperwing. **Breeding:** chestnut from breast to underparts with no barring. Female is larger than male, longer bill, resembles non-breeding. **Non-breeding:** underparts pale grey-brown with brown markings on breast and flanks. **Juvenile:** like non-breeding, but upperparts grey-brown notched with triangular buffish-white. **Voice:** "kek-kek". **Similar species:** Black-tailed Godwit in flight shows white wing-bar; at rest, visible tibia are longer; breeding Black-tailed has black bars from breast to flanks; non-breeding has paler upperparts. See Asiatic Dowitcher. **Habitat:** breeds in lowland tundra; in non-breeding period prefers sandflats. **Distribution:** breeds in North Asia; moves to South and South-East Asia. SU

ASIATIC DOWITCHER [Asian Dowitcher] *Limnodromus semipalmatus* L 33cm. Long black straight bill with swollen tip; long legs. Bill black. Eye-stripe distinct. Legs grey-brown; whole toes project beyond tail in flight. Lower back, rump, uppertail-coverts, tail are white with blackish-brown barring; they look blackish. No white bar on upperwing. **Breeding:** centre of belly white. Blackish-brown barring on flanks. Upperparts blackish fringed with pale-brown. Female duller. Undertail-coverts white barred with brown. **Non-breeding:** upperparts blackish-grey with pale fringes. Breast and neck washed grey with fine brown streaks. Belly white. **Juvenile:** like non-breeding, but neck and breast yellowish-brown; upperparts blackish with brownish fringes. Undertail-coverts white barred with brown. **Voice:** "chep-chep" or "kiaow" (soft moaning). **Similar species:** Bar-tailed Godwit is larger, has two-toned, uptilted bill, but no bold eye-stripe; no barring on undertail-coverts of breeding adult, juvenile. **Habitat:** breeds in grassy wetlands; otherwise prefers mudflats. **Distribution:** breeds in Central Asia; moves to South-East Asia in non-breeding period. Numbers few; species' ecology still not well-known. SU

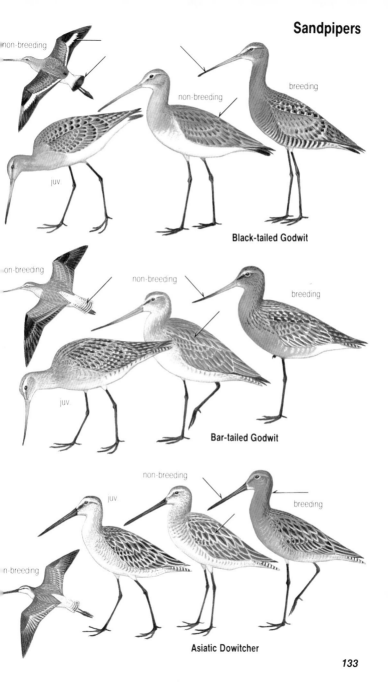

Sandpipers

non-breeding

non-breeding

breeding

juv.

Black-tailed Godwit

non-breeding

non-breeding

breeding

juv.

Bar-tailed Godwit

non-breeding

juv.

non-breeding

breeding

non-breeding

Asiatic Dowitcher

SHORT-BILLED DOWITCHER *Limnodromus griseus* L 28cm. Long straight bill. Back, rump, uppertail-coverts, tail are white with fine black barring, look whitish. On upperwing, coverts and secondaries have whitish trailing edge. Underwing-coverts, axillaries white with light-brown barring. Legs greyish-green. **Breeding:** feathers on upperparts have black centres with narrow rufous edges and whitish tips. Wing-coverts grey-brown with whitish fringes. Underparts from neck to breast are chestnut-red, heavily spotted with brown; centre of belly normally white, but some birds have whole underparts chestnut-red. **Non-breeding:** upperparts, breast plain greyish. Underparts white. Demarcation between grey breast and white belly indistinct. **Juvenile:** plumage from head to upperparts broadly edged chestnut-buff. Tertials have black centres, irregular chestnut-buff markings. Face, neck and breast washed chestnut-buff. **Voice:** gentle "tu-tu-tu". **Similar species:** see Long-billed Dowitcher. **Habitat:** intertidal mudflats. **Distribution:** breeds mainly in North America; rare visitor to East Asia. SU

LONG-BILLED DOWITCHER *Limnodromus scolopaceus* L 29cm. Very similar to Short-billed Dowitcher. At all times, Long-billed calls high-pitched "keek" instead of gentle "tu-tu-tu" by Short-billed; prefers fresh or brackish water instead of intertidal mudflats. Light bars on tail usually much narrower than black bars, while light bars usually wider than black bars in Short-billed. **Breeding:** all underparts red; foreneck densely spotted; upper breast barred. **Non-breeding:** breast and upperparts darker than on Short-billed. Demarcation between grey breast and white belly relatively distinct. **Juvenile:** grey from head to neck; breast washed-buff. Plumage of upperparts narrowly edged dull-chestnut. Tertials uniform dark-brown. **Distribution:** breeds in North America; rare visitor to East Asia. SU

WESTERN CURLEW [Curlew, Eurasian Curlew] *Numenius arquata* L 60cm. Long down-curved bill. Lower back, rump, uppertail-coverts are white, conspicuous in flight. No white bar on upperwing. Underwing white. Lower part of underparts mostly white. **Breeding:** feathers of upperparts have dark greyish-brown centres and pale brown fringes. Breast washed buffish-brown. **Non-breeding:** like breeding, but general tone of upperparts, breast is buff rather than brown. **Juvenile:** like adult, but breast more buff; flanks lightly streaked. When newly fledged, bill shorter. **Voice:** "coorlew". **Similar species:** see Far Eastern and Slender-billed Curlews, Whimbrel. **Habitat:** breeds in wet grasslands; otherwise, coasts, mudflats. **Distribution:** breeds in Central Asia; moves to South and South-East Asia and south part of East Asia in non-breeding period. SU

FAR EASTERN CURLEW [Eastern Curlew] *Numenius madagascariensis* L 62cm. Similar to Western Curlew. Separated by having deeper brown feathers overall; dark-brown back, rump, uppertail-coverts with black barring; white underwings with dense barring; brown underparts. Adult female has longest bill of any wader. **Breeding:** feathers of upperparts have dark-brown centres, rufous notched edges. Breast and flanks finely streaked; streaks dense on breast. **Non-breeding:** overall duller than breeding plumage. **Juvenile:** when newly fledged have shorter bills. **Voice:** "coor-lew". **Similar species:** care needed to distinguish from juvenile Bristle-thighed Curlew. **Habitat:** breeds in peaty marshes; in non-breeding period, coasts and mudflats. **Distribution:** breeds in north part of East Asia; moves to south part of South-East Asia and Australia. SU

breeding

Short-billed Dowitcher

juv.

non-breeding

breeding

reeding

Long-billed Dowitcher

breeding

non-breeding

juv.

Far Eastern Curlew

non-breeding

non-breeding

Western Curlew

LITTLE CURLEW *Numenius minutus* L 30.5cm. Small curlew. Bill slender, not very long, slightly down-curved, black except for pinkish-brown basal half of lower mandible. Rear part of eye-stripe extends back from below eye. Strong buff tinge overall, but from belly to undertail-coverts white. In flight, from rump to uppertail-coverts pale-brown with blackish-brown barring, looks darker than Whimbrel. **Juvenile:** like adult, but streaking of breast and flanks less pronounced; buff of upperparts paler. **Voice:** in flight, triple call of "kwit-kwit-kwit". **Similar species:** juvenile Whimbrel with short bill has whitish rump, and eye-stripe seems to pass straight through eye, not emerge from below. **Habitat:** mudflats, rice-fields, grasslands. **Distribution:** breeds in North Asia; migrates to South-East Asia and down to Australia.   KS

WHIMBREL *Numenius phaeopus* L 43cm. Long down-curved bill black except flesh-coloured base to lower mandible. Legs bluish-grey. Bold dark lateral crown-stripes. In flight, lower back and rump white with only faint brown barring. **Juvenile:** like adult, but breast more buff with finer streaking; upperparts with clearer buff spots and notches. **Voice:** whistled "hoi-pi-pi-pi-pi". **Similar species:** Bristle-thighed Curlew has more conspicuous spots on upperparts, pale orange-brown uppertail-coverts. See Little, Western and Slender-billed Curlews. **Habitat:** mudflats, rice-fields, river-banks, grassland. **Distribution:** breeds in North Asia; moves to West and South-East Asia in non-breeding period.   KS

BRISTLE-THIGHED CURLEW *Numenius tahitiensis* L 42cm. Long bill slightly thicker than Whimbrel, black except flesh-coloured base. Body rather cinnamon. Dark lateral crown-stripes. In flight, lower rump and uppertail-coverts cinnamon, unbarred. Shafts of thigh-feathers project several centimetres beyond feathers themselves, but hard to see in the field. **Juvenile:** breast more buffish, often unstreaked; cinnamon-buff spots on upperparts are larger. **Voice:** "kweeyo, peeyo". **Similar species:** see Whimbrel and Little Curlew. Juvenile Far Eastern Curlew can be confused when bill still short, but has dark rump, no lateral crown-stripes. **Habitat:** grasslands, mudflats. **Distribution:** breeds locally in north-west part of North America; migrates to islands of South Pacific. Recorded from part of East Asia as rare visitor during migration.   KS

SLENDER-BILLED CURLEW *Numenius tenuirostris* L 38.5cm. Distinguished from other medium-sized curlews by lack of crown-stripe and lateral crown-stripes, and by markedly whiter plumage. Long bill is black except pinkish-brown base, slightly more slender than Whimbrel's. Supercilium paler than Western Curlew, contrasting with dark crown. Breast almost pure-white with clearly defined dark-brown streaks. Flanks white with bold round blackish-brown spots of various shapes, some heart-shaped. In flight, lower back to uppertail-coverts white, with some brown streaks on uppertail-coverts. **Breeding:** scapulars sometimes with grey and rufous tinge. **Non-breeding:** very like breeding, but fewer round spots on flanks. **Juvenile:** markings on flanks more like streaks than spots, brown in colour. **Voice:** usually silent, but sometimes 'coor-lew" like Western Curlew. **Similar species:** see Whimbrel, Western Curlew. **Habitat:** marshes, mudflats, grasslands. **Distribution:** breeds in north part of West Asia; moves to South Europe and North Africa in non-breeding period. Uncertain record from Japan.   KS

Sandpipers

Little Curlew

Whimbrel

juv.

Bristle-thighed Curlew

non-breeding

non-breeding

Slender-billed Curlew

137

SPOTTED REDSHANK [Dusky Redshank] *Tringa erythropus* L 33cm. Long slender bill; long legs. No white bar on upperwing. **Breeding:** head, neck, underparts all-black. Upperparts black but spotted and notched white. Legs dark brown-red. **Non-breeding:** upperparts grey, fringed and notched white. Supercilium white, extends behind eye. Lores black. Underparts white. Legs orange-red. **Juvenile:** upperparts spotted and notched white. White supercilium distinct in front of eye. Underparts finely barred with grey. **Voice:** "chu-it". **Similar species:** see Common Redshank. **Habitat:** breeds in open or lightly wooded tundra; otherwise, freshwater marshes. **Distribution:** breeds in North Asia; moves to South and South-East Asia. SU

COMMON REDSHANK [Redshank] *Tringa totanus* L 28cm. Relatively long stout bill; long legs. On upperwing, primaries black; inner primaries white-tipped; secondaries white. **Breeding:** crown grey-brown with black streaks; upperparts grey-brown with black shaft-streaks and barring and warm-brown notching. Underparts have dark-brown spots. Legs bright orange-red. **Non-breeding:** similar to non-breeding Spotted Redshank, but has different wing pattern and colouration of bill; indistinct supercilium; underparts white with some streaks. Legs orange-red. **Juvenile:** upperparts warm-brown with buff notches and fringes. Underparts from breast down are streaked with light brown. **Voice:** noisy; calls "teu-teu-hu". **Habitat:** breeds on coastal salt-marshes, inland marshes; otherwise coastal wetlands. **Distribution:** breeds from Central Asia to north part of East Asia; moves to South and South-East Asia, south part of East Asia. SU

COMMON GREENSHANK [Greenshank] *Tringa nebularia* L 35cm. Bill somewhat up-turned; legs long. Lower back, rump, uppertail-coverts white. No white bar on upperwing. Underwing white but finely barred brown. In flight, legs project noticeably beyond tail. Colour of legs variable, grey to pale-olive. **Breeding:** head, neck, breast blackish-brown and heavily streaked. Scapulars blackish with finely notched white edges. Tertials have brownish-grey centres and white edges notched with small black dots. **Non-breeding:** head, neck look pale. Coverts, scapulars are grey, finely fringed white with dark subterminal crescents. Fine streaks from breast to sides of neck and flanks. **Juvenile:** upperparts browner than adult with pale buff. **Voice:** whistled "teu-teu-teu". **Similar species:** see Spotted Greenshank. **Habitat:** breeds in lightly wooded marshes of taiga; otherwise mudflats and open coasts. **Distribution:** breeds in North Asia; moves to South and South-East Asia, south part of East Asia. SU

SPOTTED GREENSHANK [Nordmann's Greenshank, Armstrong's Sandpiper] *Tringa guttifer* L 31cm. Very similar to Common Greenshank. At all times, separated by having thick, almost straight bill; relatively short dull ochreous-yellow legs; white underwing. In flight, legs project a little beyond tail. **Breeding:** head, neck, breast are blackish-brown, heavily spotted. Scapulars grey, notched with triangular white spots. Tertials dark-grey, outer edges notched with deep triangular white. **Non-breeding:** head, neck washed grey with fine streaks. Scapulars, wing-coverts, tertials are pale ashy-grey, look paler and more uniform than Common. Coverts, scapualrs finely fringed white. Underparts from breast downwards are white. **Juvenile:** upperparts browner than adult **Voice:** "kwork" or "gwaak". **Habitat:** coastal marshes, sandy mudflats. **Distribution:** only known breeding place is Sakhalin (Russia); moves to South-East Asia; very rare. SU

Sandpipers

non-breeding

breeding

non-breeding

juv.

Spotted Redshank

non-breeding

juv.

non-breeding.

breeding

Common Redshank

n-breeding

non-breeding

juv.

breeding

Common Greenshank

on-breeding

juv.

breeding

non-breeding

Spotted Greenshank

MARSH SANDPIPER *Tringa stagnatilis* L 25cm. Slender straight black bill; extremely long, greyish-green legs. Lower back, rump, uppertail-coverts white. Tail white with fine brown barring. Underparts white. No white bar on upperwing. Underwing white except black flight-feathers. **Breeding:** upperparts greyish-brown, notched buffish-grey with black shaft-streaks. Supercilium indistinct. Dense dark-brown streaking from head to breast. Legs yellowish. **Non-breeding:** from crown to upperparts fairly plain brownish-grey with whitish fringes. Supercilium white, distinct. **Juvenile:** like non-breeding, but upperparts browner with buffish or whitish fringing. **Voice:** "pi-pi-pi" or "plew". **Similar species:** Common Greenshank is large, calls "teu-teu-teu", has thick, upturned, partly greenish-grey bill. Wood Sandpiper has relatively short legs, distinct streaks on neck and breast, and dark lower back. **Habitat:** breeds in grassy marshes; outside breeding season, inland lakes, marshes. **Distribution:** breeds in Central Asia; moves to South and South-East Asia.   SU

GREATER YELLOWLEGS *Tringa melanoleuca* L 35cm. Long bill, somewhat upturned. Legs long, orange-yellow. Rump, uppertail-coverts are white, in flight appear separate from elongated blackish tertials. No white bar on upperwing. Underwing whitish. **Breeding:** head and neck streaked dark-brown; breast, flanks have distinct black spots. Scapulars, tertials, mantle are blackish-brown, spotted white. **Non-breeding:** upperparts brownish-grey, notched and fringed white. Dark streaks on breast and flanks. **Juvenile:** like non-breeding, but upperparts warmer brown, in places notched and fringed pale-buff. Brown streaks on neck, breast. **Voice:** piercing "teu-teu-teu". **Similar species:** Greenshank has greyish-green legs; in flight, lower back white. See Lesser Yellowlegs. **Habitat:** marshes inland. **Distribution:** breeds in North America; rare visitor to East Asia.   SU

LESSER YELLOWLEGS *Tringa flavipes* L 25cm. Slender straight bill; long orange-yellow legs. Rump, uppertail-coverts are white; tertials, being short, appear joined to white uppertail-coverts in flight. No white bar on upperwing. Underwing whitish. **Breeding:** head, neck, breast have brown streaks. Fewer streaks on flanks than Greater Yellowlegs. Scapulars, tertials, mantle blackish, spotted white. **Non-breeding:** upperparts brownish-grey, faintly spotted white. Breast brownish-grey, faintly streaked. **Juvenile:** like non-breeding, but warmer brown and in places spotted bright-buff. Breast washed-grey, faintly streaked brown. **Voice:** "tew-tew". **Similar species:** Greater Yellowlegs is larger, has different bill-shape and voice; but identification requires great care. Wood Sandpiper has relatively short legs, bill and neck, browner plumage and longer, more distinct supercilium. **Habitat:** inland and coastal wetlands. **Distribution:** breeds in North America; rare visitor to East Asia.   SU

Sandpipers

juv.

non-breeding

breeding

non-breeding

Marsh Sandpiper

juv.

non-breeding

non-breeding

breeding

Greater Yellowlegs

juv.

non-breeding

non-breeding

breeding

Lesser Yellowlegs

141

GREEN SANDPIPER *Tringa ochropus* L 24cm. Underparts, rump, upper-tail-coverts are white, contrast strongly with upperparts in flight. Tail white with 2-3 broad black bars. Supercilium short, joins white eye-ring. Legs blackish-green, do not project much beyond tail in flight. **Breeding:** crown nape, breast are white, heavily streaked dark-brown. **Non-breeding:** head and breast paler than breeding, streaks slightly darker. **Juvenile:** like non-breeding, but upperparts and breast browner; spots on scapulars, tertials are more buff-coloured, not conspicuous like adult's. **Voice:** ringing "weet tweet". **Similar species:** Common Sandpiper is smaller, lacks white rump, has white bar on upperwing. See Wood Sandpiper. **Habitat:** breeds in forests with marshes; otherwise inland freshwater. **Distribution:** breeds in south part of North Asia; moves to South, South-East and East Asia.　　SL

WOOD SANDPIPER *Tringa glareola* L 22cm. Underwing, rump, upper tail-coverts white. Tail white with dark-brown barring. Supercilium white and distinct, extends behind eye. Narrow white eye-ring. Long legs greenish-yellow, project a fair bit beyond tail in flight. **Breeding:** breast buffish-white with bold dark-brown streaks. Barring on flanks. **Non-breeding:** upperparts more grey-brown; breast darker with obscure brown streaks; no barring on flanks. **Juvenile:** upperparts dark warm-brown spotted and fringed with bright buff-brown. Breast grey-brown. No bars on flanks. **Voice:** "chip, chip, chip". **Similar species:** Green Sandpiper is sturdier, has richer colour on upperparts contrasting more strongly with underparts; also different flight-pattern and voice, broader wings, dark olive-brown underwing, shorter blackish-green legs. **Habitat:** breeds in forests with marshes; otherwise inland freshwater. **Distribution:** breeds in North Asia; moves to South, South-East and East Asia.　　SL

GREY-TAILED TATTLER [Grey-rumped Sandpiper] *Heteroscelus brevipes* L 25cm. Upperparts including wings, tail, are plain slate-grey. Supercilium white; lores dark. Underwings slate-grey; axillaries dark-grey. Legs yellow At rest, wings not longer than tail. Uppertail-coverts finely fringed white but this can rarely be observed in the field. **Breeding:** dark-grey barring on breast, flanks, edges of undertail-coverts; but no barring on belly, vent **Non-breeding:** barring disappears. **Juvenile:** underparts like non-breeding but faint grey barring on breast, flanks. Wing-coverts, tertials, scapulars have whitish spots. **Voice:** "tu-whip". **Similar species:** see Wandering Tattler. **Habitat:** breeds in stony river-beds in mountain areas; otherwise on mudflats, coasts. **Distribution:** breeds in north part of East Asia; moves to south part of South-East Asia.　　SL

WANDERING TATTLER *Heteroscelus incanus* L 28cm. Very similar to Grey-tailed Tattler; upperparts including wings, tail, slightly plainer and darker. Supercilium white, but narrower than Grey-tailed. Lores not as dark as Grey-tailed. Underwing dark-grey. Legs yellow. At rest, wings longer than tail. Uppertail-coverts plain grey. **Breeding:** unlike Grey-tailed underparts heavily barred dark-grey right up to tips of undertail-coverts **Non-breeding:** barring disappears. Usually supercilium does not extend behind eye, unlike Grey-tailed. **Juvenile:** like Grey-tailed, but latter has bolder white spots on upperparts, and supercilium extending clearly behind eye. **Voice:** unlike Grey-tailed, calls "pi-pi-pi-pi". **Habitat:** rocky coasts. **Distribution:** breeds in North America; observed in East Asia eastern South-East Asia en route to Australia.　　SL

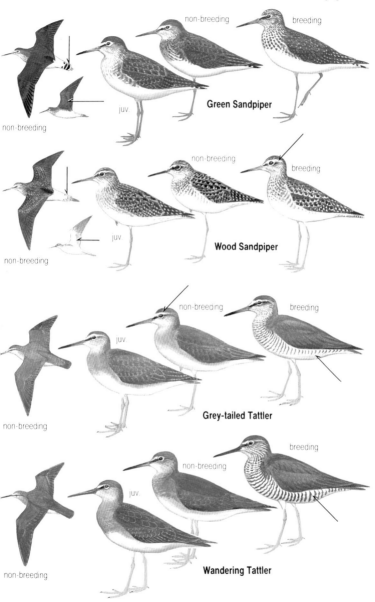

non-breeding

juv.

non-breeding

breeding

Green Sandpiper

non-breeding

juv.

non-breeding

breeding

Wood Sandpiper

non-breeding

juv.

non-breeding

breeding

Grey-tailed Tattler

non-breeding

juv.

non-breeding

breeding

Wandering Tattler

TEREK SANDPIPER *Xenus cinereus* L 23cm. Distinguished by longish upturned bill, short yellow-orange legs. Feeds actively, often runs. Upperparts grey-brown. Underparts, underwing white. Supercilium relatively clear and white in front of eye, but indistinct behind eye. All feathers of upperparts have narrow blackish shaft-streaks. Secondaries blackish-brown with broad white tips. **Breeding:** broad black shaft-streaks on scapulars form conspicuous black scapular lines. Grey streaks on breast. **Non-breeding:** almost all birds lose black scapular lines. Breast becomes paler with less distinct streaks. **Juvenile:** like breeding, but upperparts darker grey-brown with obscure dark subterminal bars and buff fringes. Black scapular lines present, but indistinct. **Voice:** fluting "twit-twit". **Similar species:** Spotted Greenshank larger with straight thick bill; white from lower half of back to rump, uppertail-coverts and tail. Grey-tailed Tattler somewhat larger with darker upperparts, straight bill, no white on upperwing in flight. **Habitat:** breeds near large rivers and freshwater lakes; otherwise on mudflats, estuaries. **Distribution:** breeds in North Asia; moves to South and South-East Asia.   SU

COMMON SANDPIPER *Actitis hypoleucos* L 20cm. Distinguished by habits of bobbing head up and down while walking, and flicking wings in flight. Upperparts dark grey-brown with narrow shaft-streaks crossed by black barring. Underparts white, with white peak in front of the wing. Supercilium white. In flight, shows clear white wing-bar, white tip and sides to tail. Legs yellowish-brown. **Breeding:** white from neck to breast with brown streaks forming breast-band. **Non-breeding:** upperparts paler; streaks on breast become less clear. **Juvenile:** like non-breeding, but feathers of upperparts fringed pale-buff. **Voice:** "tirii-tirii". **Habitat:** rivers, lakes, marshes etc. **Distribution:** breeds in North and East Asia; moves to South and South-East Asia in non-breeding period, south part of East Asia; resident in central part of East Asia.   SU

RUDDY TURNSTONE [Turnstone] *Arenaria interpres* L 22cm. Short bill, somewhat upturned; short orange-red legs. **Breeding:** male's head and breast white with distinctive pattern of black stripes; each bird has slightly diffrent head-pattern. Upperparts chestnut with black and white markings. Underparts white. Female's head duller with less white; more streaks on crown. **Non-breeding:** both sexes lose chestnut colour; head uniformly dark-brown. Legs dark-orange. **Juvenile:** like non-breeding, but pale patches on head; upperparts browner with buffish-white fringes to feathers. **Voice:** "tuk-tukatuk". **Habitat:** rocky coasts, sandy beaches; sometimes inland during migration. **Distribution:** breeds in the Arctic; moves to South and South-East Asia, south part of East Asia.   SU

BUFF-BREASTED SANDPIPER *Tryngites subruficollis* L 20cm. Face, underparts buff in all plumages. Bill slender, black. Head has distinctive rectangular shape. Dark eyes stand out against pale face. Upperparts have black shaft-streaks and buff-brown fringes. Underwing white. Legs orange-yellow. **Juvenile:** like adult, but mantle, scapulars and coverts whitish-buff and strongly fringed, giving more scaly appearance than adult. **Habitat:** grasslands. **Distribution:** rare visitor to East Asia from North America.   SU

Sandpipers

non-breeding

non-breeding

breeding

juv.

Terek Sandpiper

non-breeding

non-breeding

breeding

juv.

Common Sandpiper

non-breeding

♀ breeding

juv.

♂ breeding

Ruddy Turnstone

♂ breeding

juv.

juv.

Buff-breasted Sandpiper

WILSON'S PHALAROPE *Phalaropus tricolor* L 23cm. Least marine of the phalaropes; different shape from Red-necked and Grey, with longer, more slender body and black bill. Pecks food from water-surface while swimming; or feeds with distinctive pecking action while walking rapidly over mud. In flight, long legs project beyond tip of tail; no white wing-bar square white area on rump. **Breeding:** legs black. Female has pale-grey crown and nape; white patch above eye; black eye-stripe continues down side of neck, becomes chestnut-red on side of mantle; chestnut-red and pale-grey form V-stripes on mantle. Male's upperparts are blackish-brown instead of pale-grey; sides of neck duller. **Non-breeding:** upperparts pale-grey. Pale-grey eye-stripe less bold than other phalaropes. Legs yellow. **Juvenile:** upperparts blackish-brown, fringed buff, giving scaly appearance. Legs pinkish-yellow. **Similar species:** Red-necked and Grey Phalaropes smaller, stubbier, with shorter bills, dark-grey legs, and in flight, white wing-bars but no white on rump. **Habitat:** lakes, marshes mudflats. **Distribution:** breeds in North America; winters in South America a few records from East Asia. KS

RED-NECKED PHALAROPE *Phalaropus lobatus* L 18.5cm. Smallest phalarope. Slender longish black bill. Legs blackish with clearly lobed toes. In flight, white wing-bar; white sides to rump. **Breeding:** bold golden-buff lines along outer edges of mantle and scapulars. Female has dark grey crown and hindneck, small white patch above eye, conspicuous chestnut-red sides of neck. Male has duller upperparts and, usually, white supercilium. **Non-breeding:** conspicuous blackish mark through eye upperparts grey with white fringes. Obscure whitish lines along outer edges of mantle and scapulars. **Juvenile:** similar pattern to non-breeding adult, but dark-brown replaces grey. Bold orange-buff lines along outer edges of mantle, scapulars. **Similar species:** Grey Phalarope smaller with stubbier bill; when breeding, bill yellow with black tip, underparts chestnut-red; in flight, identification difficult in non-breeding and juvenile plumages. See Wilson's Phalarope. **Habitat:** seas, rice-fields, rivers; sometimes inland wetlands during migration. **Distribution:** breeds in the Arctic winters on seas of South-East Asia; most migrate over the sea, few overland. KS

GREY PHALAROPE *Phalaropus fulicarius* L 21cm. Short thick bill, usually yellow at base. Legs brownish with clearly visible, yellowish lobes on toes. In flight, white wing-bar; white sides to rump. **Breeding:** female chestnut red from throat to underparts; conspicuous white patch around eye. Male duller than female. **Non-breeding:** conspicuous blackish mark through eye. Upperparts uniformly pale-grey. **Juvenile:** similar pattern to non-breeding adult, but upperparts blackish-brown with buff-brown fringes. **Similar species:** see Wilson's and Red-necked Phalaropes. **Habitat:** seas, marshes near coasts; less likely than Red-necked Phalarope to be found inland or close to shore. **Distribution:** breeds in the Arctic; migrates over sea to the waters off Chile. KS

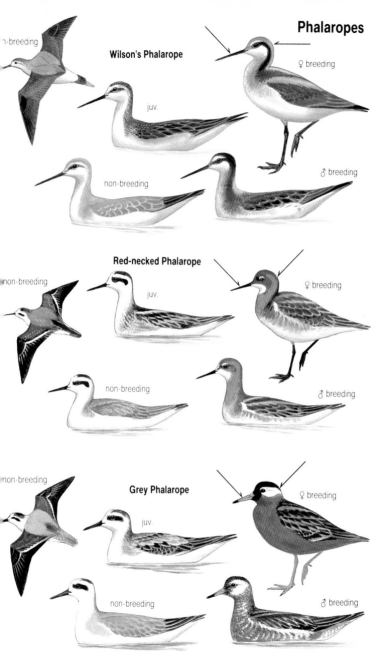

Phalaropes

Wilson's Phalarope

non-breeding

juv.

♀ breeding

non-breeding

♂ breeding

Red-necked Phalarope

non-breeding

juv.

♀ breeding

non-breeding

♂ breeding

Grey Phalarope

non-breeding

juv.

♀ breeding

non-breeding

♂ breeding

EURASIAN WOODCOCK [Woodcock] *Scolopax rusticola* L 34cm. Larger, more chunky than snipes. Head triangular in shape; thick black cross-bars on rear crown and hindneck. In flight, wings broad with rounded tips. Usually seen at dawn or dusk, in flight or feeding at the forest edge. **Voice:** usually silent when flushed; in breeding season roding male at dusk calls "chikit, chikit, boo, boo". **Similar species:** Wood Snipe smaller, with striped crown. See Amami Woodcock. **Habitat:** woods, bamboo-groves, farmlands. **Distribution:** breeds in Central and East Asia; moves to South, South-East and south part of East Asia.   KS

AMAMI WOODCOCK *Scolopax mira* L 36cm. Very similar to Eurasian Woodcock, but: — longer tarsus resulting in visible knee when standing, while the bird leans forward more. Peak of head is at forecrown; eye-stripe and cheek-stripe appear almost parallel; bars on rear crown thicker than those on top of crown; body less reddish-brown, more dark olive-brown; greater coverts and tertials uniformly dark olive-brown except for pale brown notches on feather edges. From May to September, patch of bare pink skin appears around eye. **Voice:** "quak-quak, gway" when flushed; unlike Eurasian Woodcock, display in breeding season performed on the ground with "coo-coo" calls. **Similar species:** Eurasian Woodcock has shorter tarsus; top of head at mid-crown; eye-stripe and cheek-stripe angled together towards hindneck; crown bars thickest on top of crown; brown greater coverts and tertials with large, dark brown, oval markings running across them. **Habitat:** woods, sugar-cane fields. **Distribution:** endemic to Amami Islands, Okinawa Island, Japan.   KS

RUFOUS WOODCOCK *Scolopax saturata* L 30cm. Crown rufous with black bars across head and nape; upperparts reddish-brown with black blotches and bars; primaries blackish and spotted rufous; tail black; underparts barred black and rufous. Bill brownish-black and tinged with pinkish at tip and base; iris brown; legs dark grey. Hides during the day by sitting on the ground and flies to feeding grounds in open country at night. **Voice:** harsh "do-do-do-do" and "krrr-krrr-krrr". **Similar species:** see Obi Woodcock. **Habitat:** montane forest near lakes, forest edges and grasslands at 1700-4000m above sea level. **Distribution:** resident in Indonesia (Java, Sumatera Islands and New Guinea.)   DMP

SULAWESI WOODCOCK *Scolopax celebensis* L 32cm. Head buff-brown with black bars on crown; a pale yellowish-brown band finely barred with black on hindneck; upperparts blackish-brown with small rufous spots and bars; underparts buffish-ochre with some black bars on cheek, breast and flanks; tail greyish. Bill bluish-grey; iris brown; legs grey. **Similar species:** see Obi Woodcock. **Habitat:** montane forest at 1700-2300m above sea level. **Distribution:** endemic to Sulawesi Island, Indonesia.   DMP

OBI WOODCOCK *Scolopax rochussenii* L 33cm. Forehead yellowish-brown with broad black bands on crown and hindneck; a black stripe extending from bill to eyes; upperparts blackish-brown with buff spots and bars; underparts buff with black bars on breast and flanks; tail blackish with lighter tip and buff tinges. Bill bluish-grey; iris brown; legs grey. **Similar species:** Rufous Woodcock has heavier black bars on underparts. Sulawesi Woodcock is finely marked on upperparts. **Habitat:** hill forest. **Distribution:** endemic to Obi and Batjan Islands, Indonesia.   DMP

Eurasian Woodcock

Amami Woodcock

Rufous Woodcock

Sulawesi Woodcock

Obi Woodcock

SOLITARY SNIPE *Gallinago solitaria* L 30cm. Can be distinguished from almost all snipes by being found alone in marshy areas on hills and mountains. Also by whitish face, gingery tinge to sides of breast, and whitish colour of longitudinal stripes on crown and upperparts. Tip of bill black, base brownish. In flight, whitish trailing edge to secondaries, inner primaries is extremely narrow, difficult to see. In hand, tail-feathers usually 20. **Voice:** hoarse "gwet" when flushed. **Similar species:** Wood Snipe has rather round-tipped wings, entire belly barred, much darker body and thicker base of bill. See Japanese, Pintail, Swinhoe's and Common Snipes. **Habitat:** streams, rice-fields, marshes in hilly and mountainous regions. **Distribution:** resident in mountains from West Asia to South-East and East Asia, but range discontinuous. Some move to lowlands of continental South-East Asia to central part of East Asia in non-breeding period. KS

WOOD SNIPE *Gallinago nemoricola* L 31cm. Darkest snipe, most heavily marked below, often no white on belly — appearing both structurally and in colouration like a small Eurasian Woodcock. Flight similar on broad wings, slow wingbeat. Hindneck blackish; mantle and scapulars blackish-brown fringed with greyish-buff; wing-coverts dark-brown spotted and barred greyish-buff. **Voice:** flushes silently, occasionally with a low croaking note like "tok-tok". **Habitat:** breeds in mountain forests in the eastern Himalayas; moves to lower elevations in the same regions in non-breeding period. **Distribution:** resident in east part of South Asia and west part of South-East Asia. BB

GREAT SNIPE *Gallinago media* L 28cm. Larger and stouter than Common Snipe with shorter bill, otherwise very similar. In flight, typically shows two whitish lines along tips of medium and greater coverts; white on outer tail feathers conspicuous and diagnostic; underwings dark. White flanks and belly strongly barred. White in tail barred with light-brown in juvenile birds. **Voice:** low guttural croak on flushing. **Habitat:** breeds in wooded tundra; otherwise in marshes. **Distribution:** breeds in north part of Europe; rare visitor to South Asia in non-breeding period. BB

JACK SNIPE *Lymnocryptes minima* L 20cm. Much smaller than other snipes, about same size as Dunlin. Bill much shorter. Crown with dark centre; supercilium split above the eye. Greenish gloss to upperparts. Tail brown, lacks rufous and white bands on tails of other snipes. When feeding, often makes unique a bobbing motion. Stays still until almost trodden on; even when flushed, does not fly far. In flight, shows white bar on tips of secondaries and inner primaries; tail wedge-shaped. In hand, tail-feathers 12; central ones have pointed tips. **Voice:** usually silent when flushed. **Similar species:** Common Snipe and other snipes are larger with much longer bills and have rufous on tail, but do not have broad split supercilium. **Habitat:** rice-fields, lotus ponds, marshes. **Distribution:** breeds in broad belt across northern latitudes of Asia; moves to South Asia and part of South-East Asia in non-breeding period. KS

Snipes

Solitary Snipe

Wood Snipe

Great Snipe

Jack Snipe

151

JAPANESE SNIPE [Latham's Snipe] *Gallinago hardwickii* L 29cm. Large and bulky snipe with relatively long wings, tertials and tail. Can be distinguished from similar Swinhoe's Snipe by latter's longest primary being on average 13mm longer than tertials at rest, while in Japanese Snipe both about the same length. Pintail Snipe's tail projects slightly beyond tip of closed wings; in Japanese Snipe tail projects well beyond. Common Snipe has conspicuous white trailing edge to secondaries and inner primaries in flight; Japanese Snipe only has faintly pale trailing edge to secondaries. In hand, tail-feathers usually 16 or 18. **Voice:** "get" when flushed. **Similar species:** adult Great Snipe has conspicuous broad white bands on tips of median, greater and primary coverts; outer tail-feathers conspicuously white. **Habitat:** breeds in grasslands; on migration frequents rice-fields, lotus ponds, marshes, river-banks. **Distribution:** breeds in Japan; spends non-breeding period in East Australia. KS

PINTAIL SNIPE *Gallinago stenura* L 26cm. Extremely similar to Swinhoe's Snipe except for tail structure; in flight under ideal conditions, can be seen that toes project farther beyond tip of tail. Both inner and outer margins of lower scapulars, at least towards the tips, are pale buff, producing a scalloped rather than streaked appearance like Common Snipe. In flight, extremely narrow pale trailing edge to tips of secondaries; underwing-coverts densely barred, appearing uniform grey. In hand, tail-feathers usually 26 or 28; outer 6–8 pairs like pins. **Voice:** short rasping "squik" or "ketk" when flushed. **Similar species:** Common Snipe has different pattern to scapulars, tail much longer than closed wings, large white area on underwing and conspicuous white trailing edge to secondaries. See Japanese, Swinhoe's and Great Snipes. **Habitat:** rice-fields, lotus ponds, marshes, river-banks, grasslands. Similar to Common Snipe, but often found in drier places and often found together. **Distribution:** breeds widely across North Asia; spends non-breeding period in South and South-East Asia, and south part of East Asia. KS

SWINHOE'S SNIPE *Gallinago megala* L 28cm. At rest, tertials on average 13mm shorter than longest primary; similar in size to Japanese Snipe. In flight, toes project only slightly beyond tail-tip; faint pale line on trailing edge of secondaries. In hand, tail-feathers usually 20 or 22. **Voice:** "chrap" when flushed although calls less frequently than Common and Pintail Snipe. **Similar species:** see Pintail, Japanese, Common and Great Snipes. **Habitat:** rice-fields, lotus ponds, marshes, river banks. **Distribution:** breeds in central latitudes of North Asia; spends non-breeding period in South and South-East Asia, and south part of East Asia. KS

COMMON SNIPE [Fantail Snipe] *Gallinago gallinago* L 26cm. Longish bill. In flight, distinguished from all other snipes by conspicuous white trailing edge to secondaries and inner primaries; also by largely white underwing-coverts. In hand, tail-feathers usually 14. **Voice:** long nasal "jayt" when flushed. **Similar species:** see Pintail, Japanese, Swinhoe's and Great Snipes. **Habitat:** rice-fields, lotus ponds, marshes, river banks. **Distribution:** breeds in broad belt across north of Asia; spends non-breeding period in East Asia, South-East Asia and South Asia; generally the commonest and most widely distributed snipe in these areas. KS

Snipes

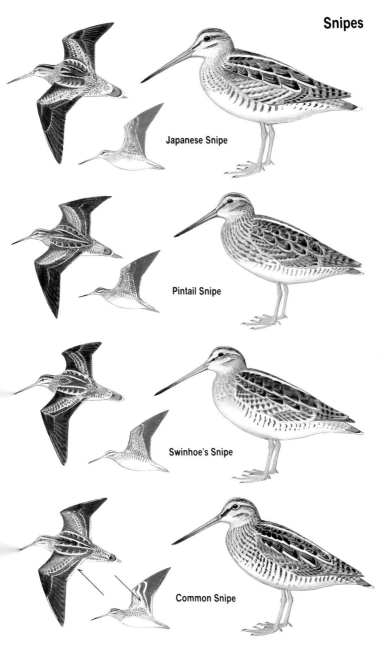

Japanese Snipe

Pintail Snipe

Swinhoe's Snipe

Common Snipe

RED KNOT [Knot] *Calidris canutus* L 24cm. Round body; together with larger Great Knot, distinctly larger than other *Calidris* species. Longish black bill; yellowish-green legs. In flight, lower rump and uppertail-coverts appears whitish and paler than mantle with numerous dark bars; narrow but conspicuous white wing-bar. **Breeding:** face, breast and upper belly reddish-brown; upperparts dark with rufous fringes. **Non-breeding:** upperparts pale grey with very narrow blackish shaft-streaks and thin whitish fringes; underparts whitish; breast and upper belly faintly streaked. **Juvenile:** coverts, scapulars and tertials have whitish fringes and black subterminal lines, forming distinct scaling on upperparts. **Voice:** short, nasal "krut". **Similar species:** Great Knot is larger and heavier, has longer bill slightly decurved at tip; lower rump and uppertail-coverts are whiter; closed primaries project beyond tail-tip (Red Knot's are about equal in length). See Curlew Sandpiper in breeding plumage. **Habitat:** mudflats, inlets. **Distribution:** breeds in North Asia; spends non-breeding period in South and South-East Asia; passage migrant further north.   KS

GREAT KNOT [Eastern Knot] *Calidris tenuirostris* L 27cm. Larger than Red Knot with longer body; relatively long black bill slightly decurved at tip; legs dark green. In flight, lower rump and uppertail-coverts whitish; narrow white wing-bar. **Breeding:** head and neck covered in fine black streaks; upperparts light brown with conspicuous chestnut patches on scapulars, sometimes tertials; underparts white with distinctive heavy black bars or spots on neck, breast and flanks, often forming breast-band. **Non-breeding:** blackish marks on sides of breast more distinct than Red Knot's; faint breast-band formed by narrow streaks. **Juvenile:** upperparts more contrasting than non-breeding; scapulars have black centres; wing-coverts and tertials edged white. Breast covered with brown streaks and spots. **Voice:** "kit-kit". **Similar species:** see Red Knot. **Habitat:** mudflats, inlets. **Distribution:** breeds in North Asia; spends non-breeding period in South and South-East Asia; passage migrant further north.   KS

RUFF *Philomachus pugnax* L 29cm (male). 22.5cm (female). Shortish bill slightly decurved, dark brown/orange-yellow. Longish legs variable in colour (yellow, red etc). Longish neck; head looks small. Some back-feathers often stand up. In flight, distinctive white oval patches on sides of long uppertail-coverts; narrow wing-bar. **Breeding:** In male, display plumes from head to breast form unmistakable ruff, variable in colour (white, black, rufous etc). Females also variable, much smaller than male; feathers on upperparts usually black-centred, and conspicuous black blotching on breast and flanks. **Non-breeding:** both sexes like breeding female, but plainer above and below; upperparts grey-brown with dark centres to feathers; underparts white to buff-brown; some birds have particularly white heads and necks (these are almost all males). **Juvenile:** feathers on upperparts are blackish-centred with distinct buffish fringes, giving scaly effect; buff from face to underparts. **Voice:** usually silent, but sometimes calls "kwat-kwat, kway". **Similar species:** see Sharp-tailed Sandpiper. Red-legged female Ruff resembles Redshank, but distinguished by rather uniformly patterned head and large light/dark markings on breast and upperparts. **Habitat:** rice-fields, mudflats, marshes. **Distribution:** breeds in north part of North Asia; spends non-breeding period in South Asia; uncommon passage migrant from South-East Asia northwards.   KS

Sandpipers

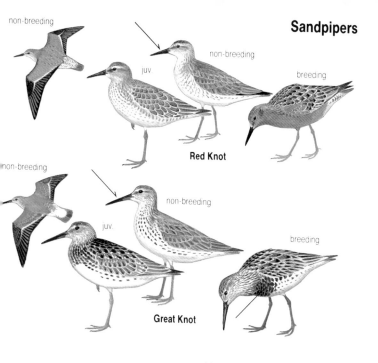

non-breeding

juv.

non-breeding

breeding

Red Knot

non-breeding

juv.

non-breeding

breeding

Great Knot

non-breeding

♂ breeding

♂ breeding

♂ breeding

♀ juv.

♀ breeding

♂ juv.

♂ non-breeding

Ruff

WESTERN SANDPIPER *Calidris mauri* L 15.5cm. Longish black bill slightly decurved. Toe webbing diagnostic if visible. In flight, distinct white patches on sides of rump and uppertail-coverts; narrow white wing-bar. **Breeding:** sides of crown, ear-coverts reddish-brown; distinctive dark spots and chevrons on breast, flanks, sometimes extending to sides of undertail-coverts. **Non-breeding:** upperparts pale grey; white underparts with pointed dark streaks on sides of breast. **Juvenile:** rufous fringes on upper scapulars form conspicuous line. **Voice:** like Rufous-necked Stint, but more high-pitched. **Similar species:** see Rufous-necked Stint. **Habitat:** mudflats, inlets. **Distribution:** breeds in eastern tip of North Asia and North America; rare vagrant to East Asia. KS

RUFOUS-NECKED STINT [Eastern Little Stint] *Calidris ruficollis* L 14.5cm. Shortish black bill. In flight, white sides to rump and uppertail-coverts; white wing-bar. **Breeding:** from crown to throat and upper breast rufous and (except crown) unmarked; on upperparts, rufous fringes to scapulars, while wing-coverts and tertials usually rather pale brown-grey with narrow whitish fringes. **Non-breeding:** upperparts grey-brown with narrow dark shafts. **Juvenile:** upperparts very variable; dark anchor-shaped subterminal marks on lower scapulars; wing-coverts and tertials grey-brown with pale rufous to pale grey fringes (not rufous to pale buff fringes like Little Stint). **Voice:** "chui-chui-chiriri-chiriri". **Similar species:** see Little and Long-toed Stints, Western Sandpiper. **Habitat:** mudflats, rice-fields, lotus ponds. **Distribution:** breeds in north part of North Asia; spends non-breeding period from East to South-East Asia. KS

LITTLE STINT *Calidris minuta* L 13cm. Very similar to Rufous-necked Stint, but tip of black bill is more pointed, legs slightly longer, body looks slightly shorter and fatter. Wing-pattern in flight is the same as Rufous-necked Stint. **Breeding:** throat white; sides of breast normally bright orange-brown with small dark streaks at sides; all upperparts with blackish centres and bright rufous fringes to feathers. **Non-breeding:** extremely like Rufous-necked Stint. Dark shafts of scapulars usually broader, but some have narrow shafts like typical Rufous-necked. **Juvenile:** white fringes to upper scapulars produce distinctive V pattern on mantle meeting on lower back, the only black-legged stint to show this feature; wing-coverts and tertials blackish with rufous to pale buff fringes. **Voice:** short distinctive "tit, tit". **Similar species:** see Rufous-necked Stint. **Habitat:** mudflats, rice-fields, river banks. **Distribution:** breeds in north part of North Asia; spends non-breeding period in South Asia. KS

TEMMINCK'S STINT *Calidris temminckii* L 13cm. Legs variable (yellow, greenish-grey, occasionally blackish). In flight, white patches on sides of black rump; short narrow white wing-bar; white outer tail-feathers diagnostic when visible. **Breeding:** breast rather dark and uniform; upperparts usually rather dark, relatively dull-coloured. **Non-breeding:** upperparts uniform dark grey-brown; faint supercilium; breast dark grey-brown band, but sometimes broken in the middle. **Juvenile:** upperparts dark grey-brown with narrow pale fringes; scapulars have narrow dark subterminal fringes. **Voice:** distinctive thin trill "chiriririt". **Similar species:** differs from other stints in rather uniform dark breast. **Habitat:** rice-fields, river banks, marshy areas. **Distribution:** breeds in north part of North Asia; spends non-breeding period in South, South-East and East Asia. KS

Sandpipers

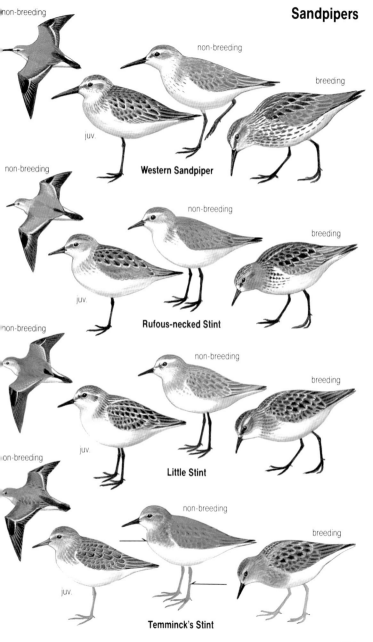

non-breeding

non-breeding

breeding

juv.

Western Sandpiper

non-breeding

non-breeding

breeding

juv.

Rufous-necked Stint

non-breeding

non-breeding

breeding

juv.

Little Stint

non-breeding

non-breeding

breeding

juv.

Temminck's Stint

SANDERLING *Calidris alba* L 20.5cm. Thick shortish black bill; black legs. In flight, white patches on sides of rump and uppertail-coverts; conspicuous broad white wing-bar. Usually feeds in flocks, dashing to and fro where the waves break on sandy shores. **Breeding:** head, neck and breast deep chestnut with small, dark-brown streaks, contrasting with white underparts. **Non-breeding:** upperparts very pale grey; face whitish; blackish lesser and primary coverts usually form black patch at bend of closed wing. **Juvenile:** upperpart feathers with black centres and pale fringes; breast buff with fine streaks at sides. **Voice:** sharp "quiriri-quiriri, queee". **Similar species:** Dunlin has longer, somewhat decurved bill. **Habitat:** sandy shores, mudflats, inlets. **Distribution:** breeds in north part of North Asia; spends non-breeding period in South Asia, South-East Asia and south part of East Asia; passage migrant further north. KS

BAIRD'S SANDPIPER *Calidris bairdii* L 15.5cm. Black, slightly longish bill, sometimes with base tinged greenish; legs short and black. Tip of closed primaries project beyond tail-tip. In flight, narrow whitish sides of dark rump and uppertail-coverts; extremely narrow, short, white wing-bar. **Breeding:** crown brown with buffish streaks; upperneck and breast finely streaked brown. **Non-breeding:** colouring less distinct; upperparts and breast-band greyish. **Juvenile:** feathers on upperparts with dark-brown centres with buffish fringes, forming neat scaly pattern; neck and breast buffish with brown streaks. **Voice:** "prreep, krree". **Similar species:** Rufous-necked Stint smaller with shorter, thicker bill. **Habitat:** mudflats, inlets, rice-fields. **Distribution:** breeds in northern tip of North Asia, but mainly from North America; rare visitor to East Asia during migration. KS

PECTORAL SANDPIPER *Calidris melanotos* L 21cm. Black bill rather long and thin, slightly decurved, paler at base. Legs yellowish-green. Distinguished by sharp demarcation between breast, always heavily streaked brown, and white belly. In flight, whitish sides to blackish rump; very narrow white wing-bar and trailing edge to inner secondaries. **Breeding:** crown and upperparts edged rufous; male's breast dark brown mottled with whitish. **Non-breeding:** upperparts less contrasting. **Juvenile:** even brighter than breeding; white edging on mantle and scapulars forms white V. **Voice:** soft trilling "krreet, chui-tsoo". **Similar species:** juvenile Sharp-tailed Sandpiper has far fewer streaks on breast, no sharp demarcation from whitish belly. **Habitat:** inlets, rice-fields. **Distribution:** breeds in north part of North Asia; recorded in East Asia during migration. KS

SHARP-TAILED SANDPIPER *Calidris acuminata* L 19cm. Slightly bigger than Dunlin. Black bill slightly down-curved, yellowish tinge at base; legs yellowish-green. Distinguished by sharp contrast between dark rufous cap and long white supercilium. In flight, white lateral uppertail-coverts with dark shaft-streaks; faint white wing-bar. **Breeding:** throat, foreneck and breast densely spotted; chevron-like markings on breast and flanks. Upperparts become deeper rufous. **Non-breeding:** faint streaks on sides of neck and breast. **Juvenile:** cap and ear-coverts bright rufous; strong rufous tinge to upperparts. **Voice:** rather quiet, soft "krrit, prreet, tweep-tweep". **Similar species:** see Ruff and Pectoral Sandpiper. **Habitat:** rice-fields, inlets. **Distribution:** breeds in north part of North Asia; spends non-breeding period in south part of South-East Asia; passage migrant further north. KS

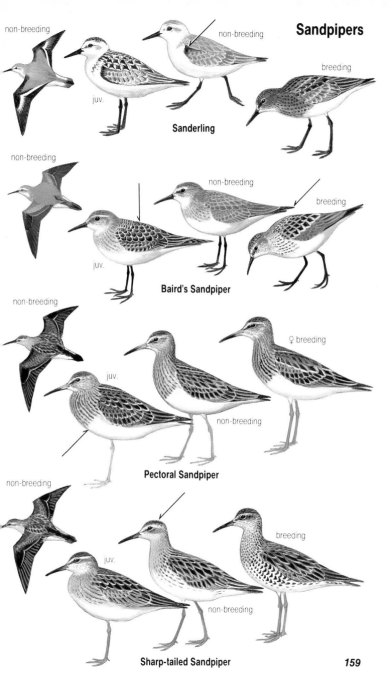

Sandpipers

non-breeding

non-breeding

breeding

juv.

Sanderling

non-breeding

non-breeding

breeding

juv.

Baird's Sandpiper

non-breeding

juv.

♀ breeding

non-breeding

Pectoral Sandpiper

non-breeding

juv.

breeding

non-breeding

Sharp-tailed Sandpiper

159

LONG-TOED STINT *Calidris subminuta* L 14cm. Small version of Sharp-tailed Sandpiper. Thin black bill; legs yellowish-green. Sides of breast rather heavily and distinctly streaked; distinct whitish supercilium; dark area of forehead comes down to base of bill, meets dark line on lores. When alarmed, attains more upright stance than other stints, neck looks longer. In flight, distinct white sides of rump and uppertail-coverts; faint white wing-bar; toes project a little beyond tail-tip. **Breeding:** cap rufous; upperparts fringed with rufous, especially broad on tertials. **Non-breeding:** upperparts dark grey with no warm colour tones, feathers have broad dark centres. **Juvenile:** like adult, but has rufous cap and split supercilium, white edging to mantle forms white V on back. **Voice:** rather musical trilling "churiri, kuriri". **Similar species:** Rufous-necked Stint has black legs. Temminck's Stint has obscure supercilium, white outer tail-feathers; different shape. See Sharp-tailed Sandpiper. **Habitat:** rice-fields, muddy fish-ponds, marshy areas and other inland wetlands. **Distribution:** breeds in south part of North Asia; spends non-breeding period in South Asia and South-East Asia; passage migrant further north. KS

ROCK SANDPIPER *Calidris ptilocnemis* L 21.5cm. Black bill, yellowish-green at base; legs yellow to yellowish-green. In flight, whitish sides to blackish rump and uppertail; distinct white wing-bar. **Breeding:** crown dark brown with chestnut fringes; distinct dark patch on rear ear-coverts; mantle, scapulars and tertials with dark-brown centres and chestnut and buff fringes. Dark brown streaks from breast to belly; streaks on lower breast are larger, often merge to form large black patch. **Non-breeding:** head grey; supercilium short, white; upperparts uniform deep grey with white fringes to wing-coverts. Breast grey; dense black spots from breast to flanks. **Juvenile:** feathers on upperparts with dark-brown centres and chestnut and buff fringes; wing-coverts grey-brown with buff edging. Breast buffish with grey-brown streaks. **Voice:** "chui". **Similar species:** see Dunlin. **Habitat:** rocky coasts, breakwaters. **Distribution:** breeds in eastern tip of North Asia; spends non-breeding period in parts of East Asia; passage migrant further north. KS

SPOON-BILLED SANDPIPER *Eurynorhynchus pygmeus* L 15cm. Very similar to Rufous-necked Stint, but has distinctive black spatulate bill; bill-shape may however be hard to make out when viewed sideways on. Feeding action also distinctive: sweeps bill from side to side in water or mud. Legs black. In flight, white sides to rump and uppertail-coverts; relatively distinct white wing-bar. **Breeding:** face, neck and upper breast almost all reddish like Rufous-necked Stint, but has no grey on lower scapulars, and face is richer strawberry colour. **Non-breeding:** distinct white supercilium; upperparts grey-brown with darker shaft-streaks; wing-coverts with grey centres and narrow white fringes. **Juvenile:** conspicuous dark patch runs from lores through eyes to ear-coverts; upperparts blackish-brown with whitish feather fringes, forming distinctive pattern and looking more black-and-white than juvenile Rufous-necked Stint. **Voice:** "pii-pii", but mostly silent. **Similar species:** see Rufous-necked Stint and Sanderling. **Habitat:** mudflats, inlets. **Distribution:** breeds in eastern tip of North Asia; spends non-breeding period in east part of South Asia and west part of South-East Asia; passage migrant further north. KS

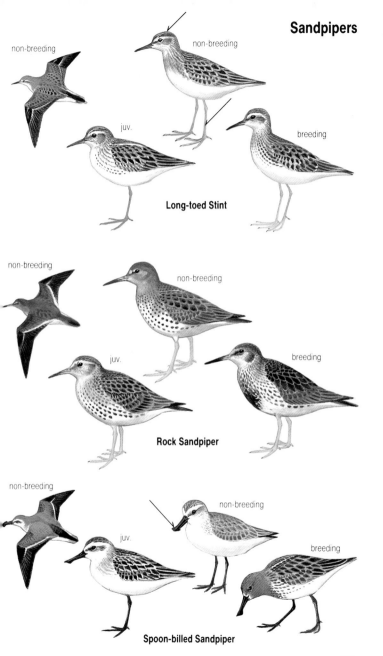

Sandpipers

non-breeding

non-breeding

juv.

Long-toed Stint

breeding

non-breeding

non-breeding

juv.

breeding

Rock Sandpiper

non-breeding

juv.

non-breeding

breeding

Spoon-billed Sandpiper

DUNLIN *Calidris alpina* L 18.5cm. Longish black bill, somewhat down-curved at tip; legs black. In flight, distinct white sides to rump and uppertail-coverts; clear white wing-bar. **Breeding:** distinguished by large black patch on centre of belly. Mantle and scapulars with blackish feather centres and chestnut fringes. **Non-breeding:** upperparts uniform grey-brown; underparts white with faint grey-brown streaks on sides of breast. **Juvenile:** mantle and scapulars blackish-brown with chestnut edging; belly and flanks white with dark brown streaks. **Voice:** distinctive trill; "tree-t-tree". **Similar species:** Curlew Sandpiper has longer legs, longer and more curved bill; lower rump and uppertail-coverts form square white area. See Broad-billed Sandpiper and Sanderling. **Habitat:** mudflats, inlets, river banks. **Distribution:** breeds in north part of North Asia; spends non-breeding period in South and East Asia. KS

CURLEW SANDPIPER *Calidris ferruginea* L 20.5cm. Black bill longer than Dunlin's, somewhat down-curved; legs black. In flight, lower rump and uppertail-coverts form all-white square (partly barred brown in breeding season); clear white wing-bar; toes project beyond tail-tip. **Breeding:** head, neck and almost all underparts are very conspicuous vinous-red. Blackish scapulars have vinous-red fringes, white tips. **Non-breeding:** upperparts uniform grey-brown with pale fringes on wing-coverts. **Juvenile:** upper parts dark brown with pale fringes and dark subterminal bands. **Voice** "chip, chirrip". **Similar species:** Broad-billed Sandpiper has split supercilium. See Dunlin. **Habitat:** mudflats, rice-fields, inlets. **Distribution:** breeds in north part of North Asia; spends non-breeding period from West Asia to South-East Asia. KS

BROAD-BILLED SANDPIPER *Limicola falcinellus* L 17cm. Distinguished by split supercilium. Longish black bill with slightly decurved tip; bill width hard to make out in the field. Legs black. In flight, white sides to dark rump and uppertail-coverts; narrow but distinct white wing-bar. **Breeding:** crown blackish-brown; conspicuous white split supercilium; white line formed by feather-edges on mantle and scapulars; black streaks on white foreneck, breast and flanks. **Non-breeding:** upper supercilium sometimes indistinct; upperparts grey-brown with dark shaft-streaks and white fringes; sometimes with black patch at bend of closed wing. **Juvenile:** like breeding, but fringes on upperparts pale chestnut and whitish; thin brown streaks on pale brown breast. **Voice:** "jooree, jirree-jirree, choi-choi-choi". **Similar species:** see Dunlin, Curlew Sandpiper. **Habitat:** mudflats, inlets, rice-fields, marshy areas. **Distribution:** spends non-breeding period from West Asia to South-East Asia. KS

STILT SANDPIPER *Micropalama himantopus* L 20.5cm. Long thin black bill, slightly down-curved. Rather long, yellowish-green legs. In flight, lower rump and uppertail-coverts form white square (partly barred brown in non-breeding period); no clear wing-bar; toes project beyond tail-tip. **Breeding:** lores, ear-coverts and nape chestnut; neck and upper breast densely streaked brown; from lower breast to undertail-coverts densely barred. **Non-breeding:** upperparts uniform grey-brown with white fringed wing-coverts. **Juvenile:** fringed on upperparts with rufous or buff. **Voice** "kirr, guriri". **Similar species:** Marsh Sandpiper has straight bill, pale tail. **Habitat:** marshy inland areas, coastal pools. **Distribution:** vagrant from North America; only a few records from East Asia. KS

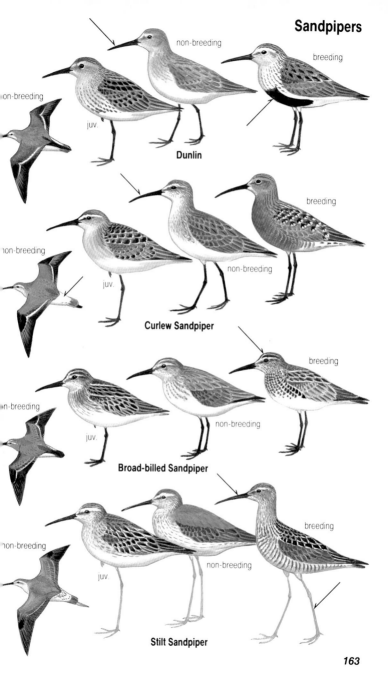

Sandpipers

non-breeding

breeding

non-breeding

juv.

Dunlin

breeding

non-breeding

non-breeding

juv.

Curlew Sandpiper

breeding

non-breeding

non-breeding

juv.

Broad-billed Sandpiper

breeding

non-breeding

non-breeding

juv.

Stilt Sandpiper

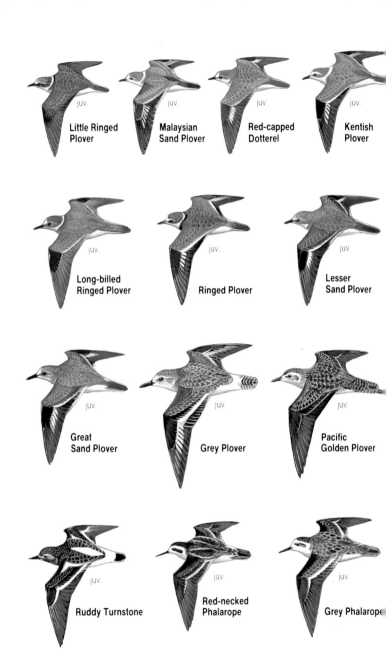

Little Ringed Plover — juv.

Malaysian Sand Plover — juv.

Red-capped Dotterel — juv.

Kentish Plover — juv.

Long-billed Ringed Plover — juv.

Ringed Plover — juv.

Lesser Sand Plover — juv.

Great Sand Plover — juv.

Grey Plover — juv.

Pacific Golden Plover — juv.

Ruddy Turnstone — juv.

Red-necked Phalarope — juv.

Grey Phalarope — juv.

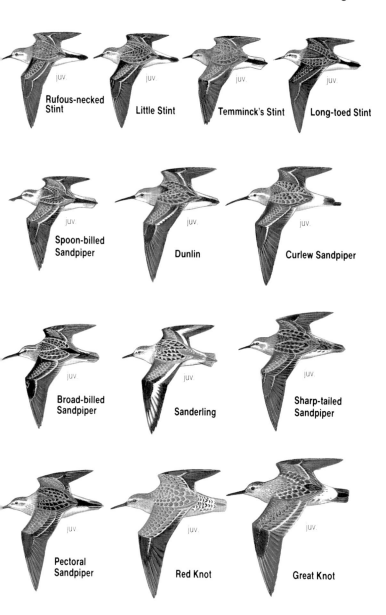

Rufous-necked Stint

Little Stint

Temminck's Stint

Long-toed Stint

Spoon-billed Sandpiper

Dunlin

Curlew Sandpiper

Broad-billed Sandpiper

Sanderling

Sharp-tailed Sandpiper

Pectoral Sandpiper

Red Knot

Great Knot

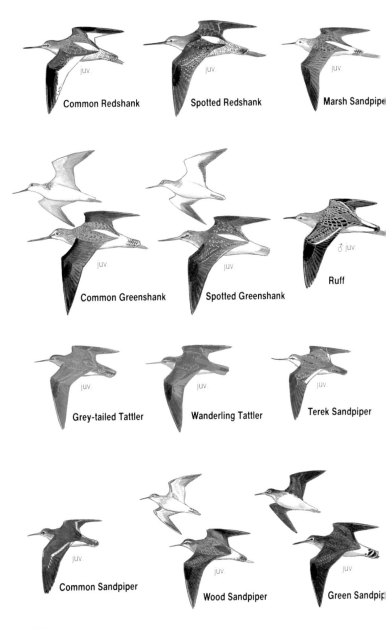

Common Redshank

Spotted Redshank

Marsh Sandpiper

Common Greenshank

Spotted Greenshank

Ruff

♂ juv.

Grey-tailed Tattler

Wanderling Tattler

Terek Sandpiper

Common Sandpiper

Wood Sandpiper

Green Sandpiper

Shorebirds in Flight

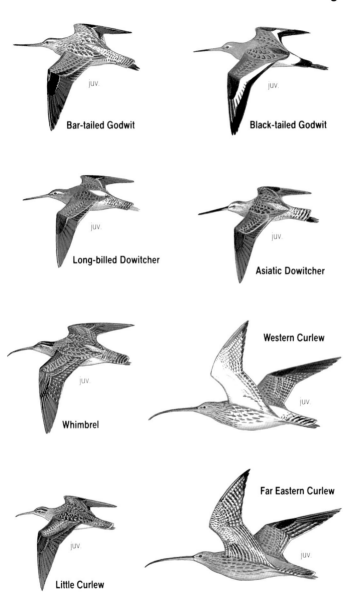

Bar-tailed Godwit

juv.

Black-tailed Godwit

juv.

Long-billed Dowitcher

juv.

Asiatic Dowitcher

juv.

Whimbrel

juv.

Western Curlew

juv.

Little Curlew

juv.

Far Eastern Curlew

juv.

Gulls

Family *Laridae,* Subfamily *Larinae* (World: 48 species; Asia: 19 species) Stocky birds with long wings, shorter bills and legs. Mainly coastal, but also found inland waters. Gregarious. Sexes similar.   SU

SOOTY GULL *Larus hemprichii* L 46cm. **Breeding:** head blackish-brown with stout yellow bill with red and black bands on tip; collar white; rump, uppertail-coverts and tail white. Legs green-yellow. **Non-breeding:** white collar reduced in size or lacking. **Juvenile:** pale brownish-grey upperparts with blue-grey bill tipped black; tail mostly black; legs dull grey. **1st imm. non-breeding:** mantle and back brownish-grey; upperwing-coverts fringed with pale; tail mostly black. **2nd imm. non-breeding:** head and breast pale brownish-grey; mantle and upperwings grey; tail mostly white with narrow black subterminal band; bill dull yellowish-green tipped black. **Habitat:** coasts, estuaries. **Distribution:** breeds around Arabian Peninsula and in Pakistan; moves to western South Asia in non-breeding period.   SU

JAPANESE GULL [Black-tailed Gull] *Larus crassirostris* L 45cm. **Breeding:** upperparts and wings blackish-grey; rump and uppertail-coverts white; tail has conspicuous black band. Bill yellow with red and black bands on tip; legs yellow. **Non-breeding:** brown streaks from crown to nape. **Juvenile:** generally blackish-brown; primaries black; tail black; white uppertail-coverts conspicuous in flight; bill flesh-coloured with black tip. **Voice:** "miyaao", "kwaao". **Similar species:** Slaty-backed Gull is large, has dark-pink legs, no black tail-band. **Habitat:** coasts. **Distribution:** East Asia.   SU

MEW GULL [Common Gull] *Larus canus* L 42cm. **Breeding:** Upperwings blue-grey with thin white leading edge and broader trailing edge. Outer few primaries mostly black with white tips and with a white mirror. Bill and legs yellowish-green; iris dark; orbital ring red. **Non-breeding:** brown streaks on head, nape and sides of breast. **Juvenile:** forehead white; head streaked brown; upperparts brown fringed paler; rump buff with dark streaks; outer primaries blackish-brown, grey inner primaries and secondaries with dark trailing edge; underwing white streaked brown; tail white with black subterminal band; underparts white with some brownish streaking on breast and flanks; undertail-coverts barred brown. Bill pink with black-pink; legs flesh-pink. **1st imm. non-breeding:** like juvenile, but streaks on crown lighter, grey back, rump and underparts whiter. **2nd imm. non-breeding:** head whiter; small white mirrors on blackish primaries; tail white. Legs blue-grey. **Voice:** a mewing "kee-er". **Similar species:** see Eastern Mew, Indian Black-headed and Herring Gulls. **Habitat:** Coastal and inland fields. **Distribution:** breeds in west part of North Asia; moves to South Asia.   TM

EASTERN MEW GULL *Larus kamtschatchensis* L 45cm. Very like Mew Gull. Eastern is larger and has paler iris. Non-breeding Mew Gull has dark subterminal band on bill, whereas bill of Eastern is all-yellow. **Similar species** (same as for Mew Gull): differs from Herring Gull in flight in having neater bill, narrower wings and, in case of adult, larger mirrors; at rest in having small, narrow bill and rounded head. **Habitat:** coasts, inland lakes/marshes. **Distribution:** resident in east part of North Asia and East Asia; northern breeders move south in non-breeding period.   SU

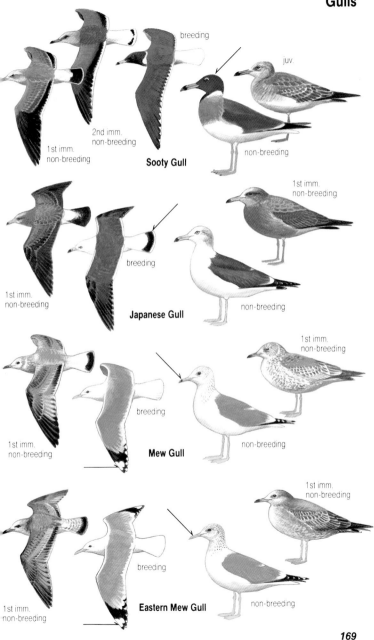

Gulls

breeding

juv.

2nd imm.
non-breeding

1st imm.
non-breeding

Sooty Gull

non-breeding

1st imm.
non-breeding

1st imm.
non-breeding

breeding

Japanese Gull

non-breeding

1st imm.
non-breeding

1st imm.
non-breeding

breeding

Mew Gull

non-breeding

1st imm.
non-breeding

1st imm.
non-breeding

breeding

Eastern Mew Gull

non-breeding

1st imm.
non-breeding

HERRING GULL *Larus argentatus* L 60cm. Long, yellow bill with red spot near gonys. Iris yellow. Race *vegae* is observed in East Asia, *mongolicus* from south part of East Asia to South-East and South Asia, and *heuglini* in South Asia. Race *vegae* has pink or bright pink legs at all ages; *mongolicus* usually yellow legs, but some apparently pink; *heuglini* adult has pink legs, but other ages yellow. The following describes race *vegae*. **Breeding:** upperparts and upperwings blue-grey; outer primaries black with white tips and one or two mirrors. **Non-breeding:** streaked from head to upper breast. **2nd imm. non-breeding:** grey mantle and scapulars contrast with wings; bill flesh-coloured with black tip. **1st imm. non-breeding:** uniformly dark; tail-band contrasts with whitish base of tail and rump. Inner webs of inner primaries are pale. Bill black. **Similar species:** see Slaty-backed Gull, which has more blackish upperparts and upperwings than race *vegae,* more greyish underwing flight-feathers. Lesser Black-backed Gull similar to race *heuglini,* but smaller with shorter legs. **Habitat:** coasts, rivers, lakes, marshes. **Distribution:** breeds in east part of North Asia, East Asia; moves to East, South-East and South Asia.   SU

SLATY-BACKED GULL *Larus schistisagus* L 61cm. Straight bill; rounded head. **Breeding:** upperparts and upperwings are uniformly blackish-grey. Head white; iris yellow; bill yellow with red spot near gonys. Legs reddish-pink. **Non-breeding:** head streaked brown, particularly densely around eyes; streaks also on upper breast. **2nd imm. non-breeding:** mantle and scapulars change from dark grey to adult's blackish-grey. Outer primaries same as first year, but inner primaries and whole inner wing uniformly pale except dark band on secondaries. Dark tail contrasts with white rump. **1st imm. non-breeding:** like Herring Gull, but no pale area on inner primaries, and less patterning on coverts. Whole tail blackish; iris brown; bill black; legs pink. **Similar species:** see Japanese Gull. **Habitat:** coasts, estuaries. **Distribution:** breeds in east part of North Asia and north part of East Asia; northern breeders moves south.   SU

GLAUCOUS-WINGED GULL *Larus glaucescens* L 64cm. Resembles Glaucous Gull, but first year has black bill, and wing-tips of adult are grey, of other ages pale brown. **Breeding:** upperparts and upperwings blue-grey; iris brown; bill yellow with red spot near gonys. **Non-breeding:** pale brown streaks on head and upper breast; primaries grey. **2nd imm. non-breeding:** uniformly dingy grey; mantle and scapulars change to adult's grey. Bill nearly black; iris dark. **1st imm. non-breeding:** bill black; at rest, colour of wing-tips similar to, or darker than tertials and rest of upperparts. **Similar species:** see Glaucous Gull. **Habitat:** coasts. **Distribution:** breeds in far east part of North Asia; moves to north part of East Asia.   SU

GLAUCOUS GULL *Larus hyperboreus* L 71cm. **Breeding:** upperparts and upperwings whitish-grey; primaries and secondaries broadly tipped white. Iris pale yellow; bill yellow with red spot near gonys; legs pink. **Non-breeding:** as breeding, except for orange-brown streaks on head, upper breast. **2nd imm. non-breeding:** pale buff or whitish all over; black on bill smaller than 1st imm. non-breeding; iris pale. **1st imm. non-breeding:** bill mainly flesh-coloured, but one-third at tip is black. At rest, wing-tips clearly whiter than tertials and other upperparts. **Habitat:** coasts, estuaries. **Distribution:** breeds in east part of North Asia; moves to north part of East Asia.   SU

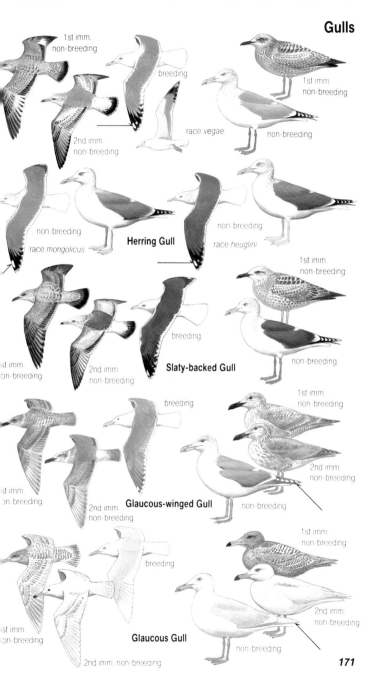

1st imm. non-breeding

2nd imm. non-breeding

breeding

race vegae

1st imm. non-breeding

non-breeding

non-breeding

race mongolicus

Herring Gull

non-breeding

race heuglini

1st imm. non-breeding

2nd imm. non-breeding

breeding

Slaty-backed Gull

1st imm. non-breeding

non-breeding

breeding

1st imm. non-breeding

2nd imm. non-breeding

Glaucous-winged Gull

non-breeding

1st imm. non-breeding

2nd imm. non-breeding

breeding

1st imm. non-breeding

2nd imm. non-breeding

Glaucous Gull

2nd imm. non-breeding

non-breeding

171

THAYER'S GULL *Larus thayeri* L 58cm. Like Herring Gull, but a little smaller, rounded head. Short bill, yellow or greenish-yellow, with orange-red spot near gonys and whitish tip. Iris usually dark; eyes large and gentle. In flight, has less black on tips of outer primaries of upperwing even than Herring Gull, and hardly any black on tips of underwing; underwing looks almost all-white except dark trailing edge to outer primaries. Legs deep pink. **Non-breeding:** generally pale brown with dark markings from head to neck. **1st imm. non-breeding:** at rest, tips of primaries are brown or dark brown, not blackish like Herring Gull; pale fringes of primaries form V-shaped pattern. In flight, shows less dark on outer primaries than Herring, since apart from tips, only outer webs are dark; underwing flight-feathers appear grey, since on secondaries also, only outer webs are dark. Bill black; legs deep pink. **Habitat:** coasts, estuaries. **Distribution:** rare visitor from North America to east part of North Asia and East Asia.   SU

LESSER BLACK-BACKED GULL *Larus fuscus* L 56cm. **Breeding:** head, neck, underparts and tail white; mantle dark slate-grey. In flight, strongly contrasting narrow white leading and trailing edges of dark wings, and white tips to black primaries conspicuous. Bill yellow with orange-red spot near gonys; iris yellow; legs bright orange-yellow. **Non-breeding:** head heavily streaked with brown. **2nd imm. non-breeding:** head white with dark streaks around eye and on crown and nape; black subterminal band on tail reduced. **1st imm. non-breeding:** head brownish-white; rump whitish and uppertail-coverts white, rest of upperparts dark brown, darker than Herring Gull; tail whiter at base and has broader and more defined blackish band than Herring Gull. Bill black; iris brown; legs dull flesh. **Habitat:** coastal and inland wetlands. **Distribution:** small numbers observed in west part of South Asia in non-breeding period.   BB

GREAT BLACK-HEADED GULL *Larus ichthyaetus* L 69cm. Large gull. At rest, wings clearly extend beyond tail. Head has distinctive shape: long, sloping forehead rises to peak behind the eyes, making whole head appear long and accentuating the length and heaviness of bill. In flight, wings appear more pointed, narrower and longer than other large gulls. **Breeding:** only large gull to have black hood. **Non-breeding:** black remains only around eyes. In flight, tips of outer primaries are white with black markings on inner webs. Legs greenish-yellow. Bill yellow with large black subterminal band and reddish tip. **2nd imm. non-breeding:** retains subterminal band on tail, but it is narrow. **1st imm. non-breeding:** brown streaks on sides of breast contrast with white underparts. Unlike other large gulls, which have brown mantle, scapulars and underparts, this species has grey mantle and scapulars, white underparts; also differs in having white tail with broad black subterminal band. **Habitat:** breeds on inland lakes; moves to coasts, lakes, rivers etc. **Distribution:** resident in Central Asia; northern breeders move to South and South-East Asia.   SU

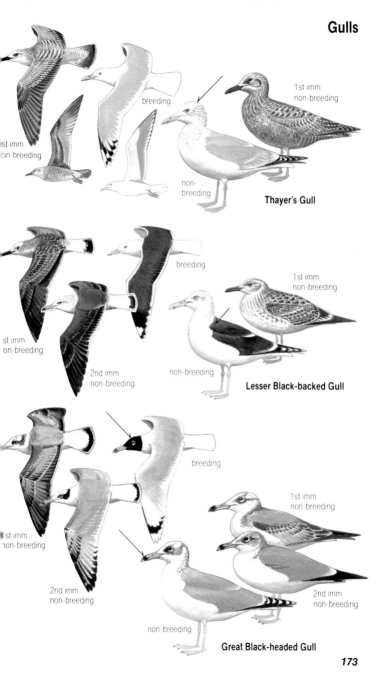

1st imm. non-breeding

breeding

non-breeding

1st imm. non-breeding

Thayer's Gull

1st imm. on-breeding

breeding

2nd imm. non-breeding

1st imm. non-breeding

non-breeding

Lesser Black-backed Gull

1st imm. non-breeding

breeding

1st imm. non-breeding

2nd imm. non-breeding

2nd imm. non-breeding

non-breeding

Great Black-headed Gull

173

INDIAN BLACK-HEADED GULL [Brown-headed Gull] *Larus brunnice-phalus* L 42cm. **Breeding:** brown hood; mantle and back pale grey with white rump; underparts white; outer two primaries black with prominent white mirror, rest of primaries white at base; underwing mostly grey with black primaries as upperwing; tail white. **Non-breeding:** like breeding, but head white with dark spot on ear-coverts. **Juvenile:** like non-breeding, but lacks white mirror, has black terminal band on white tail. **Similar species:** Black-headed Gull smaller with different wing pattern. **Habitat:** seacoasts, lakes, rivers. **Distribution:** breeds in Central Asia; moves to South Asia, South-East Asia and south part of East Asia in non-breeding period.   SU

BLACK-HEADED GULL [Common Black-headed Gull] *Larus ridibundus* L 40.5cm. W 92.5cm. In flight, leading edge of outer upperwing white; primaries on underwing almost all black. **Breeding:** hood blackish-brown down to nape; white crescents above and below eye. Longish thin dark-red bill; dark-red legs. Some birds have slight pink tinge to white underparts. **Non-breeding:** bill red with black tip. Head white with small dark crescent-shaped mark before eye and dark mark on ear-coverts. **1st imm. non-breeding:** like non-breeding adult, but tertials and part of wing-coverts dark-brown; blackish band on tip of tail; bill and legs dull flesh. In flight, upperwing shows brown carpal bar on leading edge, blackish bar on secondaries. **Similar species:** Saunders' Gull has shorter black bill, in flight shows whitish inner primaries on underwing. Slender-billed Gull has flat forehead, longish bill, no black hood in breeding plumage. See Little and Bonaparte's Gulls. **Habitat:** coasts, estuaries, mudflats, lakes, marshes, rivers. **Distribution:** breeds in central latitudes of Asia; moves to East, South-East and South Asia in non-breeding period.   KS

LITTLE GULL *Larus minutus* L 27.5cm. W 64.5cm. The smallest gull. Flight is buoyant and tern-like. In flight, dark underwing with white trailing edge stands out. **Breeding:** hood blackish; bill blackish-red, narrow; legs red. At rest, closed primaries look white. **Non-breeding:** head white, but with dark crown, ear-coverts and small crescent-shaped mark in front of eye. **1st imm. non-breeding:** like non-breeding, but tertials and part of wing-coverts are dark-brown; black band on tip of tail; legs paler. In flight, upperwing has broad blackish carpal bar on forewing, forming distinct "M" pattern, narrow dark bar on secondaries. Underwing whitish except dark-brown tips to outer primaries. **Similar species:** see Black-headed Gull. **Habitat:** coasts, lakes, marshes. **Distribution:** breeds in parts of central latitudes of East Asia; otherwise in Europe and West Africa.   KS

SAUNDERS' GULL *Larus saundersi* L 31.5cm. In flight, underwing shows whitish inner primaries, black base to outer primaries. **Breeding:** blackish hood with white crescents above and below eyes. Short black bill; legs dark-red. At rest, black tips of closed primaries interrupted by white spots. **Non-breeding:** head white with dark ear-coverts, resembling head-phones, and small crescent-shaped marks in front of eyes. **1st imm. non-breeding:** like non-breeding, but tertials and part of wing-coverts dark-brown; black band on tip of tail; legs brown. In flight, upperwing shows obscure brown carpal bar on forewing, blackish bar on secondaries. **Similar species:** see Indian Black-headed and Black-headed Gulls. **Habitat:** coasts, estuaries, mudflats, lakes, marshes. **Distribution:** breeds locally in East China; moves to East and South-East Asia in non-breeding period. KS

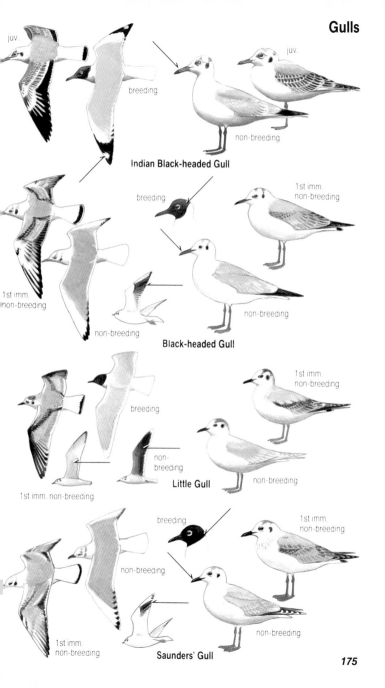

Gulls

juv.

breeding

juv.

non-breeding

Indian Black-headed Gull

1st imm. non-breeding

breeding

1st imm. non-breeding

non-breeding

1st imm. non-breeding

non-breeding

Black-headed Gull

breeding

non-breeding

1st imm. non-breeding

non-breeding

1st imm. non-breeding

Little Gull

breeding

non-breeding

1st imm. non-breeding

1st imm. non-breeding

non-breeding

Saunders' Gull

FRANKLIN'S GULL *Larus pipixcan* L 35.5cm. Relatively large white crescents above and below eyes. **Breeding:** blackish hood; red bill with thin black subterminal band. In flight, tips of primaries plain white. **Non-breeding:** head white, but from eyes to hindneck has partial blackish-brown hood flecked with white/grey. Bill black with red tip. **1st imm. non-breeding:** like non-breeding, but tertials and part of wing-coverts dark-brown; blackish band on tip of tail. In flight, blackish bar on secondaries on upperwing. **Habitat:** coasts, estuaries, rivers, lakes, marshes. **Distribution:** vagrant from North America; a few records from Japan.   KS

RELICT GULL [Relic Gull] *Larus relictus* L 45.5cm. Longish flat forehead. Longish legs with extensive tibial feathering. Walks with erect stance, thick neck extended and back at almost 45° angle to the ground. In flight, upper- and underwings show black tips to outer primaries with conspicuous white marks at the very tip. **Breeding:** blackish hood with conspicuous white crescents above and below eyes. Bill, legs dark-red. **Non-breeding:** head white with dark markings on ear-coverts and small dark patches on hindneck; white crescents above and below eyes. **1st imm. non-breeding:** like adult non-breeding, but lacks dark markings on ear-coverts, has dark crescent in front of eye; streaks on hindneck form broad band; tertials and part of wing-coverts dark-brown; black band on tip of tail. Bill colour variable, eg. black or grey-brown at base with black tip. Legs grey-brown. In flight, upperwing shows carpal bar on forewing, dark bar on secondaries and inner primaries. **Similar species:** see Black-headed and Great Black-headed Gulls. **Habitat:** estuaries, sandbanks, mudflats, sandy ground, lakes, marshes. **Distribution:** breeds locally in central latitudes of Asia; recently known to remain at mouth of Nakdong River, Rep. of Korea in non-breeding period, but non-breeding range not well known.   KS

SLENDER-BILLED GULL *Larus genei* L 42cm. Elongated forehead and bill very distinctive. In flight, shows relatively large white area along leading edge of outer upperwing. **Breeding:** head white; no blackish hood. Bill dark-red with black tip. Iris white or pale-yellow, often looks black from a distance. From head to underparts and white area on wing are faintly fringed pink. **Non-breeding:** like breeding, but some have faint dark markings on ear-coverts. **1st imm. non-breeding:** like adult non-breeding, but tertials and part of wing-coverts brown; small crescent in front of eye. Blackish band on tip of tail. In flight, pale brown carpal bar on forewing of upperwing; blackish bar on secondaries. **Similar species:** see Black-headed Gull. **Habitat:** coasts, estuaries, especially saline lakes, salt pans, marshes. **Distribution:** breeds and spends non-breeding period in West and South Asia; a few periodic records in East Asia in non-breeding period.   KS

BONAPARTE'S GULL *Larus philadelphia* L 34.5cm. Resembles Black-headed Gull, but smaller with faster wingbeat. In flight, underwing whitish with translucent outer primaries with blackish tips. **Breeding:** black hood; white crescents above and below eyes. Bill black. **Non-breeding:** head white; dark ear-coverts and small crescent in front of eye. **1st imm. non-breeding:** like non-breeding, but tertials and part of wing-coverts dark-brown. Black band on tip of tail. Legs pale flesh-coloured. In flight, upperwing shows dark-brown carpal bar and black bar on secondaries. **Habitat:** coasts, estuaries, mudflats. **Distribution:** vagrant from North America; a few records from Japan.   KS

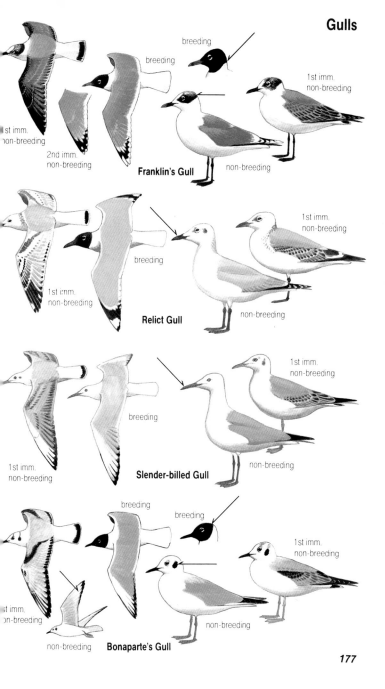

Gulls

breeding

breeding

1st imm.
non-breeding

1st imm.
non-breeding

2nd imm.
non-breeding

Franklin's Gull

non-breeding

1st imm.
non-breeding

breeding

1st imm.
non-breeding

Relict Gull

non-breeding

1st imm.
non-breeding

breeding

1st imm.
non-breeding

Slender-billed Gull

non-breeding

breeding

breeding

1st imm.
non-breeding

1st imm.
non-breeding

non-breeding

Bonaparte's Gull

non-breeding

177

Terns
Family *Laridae,* Subfamily *Sterninae* (World: 43 species; Asia 26 species) Generally smaller and more slender than gulls. Flight agile and graceful, and are also strong flyers. Unlike gulls rarely swim. Colonial breeders. Sexes similar.   SU

WHISKERED TERN *Chlidonias hybrida* L 25.5cm. This and following two species are called marsh terns; about same size as Little Tern; shallow fork in tail. Of the three species, Whiskered is the largest with longest legs and thickest base to sturdiest bill. **Breeding:** white cheeks stand out between black cap and dark-grey underparts. Vent and undertail-coverts white. Bill and legs dark-red. **Non-breeding:** black stripes on white crown, black patch on ear-coverts extends to rear-crown and hindneck, sometimes resembling non-breeding Common Tern. Rump grey. Some have dark markings on sides of breast. **Juvenile:** like adult non-breeding, but mantle, back and scapulars sepia-brown with small bold black markings. Tip of grey tail slightly darker. **Similar species:** juvenile and non-breeding White-winged Black Tern have black face-markings extending below eyes, paler rump, shallower fork in tail. Juvenile and non-breeding Black Tern have face-markings extending below eyes, and bolder dark markings on sides of breast. Common Tern is larger; at rest, primaries and tip of tail about the same length. See Gull-billed Tern. **Habitat:** coasts, estuaries, lakes, marshes, salt-pans, rice-fields. **Distribution:** breeds locally in South and East Asia; stays in South and South-East Asia in non-breeding period.   KS

WHITE-WINGED BLACK TERN [White-winged Tern] *Chlidonias leucoptera* L 23cm. Has more rounded head than other two species. **Breeding:** contrast between black from head to belly and white on wings. Bill black. Legs dark-red. In flight, striking contrast on underwing between whitish flight-feathers and black wing-coverts. **Non-breeding:** black patch from pale crown to ear-coverts extends below eyes; often between this patch and eye is a white gap. Tail white. **Juvenile:** like non-breeding, but crown blackish. Mantle, back and scapulars blackish-brown, form clear contrast in flight with pale wing-coverts, and with white rump and pale-grey tail. **Similar species:** see Whiskered Tern. Non-breeding and juvenile Black Tern has bolder dark markings on sides of breast, longer bill with sharper tip, and in flight darker mantle and back and pale rump. **Habitat:** coasts, estuaries, lakes, marshes, salt pans, rice-fields, marshes. **Distribution:** breeds in central latitudes of East Asia; moves to South and South-East Asia in non-breeding period.   KS

BLACK TERN *Chlidonias nigra* L 23cm. Bill longish with narrow pointed tip. **Breeding:** combination of black from head to belly, dark-grey upperparts, grey tail and white vent and undertail-coverts is diagnostic. Bill black. Legs blackish-red. **Non-breeding:** black patch on ear-coverts extends from blackish cap to below eyes. Upperparts much darker than White-winged Black Tern, rump greyer, bolder dark markings on sides of breast. **Juvenile:** like non-breeding adult, but mantle, back and scapulars grey-brown, rump grey. In flight, conspicuous broad dark band on leading edge of wing-coverts. **Similar species:** see Whiskered and White-winged Black Terns. **Habitat:** coasts, estuaries, lakes, marshes, salt-ponds, rice-fields. **Distribution:** breeds in central latitudes of West Asia; moves to west part of South Asia in non-breeding period in small numbers.   KS

Terns

breeding

juv.

breeding

non-breeding

Whiskered Tern

juv.

non-breeding

breeding

juv.

breeding

non-breeding

White-winged Black Tern

juv.

non-breeding

breeding

juv.

breeding

non-breeding

Black Tern

juv.

non-breeding

GULL-BILLED TERN *Gelochelidon nilotica* L 39cm. A little larger than Common Tern. Heavier body. Thick black bill. In flight, broad wings are white below with rather blackish tips to outer primaries. Shallow fork in tail. Does not plunge dive, often feeds over dry land; picks food off surface of water, vegetation etc. **Breeding:** black cap; grey upperparts and tail. **Non-breeding:** upperparts white; conspicuous black patch on ear-coverts. Some have some black streaks on hindneck. In flight, all-white except for black of primaries and ear-coverts; may resemble small whitish gull. **Juvenile:** like non-breeding adult, but rear crown and hindneck brownish, upperparts tipped brown, primaries darker. **Similar species:** Common Tern slightly smaller with narrower bill, shorter legs; at rest tips of primaries and tail about same length. Sandwich Tern has longer bill; adult has yellow tip to bill, crest on rear crown. See Whiskered Tern. **Habitat:** coasts, estuaries, lakes, marshes. **Distribution:** breeds locally in south part of Central Asia; moves to south part of Central, South-East and South Asia in non-breeding period.   KS

CASPIAN TERN *Hydroprogne caspia* L 52.5cm. Large tern, a little larger than Japanese Gull. Shallow fork in tail. In flight, dark area of outer primaries conspicuous on underwing. **Breeding:** thick red bill with dusky tip. Legs black. Slight crest on black cap. Tail grey. **Non-breeding:** like breeding, but cap blackish with white streaks; some have almost all-white head except for black patch on ear-coverts. **Juvenile:** bill dull-red. Legs blackish. Like non-breeding, but upperparts tipped brown, tail white with brown bar at tip. **Similar species:** Great Crested Tern has yellow bill; on underwing, dark area of outer primaries limited to tips only. Black-headed Gull is much smaller with narrower bill, red legs. See Lesser Crested Tern. **Habitat:** coasts, estuaries, lakes, marshes, marine islands. **Distribution:** breeds in Central Asia; moves to South Asia in non-breeding period.   KS

WHITE-CHEEKED TERN *Sterna repressa* L 32cm. **Breeding:** white line below black cap contrasts with grey lower ear-coverts and underparts. In flight, underwing coverts whitish-grey contrasting with dark-grey secondaries and primary tips. Sides of rump whiter than centre of rump and belly. **Non-breeding:** forehead white. **1st imm. non-breeding:** similar to Common Tern. Separated with care by longer and narrower wings. Rump and tail similar in colour to upperparts. Underwing coverts paler than adult but secondaries remain dark and contrast with coverts. **Similar species:** separated from immature Common and Arctic Terns by longer thinner bill, and more extensive black on head, similar to the of Roseate Tern. Underwing pattern if seen is diagnostic. **Habitat:** coastal and marine; avoids inland water. **Distribution:** small numbers stay in west part of South Asia in non-breeding period.   BB

SANDWICH TERN *Thalasseus sandvicensis* L 42cm. **Breeding:** similar to Gull-billed Tern, but black bill longer and finer, tipped with yellow; pronounced shaggy crest; wings project well beyond tail at rest. **Non-breeding:** crown white streaked with black; black stripe from eye continuing on to short black crest. In flight, mantle very pale-grey with blackish tips to primaries. **Juvenile:** like non-breeding, but dark subterminal fringes on mantle, scapulars, coverts, tertials and tail; primaries dark grey. **Habitat:** coasts, creeks. **Distribution:** breeds in north part of West Asia; moves to west part of South Asia in non-breeding period.   BB

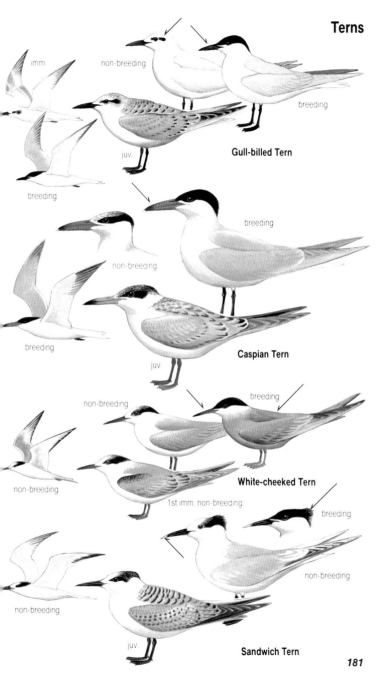

Terns

imm.

non-breeding

breeding

juv.

Gull-billed Tern

breeding

non-breeding

breeding

non-breeding

breeding

juv.

Caspian Tern

non-breeding

breeding

non-breeding

1st imm. non-breeding

White-cheeked Tern

breeding

non-breeding

non-breeding

juv.

Sandwich Tern

INDIAN RIVER TERN [River Tern] *Sterna aurantia* L 40cm. **Breeding:** forehead, crown and nape black with small white crescent-shaped patch under eye; back and wings deep grey contrasting with light grey rump, long forked tail; underparts white to greyish-white. Bill pointed, orange-yellow; legs crimson-red. **Non-breeding:** black crown and nape with white flecks; bill dark tipped. **Juvenile:** head blackish-brown with white streaks; upperparts brown and grey; underparts white. **Voice:** high-pitched melodious "kiuk-kiuk", often calls in flight. **Similar species:** Black-bellied Tern similar in non-breeding plumage but smaller and slender-billed. **Habitat:** freshwater rivers, lakes, marshes. **Distribution:** resident in South Asia and west part of South-East Asia. TM

GREATER CRESTED TERN [Large Crested Tern, Swift Tern, Great Crested Tern] *Thalasseus bergii* L 45.5cm. W 104cm. Large tern, slightly smaller than Caspian Tern, same size as Eastern Mew Gull. Thick bill slightly decurved. **Breeding:** bill yellow; black cap has shaggy crest; forehead white. Upperparts dark-grey, rump paler; underparts white. **Non-breeding:** like breeding, but white of forehead extends to lores; white streaks on blackish cap. **Juvenile:** like non-breeding, but bill dull-yellow; black on head tinged brown, comes down to sides of face. Upperparts dark-brown with white fringes to feathers. **Similar species:** Lesser Crested Tern has bright orange bill; when breeding, black extends to forehead; non-breeding and juvenile have white extending onto crown. Chinese Crested Tern has distinct black tip to yellow bill. Caspian Tern has red bill with dusky tip; dark outer primaries on underwing in flight. **Habitat:** coasts, estuaries, marine islands. **Distribution:** resident from South Asia to South-East Asia. KS

LESSER CRESTED TERN *Thalasseus bengalensis* L 40cm. **Breeding:** black crown and crest; lacking white lores and forehead of Greater Crested Tern; upperparts pale bluish-grey; underparts white. Bill bright orange; legs black. **Non-breeding:** white on head more extensive than in Greater Crested Tern. **Voice:** loud "chirruk" usually uttered when hovering to plunge. **Habitat:** coasts. **Distribution:** resident in South Asia and South-East Asia. BB

CHINESE CRESTED TERN *Thalasseus bernsteini* L 38cm. Very rare coastal tern. **Breeding:** crown and crest black; upperparts very pale grey; underparts white; upperwings grey with outer webs of outer primaries blackish; deeply forked white tail. Bill yellow with extensive black tip; legs black. **Non-breeding:** like breeding, but forehead and crown white; extreme tip of bill yellow. **Similar species:** Lesser Crested Tern has no black on bill. See Greater Crested Tern. **Habitat:** coasts. **Distribution:** resident in South-East Asia and East Asia. Extremely rare, possibly extinct. TM

Terns

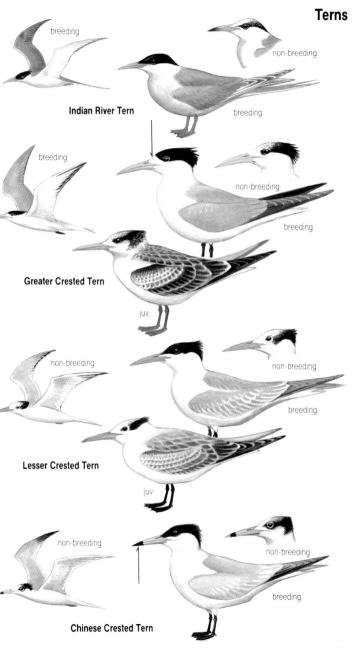

Indian River Tern

breeding

non-breeding

breeding

Greater Crested Tern

breeding

non-breeding

breeding

juv.

Lesser Crested Tern

non-breeding

non-breeding

breeding

juv.

Chinese Crested Tern

non-breeding

non-breeding

breeding

COMMON TERN *Sterna hirundo* L 33cm. Slender body, long forked tail. At rest, wings and tail look almost the same length. Outer web of outer tail-feathers black. Upperparts blue-grey; underpart white. Race *longipennis* in breeding plumage has whitish-grey underparts, black bill and legs. Race *minussensis* has orange-red bill with black tip, and red legs. **Breeding:** head has black cap. **Non-breeding:** forehead white; crown streaked white and black. **Juvenile:** resembles non-breeding, but feathers of wings, upperparts are fringed white with black subterminal band; base of lower mandible red. **Voice:** "girri, girri". **Similar species:** Common and Arctic most easily distinguished in flight. Common's outer primaries are dark above, show faint black line on trailing edges underneath; Arctic's upper- and underwings show clear black line running from outer edge of outermost primary along trailing edge of outer primaries. Common's wings look long and broad, tail short; Arctic's wings look shorter, narrower and more pointed, tail longer. Non-breeding Roseate Tern resembles Common, but upperwing is paler, underwing white. **Habitat:** coasts, lakes, rivers. **Distribution:** breeds from Central Asia across to north part of East Asia; moves to South and South-East Asia in non-breeding period.   SU

ARCTIC TERN *Sterna paradisaea* L 39cm. Similar to Common Tern, but bill, neck and legs are shorter, tail longer. Rounded head. At rest, tail extends slightly beyond wings. Outer webs of outer tail-feathers grey. **Breeding:** like Common, but underparts greyer; bill and legs red. **Non-breeding:** like Common. **Juvenile:** like Common, but no brown on upperparts; underwing pure-white. **Voice:** "kirri, kirri". **Similar species:** see Common and Roseate Terns. **Habitat:** coasts, seas. **Distribution:** breeds in high northern latitudes, migrates to high southern latitudes.   SU

ROSEATE TERN *Sterna dougallii* L 31cm. Upper- and underparts whiter than Common and Arctic; tail extremely long. At rest, tail extends well beyond wings. Adult differs from Common and Arctic in having absolutely no black trailing edge on underwing primaries. Bill is heavier, darker. **Juvenile:** distinctive, anchor-shaped marks on mantle, scapulars; crown black; legs black (unlike red legs of both Common and Arctic); underwing white with pale grey trailing edges to primaries. **Voice:** soft "chu-weet". **Similar species:** see Common and Arctic Terns. **Habitat:** coasts, oceans. **Distribution:** breeds from south part of East Asia to South-East and South Asia; northern breeders move south.   SU

ALEUTIAN TERN *Sterna aleutica* L 33cm. Proportions similar to Common Tern, but upperparts and upperwings are slaty-grey, contrast sharply with white tail and rump. Dark trailing edges to underwing secondaries. Bill and legs of adult black. **Breeding:** forehead white; whitish-grey from nape to belly. **Non-breeding:** like breeding, but underparts white. **Juvenile:** rump, uppertail-coverts, tail pale-grey; bill black with reddish tinge to lower mandible; legs yellowish-brown. **Similar species:** Little Tern is small, has orange bill and legs in breeding season. See Spectacled Tern. **Habitat:** coasts, oceans. **Distribution:** breeds in north-east part of North Asia; distribution outside breeding season not well known.   SU

Terns

juv.

breeding

race *longipennis*

non-breeding

Common Tern

breeding

breeding

race *minussensis*

juv.

non-breeding

breeding

breeding

non-breeding

Arctic Tern

breeding

juv.

breeding

breeding

non-breeding

juv.

non-breeding

Roseate Tern

breeding

breeding

non-breeding

juv.

breeding

breeding

Aleutian Tern

BLACK-NAPED TERN *Sterna sumatrana* L 30cm. In the field, appears all-white except clear black band from lores to nape. **Adult:** tail long, deeply forked. Bill black, occasionally with yellow tip; legs black. Outer web of outermost primary is black. **Juvenile:** bill slightly paler black than adult and looks shorter, thicker. **Voice:** "tsii-chee-chi". **Similar species:** all terns of the same size, when non-breeding, have similar head-pattern, so care required. Common, Arctic and Roseate Terns in non-breeding plumage are darker and have reddish legs; patterns of black on primaries are different from Black-naped Tern. **Habitat:** coasts, oceans. **Distribution:** South, South-East and East Asia.   SU

BLACK-BELLIED TERN *Sterna melanogaster* L 32cm. **Breeding:** crown and nape glossy-black; lores, cheeks and throat white; upper breast, belly and undertail-coverts vary from deep chocolate-brown to black; back and wings pale silvery-grey; tail pale-grey forked with long streamers. Bill slender and orange-red. **Non-breeding:** crown white; nape streaked black; breast and belly white or lightly speckled with black. **Juvenile:** buffy-grey with buff-white edged feathers. **Voice:** short sharp "krek-krek" repeated occasionally. **Similar species:** see Indian River Tern. **Habitat:** freshwater, rivers and lakes. **Distribution:** resident in South Asia and west part of South-East Asia.   TM

LITTLE TERN *Sterna albifrons* L 28cm. Together with Black-shafted Tern, smallest tern of the region. Upperparts and wings pale blue-grey. Rump, uppertail-coverts and tail white. **Breeding:** black cap and nape, white from forehead to behind eyes; bill yellow with black tip; legs yellowish-orange. **Non-breeding:** bill black; legs yellowish-brown. Crown turns ash-grey. **Juvenile:** upperparts grey, fringed brown; bill black with yellow base. **Voice:** "krri-krri". **Similar species:** Black-shafted Tern has black outer primaries, and grey rump, uppertail-coverts and tail; in breeding plumage, white forehead is triangular, white does not extend behind eyes, legs are brown. **Habitat:** coasts, rivers. **Distribution:** throughout the region except Central Asia.   SU

BLACK-SHAFTED TERN [Saunders' Tern] *Sterna saundersii* L 23cm. Very similar to Little Tern. Black outer primaries more extensive, usually outer 3-7 primaries black (2-3 in Little Tern); rump grey, concolorous with mantle (white and contrasting with mantle in Little Tern). Legs brown. These features also apply to adults outside the breeding season. **Voice:** a high-pitched "kiwick-kiwick-kiwick". **Habitat:** seacoast. **Distribution:** small population observed in west part of South Asia in non-breeding period. BB

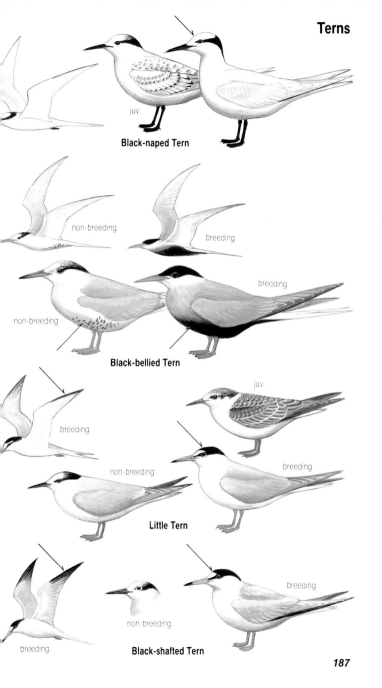

Terns

Black-naped Tern

juv.

Black-bellied Tern

non-breeding

breeding

breeding

non-breeding

Little Tern

breeding

non-breeding

juv.

breeding

Black-shafted Tern

breeding

non-breeding

breeding

SPECTACLED TERN *Sterna lunata* L 38cm. Marine Tern. White forehead continuing behind eye as narrow white supercilium. Mantle and back grey, contrast in flight with blackish-grey wings. Outer tail-feathers white; underparts white. Bill and legs black. **Juvenile:** similar pattern to adult, but demarcation of black on head is blurred. **Voice:** "kur-wak". **Similar species:** distinguished from Aleutian Tern by blacker upperparts, and especially by rump, uppertail-coverts and tail not being white. See Bridled Tern. **Habitat:** oceans, marine islands. **Distribution:** western Pacific; rare migrant to Asia.   SU

BRIDLED TERN [Brown-winged Tern] *Sterna anaethetus* L 36cm. Resembles Spectacled Tern; almost identical head-pattern. Upperparts brownish-black, in flight appear almost the same colour as blackish-brown wings, while Spectacled's upperparts contrast with blackish-grey wings. Outer tail-feathers white. Underparts slightly grey. Bill, legs black. **Juvenile:** similar pattern to adult. Upperparts browner than juvenile Spectacled. **Voice:** "wep-wep, kuruu". **Similar species:** adult differs from Sooty Tern in having supercilium extending behind eyes, grey collar separating upperparts from black crown and nape, and in not having black mantle and back; juvenile differs in having white underparts. **Habitat:** coasts, marine islands. **Distribution:** south part of East Asia, west part of South-East Asia.   SU

SOOTY TERN *Sterna fuscata* L 40cm. Resembles Bridled Tern, but white on forehead is broader, does not extend behind eyes. Upperparts and upperwings black. Underparts white. Bill and legs black. **Juvenile:** at rest, looks all-black; although belly, undertail-coverts and underwing-coverts are white, and upperwing-coverts tipped with white, plumage is otherwise nearly all black. **Voice:** "kur-wak". **Habitat:** marine islands, coasts. **Distribution:** south part of East Asia, South-East Asia, South Asia.   SU

Skimmer Family *Rynchopidae* (World: 3 species; Asia: 1 species)

Unique birds with long bills. Feeds in flight by dipping projecting tip of lower mandible into water, lightly ploughing the surface to feed on aquatic small animals. Sexes similar.   SU

INDIAN SKIMMER [Scissors-bill] *Rynchops albicollis* L 43cm. Pied plumage, long narrow wings, peculiar compressed knife-like orange bill with yellow tip to elongated lower mandible conspicuous. Forehead, sides of head and underparts contrasting with black crown and nape. In flight, a dark stripe down middle of white rump and tail. Legs bright red. Feeds actively also during moonlit nights. **Juvenile:** lighter brown above, scalloped with fulvous-white; forehead streaked white; tail tipped brown. **Voice:** a nasal "kap, kap". **Habitat:** freshwater lakes, rivers, seacoast. **Distribution:** resident in South Asia and west part of South-East Asia.   BB

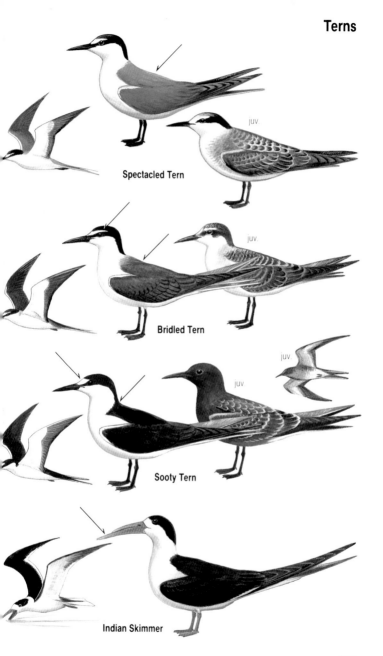

Terns

Spectacled Tern

juv.

Bridled Tern

juv.

Sooty Tern

juv.

juv.

Indian Skimmer

Terns   Family *Laridae,* Subfamily *Sterninae* (continued)

COMMON NODDY   [Brown Noddy] *Anous stolidus* L 39cm. Resemble
Lesser Noddy, White-capped Noddy. White forehead clearly demarcated
from black lores. Whitish-grey from crown to nape. Thick, black bill. Body
dark brown; tail and flight-feathers black. Legs black. On the sea look
all-black. The three *Anous* species (Common, Lesser and White-capped
Noddies) are all wholly marine; unlike forked tails of *Sterna* species, all
have heavy notched tails. **Juvenile:** forehead and crown dark (not
illustrated). **Similar species:** difficult to distinguish from Lesser and White-
capped Noddies at a distance. Closer up, differs from Lesser Noddy in
having thicker bill and clearly black lores; from White-capped in having
thicker bill, less white on head, slightly curving rather than straight line
separating lores and forehead, and dark margins producing contrast on
underwings. **Habitat:** coasts, marine islands. **Distribution:** south part of
East Asia, South-East Asia, South Asia.   SU

LESSER NODDY   *Anous tenuirostris* L 32cm. Similar to Common Noddy.
Forehead greyish-white, even extending onto nape; lores white. Separated
from larger Common Noddy by having narrower wings and blacker upper
parts and a darker underwing at a distance. **Habitat:** coasts, marine islands.
Distribution: west part of South Asia.   SU

WHITE-CAPPED NODDY   *Anous minutus* L 34cm. White of forehead is
clearly demarcated from black of lores, continues onto crown and nape.
Body all-black; underwings uniformly black. Bill black, long and thin. Tail
relatively short. **Juvenile:** forehead and crown less white than adult, clearly
demarcated from blackish nape (not illustrated). **Similar species:** differs
from Lesser Noddy in having clearly black lores, and whiter, more extensive
white on head. Ranges do not overlap. **Habitat:** coasts, marine islands.
Distribution: south part of East Asia, west part of South-East Asia.   SU

WHITE TERN   [Fairy Tern, White Noddy] *Gygis alba* L 28cm. Body almost
all-white; narrow black line around eyes. Bill slightly up-turned, black with
blue base. Second outermost tail-feathers are longest, giving distinctive
shape to tail. **Juvenile:** dark ear-coverts, rounded wings and short tail;
similar to gulls, but size, bill and large black eyes prevent confusion with
other species. **Habitat:** coasts, marine islands. **Distribution:** south part of
East Asia, South-East Asia, South Asia.   SU

Terns

Common Noddy

Lesser Noddy

White-capped Noddy

juv.

White Tern

Systematic List of the Waterbirds of Asia

1) The list is filled out under the following categories,

R (Resident) : A bird which stays and breeds in a country throughout the year.

B (Breeder) : A bird which breeds and stays in a country for several months (usually in summer), and spends the rest of the year in another country.

N (Non-breeder) : A bird which is presumed not to breed but remains in a country for several months (usually in the northern winter) and breeds elsewhere.

P (Passage migrant) : A bird which regularly passes through a country on its migration between its breeding areas and main non-breeding areas.

L (Little known) : A bird of which status is little known but which is recorded regularly in a country.

* : An asterisk indicates that the species is rare. Thus a rare breeder = B*.

E (Endangered) : A bird that is internationally endangered or threatened, based on the 1990 IUCN RED DATA BOOK.

- If a species breeds in one area and spends the non-breeding period in other area within one country, there are two classes:
  - a) If very small number of a species breed and almost all of it spend the non-breeding period in a country, it is classified as "Non-breeder" and "(Breeder)" [shortened as N(B)]. Vice versa.
  - b) If a good number of a species both breed and spend the non-breeding period within a country (but in different areas), it is classified as "Breeder" and "Non-breeder" [B/N].
- Some species are non-breeders and passage migrants to a country and so are identified as [N/P].

2) The field guide covers the following countries and areas; Republic of Russia (eastern part), Mongolia, China, D.P.R. Korea, Rep. of Korea, Japan, Taiwan, Viet Nam, Laos, Cambodia, Thailand, Malaysia, Singapore, Bhutan, Myanmar, Bangladesh, Sri Lanka, Nepal, India, Pakistan, Indonesia (excluding Irian Jaya), Brunei, Philippines and Hong Kong.

3) New information on the status of waterbirds in each country will be welcome and should be sent to WBSJ or AWB.

ENGLISH NAME	SCIENTIFIC NAME	1. BANGLADESH	2. BHUTAN	3. BRUNEI
		BAN	BHU	BRI
Red-throated Diver	*Gavia stellata*			
Black-throated Diver	*G. arctica*			
Pacific Diver	*G. pacifica*			
White-billed Diver	*G. adamsii*			
Little Grebe	*Tachybaptus ruficollis*	R	R	N*
Australian Dabchick	*T. novaehollandiae*			
Red-necked Grebe	*Podiceps grisegena*		N/P	
Great Crested Grebe	*P. cristatus*	N	N/P	
Slavonian Grebe	*P. auritus*			
Black-necked Grebe	*P. nigricollis*			
Great White Pelican	*Pelecanus onocrotalus*			
Grey Pelican	*P. philippensis*	E*		
Dalmatian Pelican	*P. crispus*	E*		
Australian Pelican	*P. conspicillatus*			
Little Black Cormorant	*Phalacrocorax sulcirostris*			
Great Cormorant	*P. carbo*	N	R/B	N
Indian Cormorant	*P. fuscicollis*	L		
Japanese Cormorant	*P. capillatus*			
Pelagic Cormorant	*P. pelagicus*			
Red-faced Cormorant	*P. urile*			
Little Pied Cormorant	*P. melanoleucos*			
Javanese Cormorant	*P. niger*	R		
Pygmy Cormorant	*P. pygmeus*			
Indian Darter	*Anhinga melanogaster*	R	*	R
Australian Darter	*A. novaehollandiae*			
Grey Heron	*Ardea cinerea*	R	P	N
Imperial Heron	*A. imperialis*	*	R	
Dusky-grey Heron	*A. sumatrana*			R
Goliath Heron	*A. goliath*	*		
Purple Heron	*A. purpurea*	R	R/B	N/(

194

6. D.P.R. KOREA	7. REP. of RUSSIA (eastern part)	8. HONG KONG	9. INDIA	10. INDONESIA	11. JAPAN	12. LAOS	13. MALAYSIA	14. MONGOLIA	15. MYANMAR	16. NEPAL	17. PAKISTAN	18. PHILIPPINES	19. REP. of KOREA	20. SINGAPORE	21. SRI LANKA	22. TAIWAN	23. THAILAND	24. VIET NAM
PRK	RUS	HGK	IND	INA	JPN	LAO	MAS	MGL	MYA	NEP	PAK	PHI	KOR	SIN	SRI	TWN	THA	VIE
N	B		*		N			P*			N*		N(P)			L		
N	B		*		N			B					N(P)			L		
N	B				N								N(P)					
N	B				N								P*					
R		R	R/B	R*	R/B	R	R			R/P	R	R	N(B*)		R	R	R/B	R
				L														
N	B	N*	N		N/B		B*				N*		N(P)					
N	B*	N	N(B)	N	N(B)		B		N	N	N		N(P)			N*	N	
N	B				N		B				N		N(P)			N*		
N		N*	N		N		B*			N	N	R*	N(P)			P*		
		N(B)								N	N							
		ER/P	EN(B)			EL	EN*	EB*	ER	EN		ER			ER	EL	EN(B)	EL
		EN	EN		EN*						EN		E*		EL			EL
				N														
				R														
N	N		R	N	R		N*	B	R	L	R	N*	P(R*)		R*(N)	P	N(B)	R
					R					R					R	R*	R	
R	R				R/N								R(N)		P*	L		
N	B				N/B								N(P)			L		
	B				R*											L		
			R															
		R	R			R	N*			N					R		R	R
									ER		E*				R		R*/B*	R
		R	R			R	N*/B	R	B	R	R				R		R*/B*	R
				L														
R		N	R/N	R	R	R	R/N	B	R	N(B)	N(B)	N	B(N)	R	R	N	R	N
										P	*							
			R		R					P			R		R		R*	N
				L											N*			
N		N/P	R	R	R/P*	R	R	B*	R	R/N	R	R	P*(N*)	B/N	R	N	R/B	R

ENGLISH NAME	SCIENTIFIC NAME	1. BAN	2. BHU	3. BRU
Great Egret	*Egretta alba*	R	N	N
Pied Heron	*E. picata*			
Intermediate Egret	*E. intermedia*	R	R/B	N
White-faced Egret	*E. novaehollandiae*			
Little Egret	*E. garzetta*	R	N	N/(R*
Swinhoe's Egret	*E. eulophotes*			EN
Reef Heron	*E. sacra*	N*		R
Cattle Egret	*Bubulcus ibis*	R		N
Indian Pond Heron	*Ardeola grayii*	R	R/N	
Chinese Pond Heron	*A. bacchus*	N*		N
Javanese Pond Heron	*A. speciosa*			
Green-backed Heron	*Butorides striatus*	R		N/P
Black-crowned Night Heron	*Nycticorax nycticorax*	R	R/B	R*
Nankeen Night Heron	*N. caledonicus*			*B/L
Magnificent Night Heron	*Gorsachius magnificus*			
Japanese Night Heron	*G. goisagi*			EN*
Malaysian Night Heron	*G. melanolophus*	R		N*
Little Bittern	*Ixobrychus minutus*	R	P	
Chinese Little Bittern	*I. sinensis*	R		N/(R
Schrenck's Bittern	*I. eurhythmus*			N
Cinnamon Bittern	*I. cinnamomeus*	R		R
Black Bittern	*I. flavicollis*	R		N*
Eurasian Bittern	*Botaurus stellaris*	N/P	P	N*
Milky Stork	*Mycteria cinerea*			
Painted Stork	*M. leucocephala*	R		
Asian Open-bill Stork	*Anastomus oscitans*	R		
Black Stork	*Ciconia nigra*	N*	P	
Woolly-necked Stork	*C. episcopus*	N*		
Storm's Stork	*C. stormi*			EL
White Stork	*C. ciconia*	N*		
Oriental White Stork	*C. boyciana*	EN*		
Black-necked Stork	*Ephippiorhynchus asiaticus*	L	R/N	
Lesser Adjutant Stork	*Leptoptilos javanicus*	ER	ER/B	EL
Greater Adjutant Stork	*L. dubius*	EN(B)	EP	
Oriental Ibis	*Threskiornis melanocephalus*	N	R/N	
Australian White Ibis	*T. molucca*			
Black Ibis	*Pseudibis papillosa*	EN		
Giant Ibis	*Thaumatibis gigantea*			

6. PRK	7. RUS	8. HGK	9. IND	10. INA	11. JPN	12. LAO	13. MAS	14. MGL	15. MYA	16. NEP	17. PAK	18. PHI	19. KOR	20. SIN	21. SRI	22. TWN	23. THA	24. VIE
N	B	R/N	R	R	R/B/N	R	N(R)	B	R	R	R	R	B(N)	N	R	N	R	N
B		P/N	R	R	B(R)	R	N		R	R	R	R	B	N	R	L / N	R(B)	N
B		R/N	R	N/R	R	R	N		R	R	R	N	R(N)	EN	R	R/P	R(B)	R
EB		EP		EN	EP*		EN					EN	EB	EN		EP		EN
R		R	EN	R	R	R	R		R			R	R*	R	N*	R	R	R
B		R	R	R	B(R)	R	N/P		R	R/B	R	R	B(N)	N	R	B	R/B	R
		R	R	R					R	R	R	R			R			
R		R	R	N	P*(B*)	R	N	P*	R			R	*	N		P	N(B)*	R
			R		N*							N					R(B)*	R
B		B/N	R	R	B(R)		R/N		R	R/B	R	R	B	N(B)	R	R/P	R	N
B		R/N	R	R	R(B)	R	R		R	R/B	R	R	B	R	R	R/P	R/N	R
			R(N)		R		R					R						EL
																		EL
		EP*		EN*	EB*(R*)		N			EN*	E*	EN*		N	EP*		R
		R/B	N	R	R		N		L	*		R		N	N*	R	R	
		R		R				P*			R						R	
B		B/N	R/N	B	R		R/N		N	B	N	R	B	B/N	R	R	R	R
B		P		N	B*	N	N			N	N*	N*	B	N		P	R	
		R	R	R	R	R	R		R	R/B	N	R	*	N(B)	R	R	R(B)	R
	P	R	R/N		*	R	N/P		R	R		R		N/P	R	L	B/N	
B	B*	N	N		B*/N	N	N*	B	N	N/P	N	N*	N		N*	P	N	N
				ER		R				N	R				R		R/B	EL
		R			N*	N		B	R	R/P	N*		N*		R	P*	R/B/N	R
N	B	N	N					B	N	N/P	N/P		N*		N*	P*	N	R
		R	R/N	N*	R		ER		R	R/B	N*	R			R		ER(B)	R
		N	ER							*	N/P				N*		L	
EN	EB	EN*	EL		EN*		EP*			N	N*		EN*			EP*	R(B)*	L
		R			R					EB/N	ER				R*		EN*	ER
		ER	ER		ER	ER				EB/N	EN	EN*			ER		EN*	ER
		EB*			ER					R	N	R	N*				R*	R
	N	R	R/N*	N*	L*				R	N	R		*	R	P		E*	R
		ER			ER	ER				ER	ER	EN					E*	EL

ENGLISH NAME	SCIENTIFIC NAME	1. BAN	2. BHU	3. BRU
Japanese Crested Ibis	*Nipponia nippon*			
Glossy Ibis	*Plegadis falcinellus*	N	P	*
White Spoonbill	*Platalea leucorodia*	R	P	
Black-faced Spoonbill	*P. minor*			EN*
Royal Spoonbill	*P. regia*			
Greater Flamingo	*Phoenicopterus ruber*			
Lesser Flamingo	*P. minor*			
Spotted Whistling Duck	*Dendrocygna guttata*			
Fulvous Whistling Duck	*D. bicolor*	R		
Wandering Whistling Duck	*D. arcuata*			*
Indian Whistling Duck	*D. javanica*	R	R/N	
Mute Swan	*Cygnus olor*			
Whooper Swan	*C. cygnus*			
Tundra Swan	*C. columbianus*			
Swan Goose	*Anser cygnoides*			
Bean Goose	*A. fabalis*			
White-fronted Goose	*A. albifrons*	N*		
Lesser White-fronted Goose	*A. erythropus*			
Greylag Goose	*A. anser*	N	P/N	
Bar-headed Goose	*A. indicus*	N	P/N	
Snow Goose	*A. caerulescens*			
Emperor Goose	*A. canagicus*			
Canada Goose	*Branta canadensis*			
Brent Goose	*B. bernicla*			
Red-breasted Goose	*B. ruficollis*			
Ruddy Shelduck	*Tadorna ferruginea*	N	N/P	
Common Shelduck	*T. tadorna*	N		
Radjah Shelduck	*T. radjah*			
Crested Shelduck	*T. cristata*			
White-winged Wood Duck	*Cairina scutulata*	ER	EL	
Comb Duck	*Sarkidiornis melanotos*	R	L	
Green Pygmy Goose	*Nettapus pulchellus*			
Cotton Teal	*N. coromandelianus*	R	*	*
Mandarin Duck	*Aix galericulata*	N*		
European Wigeon	*Anas penelope*	N		N*
American Wigeon	*A. americana*			
Falcated Teal	*A. falcata*	N*		

6. PRK	7. RUS	8. HGK	9. IND	10. INA	11. JPN	12. LAO	13. MAS	14. MGL	15. MYA	16. NEP	17. PAK	18. PHI	19. KOR	20. SIN	21. SRI	22. TWN	23. THA	24. VIE
EN					ER								EN*			EL		
		P*	R/N	R					R	P	R	R		N*	N*		N*	R
EB		N	R/N		N*			B	N	P/N	N(B)	EN*	P(N*)		R	N*	N*	EN
		EN			EN*								EP(N*)			EN	EN*	
			R	R/N*					N/P	*	R				N			
			L								N*							
			R						R	*	B*	R			N*			
			R									R						
N		P*	R	R	*	R	R	P*	R	N/P(R)	B		N	R	R	L	R/B	N
			*		*						N*					L		
N	B		*		N			B		*	N*		N			L		
N	B		*		N					*	N*		N			N*		
N	B				N*			B					N*			N*		
N	B	N*	*		N			P			N*		N			N*		
N	B		N*		N			P*	N*		N*		N			N		
	EB		EN*		EN						EN*		EN*			EN*		
		N*	N		N*			B	N	N/P	N/P		*		N*			N
			B/N		N*			B	N	P/N	N/P						N	
B			*		N*								*					
B					N*													
					N								*					
N	B				N								N			L		
	B																	
		N*	E*					B	N	B/N	N(B)		N		N*	N	N	
N		N	N(B)		N*			B	N	*	N(B)		N			N	N*	N
			N		N													
E*	E*			N*	E*								E*					
		ER*	ER		ER	ER*		ER								ER/B*	ER	
		R	R		R	R		R	N	R						R/B*		
			B*															
		P*	R	R		R	L		R	N	R			L	R	L	R/B*	N
ER		EN	E*		ER/N	N		EL	EN	E*	N		ER/N			EP(N)	EN	
N	B	N	N	N*	N	N	N*	B	N	N/P	N		N	P*	N	N	N	N
	L				N								*			L		
N	B*	N	N*	N(B)	N			B	N	N	N*		N			N*	N	N

ENGLISH NAME	SCIENTIFIC NAME	1. BAN	2. BHU	3. BRU
Gadwall	*Anas strepera*	N		
Baikal Teal	*A. formosa*			
Green-winged Teal	*A. crecca*	N	N	N*
Grey Teal	*A. gibberifrons*			
Mallard	*A. platyrhynchos*	N	N/P	N*
Spotbill Duck	*A. poecilorhyncha*	R	R/N	
Pacific Black Duck	*A. superciliosa*			
Philippine Duck	*A. luzonica*			
Northern Pintail	*A. acuta*	N	P	N*
Garganey	*A. querquedula*	N	P	N
Northern Shoveler	*A. clypeata*	N		N*
Marbled Teal	*Marmaronetta angustirostris*			
Pink-headed Duck	*Rhodonessa caryophyllacea*			
Red-crested Pochard	*Netta rufina*	N	P	
Canvasback	*Aythya valisineria*			
Common Pochard	*A. ferina*	N	P	
Redhead	*A. americana*			
Ring-necked Duck	*A. collaris*			
Australian White-eyed Duck	*A. australis*			
Baer's Pochard	*A. baeri*	EN		
Ferruginous Duck	*A. nyroca*	N		
Tufted Duck	*A. fuligula*	N	P(N)	N*
Greater Scaup	*A. marila*	N*	P(N)	
Lesser Scaup	*A. affinis*			
Long-tailed Duck	*Clangula hyemalis*			
Bufflehead	*Bucephala albeola*			
Common Goldeneye	*B. clangula*			
Smew	*Mergus albellus*			
Red-breasted Merganser	*M. serrator*			
Chinese Merganser	*M. squamatus*			
Goosander	*M. merganser*	N*	N	
White-headed Duck	*Oxyura leucocephala*			
Common Crane	*Grus grus*		N*	
Black-necked Crane	*G. nigricollis*		EN	
Hooded Crane	*G. monacha*			
Sandhill Crane	*G. canadensis*			
Manchurian Crane	*G. japonensis*			

6. PRK	7. RUS	8. HGK	9. IND	10. INA	11. JPN	12. LAO	13. MAS	14. MGL	15. MYA	16. NEP	17. PAK	18. PHI	19. KOR	20. SIN	21. SRI	22. TWN	23. THA	24. VIE
N	L	N	N		N(B)		N*	B	N	N/P	N		N	P*	N*	N*	N	N
EN	EB	EN	EN*		EN			EP			EN*		EN			EN*		EN
N	B	N	N		N(B)	N/P	N*	B	N	N/P	N		N	P*	N	N	N	N
			R	R/N					N									
N	B	N	N(B)		N/B			B	N	N/P(B)	N		N(B)			N		
R		R/N	R		R	R		B	R	N	R		R/N		N*	N(R)	N	N
			R(N)													L		
												R						
EN		EN	EN*		EN*			EP*	EN	E*	EN*		EN*			EN*	EN	EN
		N*	N(B)		N*			B*	N	N/P	N						N*	
N	B	N	N	N*	N(B)	N	N*	B	N	N/P	N		N		N*	N	N	N
N	B	N	N*		N			P*	N*		N*		N			N		N
					N*													
N			N*		N						N*		N					
					N*													
N	B	N*	N		N			B	N*	NP	N*		N			L	N	N
N	B		N		N(B)			P(B)	N*	*	N*		N			N*		
N	B	N	N*		N			P*					EN*(P*)			N*		N
EB					EN*											EL		
N	B		N(B)		N(B)			B	N	N	N		N			N*		
	EB*		EN					EB*			EN							
N	B	N*	N		N*			B	N	P(N)	N/P		N*			L	N	N
			EB/N							E*								EL
EN	EB		E*		EN			EP					EN			EL		
	B				N*													
EN	EB				ER(N*)			EP*					EN			EL		

ENGLISH NAME	SCIENTIFIC NAME	1. BAN	2. BHU	3. BRU
Japanese White-naped Crane	Grus vipio			
Sarus Crane	G. antigone	L*		
Great White Crane	G. leucogeranus			
Demoiselle Crane	Anthropoides virgo	N*	P	
Chestnut-bellied Rail	Eulabeornis castaneoventris			
Bare-eyed Rail	E. plumbeiventris			
Bald-faced Rail	E. rosenbergii			
Platen's Rail	Rallus plateni			
Wallace's Rail	R. wallacii			
Buff-banded Rail	R. philippensis			
Blue-breasted Banded Rail	R. striatus	R		R
Barred Rail	R. torquatus			
Slate-breasted Rail	R. pectoralis			
Water Rail	R. aquaticus	N/P		N*
Okinawa Rail	R. okinawae			
Red-necked Crake	Rallina tricolor			
Andaman Banded Crake	R. canningi			
Red-legged Crake	R. fasciata			L
Banded Crake	R. eurizonoides			
Band-bellied Crake	R. paykullii			N*
Yellow Rail	Coturnicops neveboracensis			
Corn Crake	Crex crex			
White-browed Rail	Porzana cinerea			R
Sooty Crake	P. tabuensis			
Little Crake	P. parva	*		
Baillon's Crake	P. pusilla	N*		N*
Spotted Crake	P. porzana			
Ruddy-breasted Crake	P. fusca	R		
Rufous-tailed Moorhen	Amaurornis olivaceus			
Sulawesi Water Hen	A. isabellinus			
Brown Crake	A. akool	L		
Elwes' Crake	A. bicolor		B(R)	
White-breasted Water Hen	A. phoenicurus	R	B(R)	R
Water Cock	Gallicrex cinerea	R	R	N
Dusky Moorhen	Gallinula tenebrosa			
Moorhen	G. chloropus	R		N(R*)
Purple Swamphen	Porphyrio porphyrio	R		*

6. RK	7. RUS	8. HGK	9. IND	10. INA	11. JPN	12. LAO	13. MAS	14. MGL	15. MYA	16. NEP	17. PAK	18. PHI	19. KOR	20. SIN	21. SRI	22. TWN	23. THA	24. VIE
EN	EB			EN				EB	R	R	R*		EN			EL	N*	N
	EB*		R	EN*/P*	R			EP*			EN/P		*					
	B		EN*	N*/P*				B	N	P	N/P							
			N	R														
				R														
				ER														
				ER														
				ER								R						
				R								R						
	R	R	R	R		R	R		R	N*		R		R	R	R	R	R
				R								R						
P	N*	B/N	B/N	B/N		R		P*	N	N*	N	R	P(N)		N*	P(R)	N	
				ER								R						
				N														
			R	R														
		L	N/R			R/N			R			R		N(B)		L	R	L
	B*	R	N/R	R			N		R	*		R		P*	N	R	N/P	L
	P*						N*						P*				N*	N
EP	EB	E*		EL				EB*			EN*		EP*		EN*			
	P*		R	E			R					R		R		L	R	
			N*								N	R						
P	B	P	B/N	B/N	R/N	N	N	B	N	N/P	N	N*	P	N	N*	P*	N/P	R
B		P/N	N	R	R	R	R		R	N	N	R	B	R	R*	R	N	R
			R	R						N(B)	R	R					R	R
			R	R														
	R*	R			R				R	R	R							L
		R							R	*								R
	R	R	R	R	R	R		R	R	R	R	P	B/N	R	R	R/B	R
B	P/B	R	N/R	B(P*)	R	N/R/P		R	N	B	R	B	N	R	B	R/B	R
			R															
B	R	R/N	R	R/B	R	R	B*	R	N	R	R	B	R	R	R	R/N	R
B	R*	R	R		R	R		R	N/P	R	R		R	R		R/B	R

ENGLISH NAME	SCIENTIFIC NAME	1. BAN	2. BHU	3. BRL
Black Coot	Fulica atra	N	P	N*
Masked Finfoot	Heliopais personata	EL		
Comb-crested Jacana	Irediparra gallinacea			
Pheasant-tailed Jacana	Hydrophasianus chirurgus	R		
Bronze-winged Jacana	Metopidius indicus	R		
Painted Snipe	Rostratula benghalensis	R	P	L
Crab Plover	Dromas ardeola	N*/P*		
Palaearctic Oystercatcher	Haematopus ostralegus	N		
Pied Oystercatcher	H. longirostris			
Ibis Bill	Ibidorhyncha struthersii		R/B	
Black-winged Stilt	Himantopus himantopus	N		N*
Australian Stilt	H. leucocephalus			N
Pied Avocet	Recurvirostra avosetta	N		
Stone-Curlew	Burhinus oedicnemus	N/P		
Great Stone Plover	Esacus recurvirostris	N*	R/B	
Great Australian Stone Plover	E. magnirostris			P*
Australian Pratincole	Stiltia isabella			
Pratincole	Glareola pratincola			
Eastern Collared Pratincole	G. maldivarum	R	P	N/P/B*
Little Pratincole	G. lactea	R		
Northern Lapwing	Vanellus vanellus	N	P	P*
River Lapwing	V. duvaucelii	R	R	
Yellow-wattled Lapwing	V. malabaricus	R		
Sociable Plover	V. gregarius	*		
White-tailed Plover	V. leucurus	N*		
Grey-headed Lapwing	V. cinereus	N		P*
Red-wattled Lapwing	V. indicus	R	R/N	
Javanese Wattled Lapwing	V. macropterus			
Masked Plover	V. miles			
Pacific Golden Plover	Pluvialis fulva	N		N/P
Grey Plover	P. squatarola	N		N/P
Ringed Plover	Charadrius hiaticula	*		P*
Long-billed Ringed Plover	C. placidus	N/P*		P*
Little Ringed Plover	C. dubius	N		N/P
Kentish Plover	C. alexandrinus	N	P	N/P
Red-capped Dotterel	C. ruficapillus			
Malaysian Sand Plover	C. peronii			R

6. PRK	7. RUS	8. HGK	9. IND	10. INA	11. JPN	12. LAO	13. MAS	14. MGL	15. MYA	16. NEP	17. PAK	18. PHI	19. KOR	20. SIN	21. SRI	22. TWN	23. THA	24. VIE
P	B	N	R/N	R	R/N	L	N*	B	R	N/P	N(B)	N*	R/N	P*	R*	N	N	N
		ER*	EN				EL		ER								ER	
			R									R						
	P	R	N*		*	R	N		R	N(B)	R	R		N	R	R	R/N	R
		R	R			R	N*		R	R	R*						R/B	R
		R/P/N	R		R	R	R		R	R	R	R		*	R	R	R	N
R	L	N	N				N*		N	*	N/P				R*		L	
		N	N		P/N				N		N		(R)/N		N	P*		
		R/N	R						R	B/N	N*							
	N/P	R	R	R	P(N/B)	R	N	B	N/P	P	R	P/N	P	N/P	R	P(B)	R/N	N
	B	N	N(B)	N	N*			B	N	P	N(B)				N	P*		N
			R		P/N*				R	R	R				R			
			R						R	B/N	R				R			
			R	R/B	R	R	R		R		R	R/B						
				N														
P		N*	L		B/P	R	P/N(B)	P*	R	P	B	R	P	P	N*	B	R(N)	R/B
			R			R	*		R	B	B		P*	P*	R		R*(N)	N
N	B	N	N		N(B')		N	B	N	N/P	N	N	N(P)	N/P		P	N	N
P	B	N*	N*		P*		N*	P*	N*		N	P	P*	P*	N*	P		N
P	B	N*		P*	R(B)	N/P	N*	N	N	P/N			P(N)	P*	P*	N*	N*	N
B	L	R/P/N	B/N	N/P	R(B)	R	N	B		R	B/N	P/N	B	N/P	R	N(R)	R/N	N/P
P		N	B/N	R/N/P	R(B)	N/P	N	B		N/P	B/N	P/N	P(B)	N/P	R	P(R)	N	N/P
			N*	R			R					P/N		N			R	N/P

ENGLISH NAME	SCIENTIFIC NAME	1. BAN	2. BHU	3 BR
Lesser Sand Plover	*Charadrius mongolus*	N		N/
Great Sand Plover	*C. leschenaultii*	N	P	N/
Caspian Plover	*C. asiaticus*			
Eastern Sand Plover	*C. veredus*			P
Dotterel	*Eudromias morinellus*			
Black-tailed Godwit	*Limosa limosa*	N		P/
Bar-tailed Godwit	*L. lapponica*	N		P'/
Little Curlew	*Numenius minutus*			P
Whimbrel	*N. phaeopus*	N		P/
Bristle-thighed Curlew	*N. tahitiensis*			
Slender-billed Curlew	*N. tenuirostris*			
Western Curlew	*N. arquata*	N		P/
Far Eastern Curlew	*N. madagascariensis*	N*		P/
Spotted Redshank	*Tringa erythropus*	N	P	P
Common Redshank	*T. totanus*	N	P	P/
Marsh Sandpiper	*T. stagnatilis*	N	P	P/
Common Greenshank	*T. nebularia*	N	N	P/
Spotted Greenshank	*T. guttifer*	EN*		
Greater Yellowlegs	*T. melanoleuca*			
Lesser Yellowlegs	*T. flavipes*			
Green Sandpiper	*T. ochropus*	N	N	P/
Wood Sandpiper	*T. glareola*	N	N	P/
Terek Sandiper	*Xenus cinereus*	N/P		P/
Common Sandpiper	*Actitis hypoleucos*	N	N	P/
Grey-tailed Tattler	*Heteroscelus brevipes*	N/P*		P/
Wandering Tattler	*H. incanus*			
Ruddy Turnstone	*Arenaria interpres*	N		P/
Wilson's Phalarope	*Phalaropus tricolor*			
Red-necked Phalarope	*P. lobatus*			P(N
Grey Phalarope	*P. fulicarius*			
Eurasian Woodcock	*Scolopax rusticola*	N*	N	P
Amami Woodcock	*S. mira*			
Rufous Woodcock	*S. saturata*			
Sulawesi Woodcock	*S. celebensis*			
Obi Woodcock	*S. rochussenii*			
Solitary Snipe	*Gallinago solitaria*	N*		
Japanese Snipe	*G. hardwickii*			
Wood Snipe	*G. nemoricola*	N*	EN	

6. PRK	7. RUS	8. HGK	9. IND	10. INA	11. JPN	12. LAO	13. MAS	14. MGL	15. MYA	16. NEP	17. PAK	18. PHI	19. KOR	20. SIN	21. SRI	22. TWN	23. THA	24. VIE
P	B	N/P	B/N	N/P	P	N/P	N	P	N	P	N	P/N	P	N/P	N	N	N	N/P
P	B	N/P	N	N/P	P	N	N	B	N	*	N	P/N	P*	N/P	N*	N	N	N/P
			N*												N*			
		P		N/P	P*		P	B*				P/N*	*	P*		P*		N
	B				P*			B			N*							
P	B	P/N	N	N/P	P		N	B	N	P	N	P/N	P	N/P	N	P	N/P	N/P
P	B	P/N	N	N/P	P		N	B			N	P/N	P	N/P	N*	P	N	N/P
P	B	P		N/P	P*			P*				N	P*			P	P*	
P	B	P	N	N/P	P		N	P*	N	P	N	P/N	P	N/P	N	N	N	N/P
					P*							P						
	LB*				*													
N	B	N/P	N	N/P	P/N	L	N	B		N/P	N	P/N	P(N)	N/P	N	N	N	N/P
P	B*	P/N		N/P	P/N		P(N)*	L				P/N	P	P*		N	P*	
P	B	N/P	N		P(N)	N	N*	P	N	N/P	N		P	N*	N*	N	N	N/P
EP	EB*	EP	EN*	EN/P	EP*		EN		EN			EP/N	EP*	EN*	EL	EP*	EN*	EN/P
	P*		N*		P*/N*													
			N*		P*/N*													
P	B	N/P	N	N*	P/N	N/P	N*	B		N/P	N	P/N	P	N*	N	N	N	N/P
B	B	N/P	N	N/P	P(N)	N/P	N	B		P/N	N/P	P/N	P	N/P	N	N	N	N/P
P	B	P	N	N/P	P	N	N	P	N	*	N	P/N	P	N/P	N	N	N	N/P
P	B	N/P	B/N	N/P	R	N/P	N	B		N/P	B/N	P/N	P(B)	N/P	N	N(R)	N	N/P
P	B	P		N/P	P		N	P				P/N	P	N/P		N	P*	N
	L				P(N*)											L		
P	B	P	N	N/P	P		N	P	N	*	N	P/N	P	N		N	N	N/P
	L				P*													
P	B	P	N	N/P	P		P*(N)	P		*	N	P/N	P			N	P	N/P*
	B				P											P		
P	B	N	B/N		B/N	N/P	N*	B	N	B/N	R	P/N*	P	N*	N*	P*	N*	N
					R													
				ER*														
P	L		N	N				B	N	P/N	N			N				
B				B										*				
			EB/N			EN			EN						EN		EN*	
			P															

ENGLISH NAME	SCIENTIFIC NAME	1. BAN	2. BHU	3. BR*
Pintail Snipe	*Gallinago stenura*	N	N	N/*
Swinhoe's Snipe	*G. megala*	N*	N	N/*
Great Snipe	*G. media*			
Common Snipe	*G. gallinago*	N	N	N/*
Jack Snipe	*Lymnocryptes minima*	N*		
Short-billed Dowitcher	*Limnodromus griseus*			
Long-billed Dowitcher	*L. scolopaceus*			
Asiatic Dowitcher	*L. semipalmatus*	EN/P*		EN/
Red Knot	*Calidris canutus*	N*		P*
Great Knot	*C. tenuirostris*	N/P		P*
Sanderling	*C. alba*	N		N/*
Western Sandpiper	*C. mauri*			
Rufous-necked Stint	*C. ruficollis*	N		N/*
Little Stint	*C. minuta*	N	N	
Temminck's Stint	*C. temminckii*	N	N	N/*
Long-toed Stint	*C. subminuta*	N/P		N/*
Baird's Sandpiper	*C. bairdii*			
Pectoral Sandpiper	*C. melanotos*			
Sharp-tailed Sandpiper	*C. acuminata*			N/*
Rock Sandpiper	*C. ptilocnemis*			
Dunlin	*C. alpina*	N/P		P*
Curlew Sandpiper	*C. ferruginea*	N		N/*
Spoon-billed Sandpiper	*Eurynorhynchus pygmeus*	EN/P		
Broad-billed Sandpiper	*Limicola falcinellus*	N		N/*
Stilt Sandpiper	*Micropalama himantopus*			
Buff-breasted Sandpiper	*Tryngites subruficollis*			
Ruff	*Philomachus pugnax*	N	N	N/*
Sooty Gull	*Larus hemprichii*			
Japanese Gull	*L. crassirostris*			
Mew Gull	*L. canus*			
Eastern Mew Gull	*L. kamtschatschensis*			
Herring Gull	*L. argentatus*	N*	P	
Thayer's Gull	*L. thayeri*			
Lesser Black-backed Gull	*L. fuscus*		P	
Slaty-backed Gull	*L. schistisagus*			
Glaucous-winged Gull	*L. glaucescens*			
Glaucous Gull	*L. hyperboreus*			
Great Black-headed Gull	*L. ichthyaetus*	N		

6. PRK	7. RUS	8. HGK	9. IND	10. INA	11. JPN	12. LAO	13. MAS	14. MGL	15. MYA	16. NEP	17. PAK	18. PHI	19. KOR	20. SIN	21. SRI	22. TWN	23. THA	24. VIE
P	B	N/P	N	N	N/P	N/P	N	B	N	P/N	P	P/N*	P	N	N	P	N	N
P		P/N	N	N/P	P		N	B	N			P/N	P*	N	N*	P	N	
		N*													N*			
P	B	N/P	N	N/P	N/P	N/P	N	B		P/N	N	P*	P	N	N	N	N	R
	B*		N		N*/P*				P		N	P	*		N	P*	N*	
	B*				P*													
	B	P*			P*/N*		N*	P*										
	B	EP	EN*	EN/P	EP*		EP	EB	EN*			EP/N			EN*	EL		EN/P
P	B	P/N	N*	N/P	P		P(N)	P*			N*	P/N	P	N	N*	P	N*	
P	B	P/N	N	N/P	P		N		N		N	P/N	P	P	N*	P	N/P	N/P
P	L	P	N	N/P	P/N		N	P*	N	*	N	P/N	P(N)	N	N	N	N	N/P
	B				P*/N*											P*		
P	B	P/N	N	N/P	P		P/N	P	N			P/N	P	N/P		N	N	N/P
	B	P	N	N*	P*/N*		N*	P	N	N	N	P			N			N/P
P	B	P/N	N	N/P	P/N	N	N	P	N	N	N	P/N	P	P	N	P	N	N/P
P	B	P/N	N	N*	P		N	P	N	*	N	P/N	P	N/P	N	P	N	N/P
	B				P*													
	B	P*	N*		P*								*			L		
P	B	P	N*	N/P	P		P*	P	N*		N*	P/N	P	P*	N*	N	N*	
	B				N*													
P	B	N	N	N*	P/N		N*	P		P/N	N		P(N)	P*	N*	N	N*	
P	B	P	N	N/P	P		N/P	P	N	P	N	P/N	P	N/P	N	N	N	N/P
EP	EB	EP	EN		EP*		EN*		EN				EP*	EN*	EN*	EP*	EN*(P)	EN/P
P	B*	P/N	N	N/P	P		N	P	N		N	P/N*	P	N/P	N*	N	N	N/P
					P*											L		
	B*		*		P*								*		N*	L		
	B	P/N	N	N*	P		N	P	N	P	P	P/N	*	N	N	P	N*	N
		N									B*							
R		N			R		P*			*	N*		R			N	N*	
	B						B		*		N*					N*		N
N	B*	N*			N					N/P	N	P/N	N		N*	N*	N	N
N	B	N	N		N		B		N/P	N	P/N	N		N*	N*	N	N	
					N*					*	N*				N			
N	B	N*			B/N						N		N			N*		
	B*	N*			N								*					
	B	N*			N			P*					N*					
	N	N			N*			B	N	N/P	N				N		N*	

ENGLISH NAME	SCIENTIFIC NAME	1. BAN	2. BHU	3. BRU
Indian Black-headed Gull	*Larus brunnicephalus*	N	N	
Franklin's Gull	*L. pipixcan*			
Relict Gull	*L. relictus*			
Black-headed Gull	*L. ridibundus*	N		N*
Slender-billed Gull	*L. genei*			
Bonaparte's Gull	*L. philadelphia*			
Little Gull	*L. minutus*			
Saunders' Gull	*L. saundersi*			
Whiskered Tern	*Chlidonias hybrida*	N(B)	P	N
White-winged Black Tern	*C. leucoptera*	N/P	P	N
Black Tern	*C. nigra*			
Gull-billed Tern	*Gelochelidon nilotica*	R	P	N
Caspian Tern	*Hydroprogne caspia*	N	P	P*
Indian River Tern	*Sterna aurantia*	R	R	
Common Tern	*S. hirundo*	N	P	N*
Arctic Tern	*S. paradisaea*		P	
Roseate Tern	*S. dougallii*			R
White-cheeked Tern	*S. repressa*			
Black-naped Tern	*S. sumatrana*	N*		R
Black-bellied Tern	*S. melanogaster*	R		
Aleutian Tern	*S. aleutica*			
Spectacled Tern	*S. lunata*			
Bridled Tern	*S. anaethetus*			B
Sooty Tern	*S. fuscata*			
Little Tern	*S. albifrons*	R		N(B*)
Black-shafted Tern	*S. saundersi*			
Greater Crested Tern	*Thalasseus bergii*	R		N/P
Lesser Crested Tern	*T. bengalensis*	R		
Chinese Crested Tern	*T. bernsteini*			
Sandwich Tern	*T. sandvicensis*			
Common Noddy	*Anous stolidus*			P*
Lesser Noddy	*A. tenuirostris*	L*		
White-capped Noddy	*A. minutus*			
White Tern	*Gygis alba*	L*		
Indian Skimmer	*Rynchops albicollis*	R		

6. PRK	7. RUS	8. HGK	9. IND	10. INA	11. JPN	12. LAO	13. MAS	14. MGL	15. MYA	16. NEP	17. PAK	18. PHI	19. KOR	20. SIN	21. SRI	22. TWN	23. THA	24. VIE
		N	B/N	N	N*	N/P	N		N	N/P	N			N*	N		N	N
N	EB	EN*		EN*	EN*			EB			N		EN*	N*	N		N	N
	B	N	N	N	N		N	B		N/P	N	P/N	N*		N*	N	N*	
		N*	N/B		N*			P*			R							
	B		*		N*			B										
EN		EN/P			* EN								EN*		EN*		EN*	EN
	B	P	R/B	N	P*	L	N(P)	B		P/N	R	P/N	*	P*	N	P	N	N
P	B	P	N	N(P)	P	L*	P/N	B	N	P	P	P/N	P*	N/P	N	P	N	N
		*			P*/N*			B										
		P	B*N	N	P*		N	B	N	N/P	N(B)	P/N		N/P	N	P*	N	N
		P/N	B*N	N	P*/N*		N	B	N*	N/P	R	P*		N	R	P*		N
		R	R			R			R	B/R	R						R*	
P	B	P	B/N	P/N	P		N	B	N	P	N	P/N	P	N/P	N	P	N(R)	N
	B	*	*		P*													
		B*	B	R/B	B		R*		N		L	R			B	B*	R*	
			B								N							
	B	B	B	R	B		R		N		R			R		B	R*	N
		R				R			R	B/R	R						*	N
B				P	P*							P*						
		B*	B	R	B		R				R*	R		N	P	B	R*	
		P*	R/N	B			R		N*		R	R			P	B*	N*	
B		P	B	R/N	B	R	N(R)	B	R	B	R	R	*	N(B)	R	B(R)	R	N
		B*									B				R			
N		P*	B/N	N/R	B		N		R		R	R		N	N	B*		
		B/N	R/N				N		N		R			N	N		N*	
			EN*									EP					EN	
		N							R*		N				N*			
		B*	R/B	B			R		R*		R*	R			P	B	R*	N
		N*													P			
			R/B	*								R			P			
		*	N*	*														*
		R/N			R				R	N	B						L*	R

Bibliography

Ali, S. and Ripley, S.D. 1983. *A Pictorial Guide to the Birds of the Indian Subcontinent.* Oxford University Press, New Delhi and Oxford.
—— and —— 1983. *Handbook to the Birds of India and Pakistan.* Compact edition. Oxford University Press, New Delhi and Oxford.
Alström, P. 1989. Identification of marsh terns in juvenile and winter plumages. *British Birds* 82: 296–319. Bedford.
—— and Olsson, U. 1985. Comments on the text and plates of 'A Field Guide to the Birds of Japan'. *Personal comm.* Sweden.
Anon. 1981. Bird topography charts. *British Birds* 74: 239–242. Bedford.
Bakewell, D.N., Carey, G.J., Duff, D.G., et al. 1989. Observations of Relict Gulls *Larus relictus* on passage at Beidaihe, People's Republic of China. *Forktail* 4: 77–87. Oriental Bird Club, Bedford.
Beehler, B.M., Pratt, T.K. and Zimmerman, D.A. 1986. *Birds of New Guinea.* Princeton University Press, Princeton.
Brazil, M.A. and Ikenaga, H. 1987. The Amami Woodcock *Scolopax mira*: its identity and identification. *Forktail* 3:3–16. Oriental Bird Club, Bedford.
Campbell, B. and Lack, E. (eds.) 1985. *A Dictionary of Birds.* T & AD Poyser, London.
Chandler, R.J. 1989. *The Macmillan Field Guide to North Atlantic Shorebirds.* Macmillan Press, London and Basingstoke.
Cheng, Tso-Hsin. 1976. *A Distribution List of Chinese Birds.* Science Publishing House, Peking. (in Chinese)
Coates, B.J. 1985. *The Birds of Papua New Guinea.* Vol. 1. Dove Publications, Australia.
Cramp, S. and Simmons, K.E.L. 1977, 1983 and 1985. *Handbook of the Birds of Europe, the Middle East and North Africa.* Vols. 1, 3 and 4. Oxford University Press, Oxford.
Delacour, J. and Scott, P. 1975. *The Waterfowl of the World.* 4 vols. Country Life, London.
Delin, H. and Svensson, L. 1988. *Photographic Guide to Birds of Britain and Europe.* Hamlyn, London.
Dunn, J.L. and Rose, B.J. 1992. A Further Note on Arctic Loon Identification. *Birding* 24: 106–107. American Birding Association, Colorado.
du Pont, J.E. 1971. *Philippine Birds.* Delaware Museum of Natural History, Delaware.
Farrand, Jr., J. 1985. *The Audubon Society Master Guide to Birding.* Vols. 1–2. Knopf, New York.
—— 1988. *Western Birds: An Audubon Handbook.* McGraw-Hill Book, New York.
Ferguson-Lees, J., Willis, I. and Sharrock, J.T.R. 1983. *The Shell Guide to*

the Birds of Britain and Ireland. Michael Joseph, London.

Flint, V.E., Boehme, R.L. and Kuznetsov, A.A. 1984. A Field Guide to Birds of the USSR. Princeton University Press, Princeton.

Fukuda, M. 1992. Identification of Great and Japanese Cormorant. Habataki 238: 4. Kanagawa Chapter of Wild Bird Society of Japan, Yokohama. (in Japanese)

Grant, P.J. 1986. Gulls: a guide to identification (2nd ed.). T & AD Poyser, Calton.

—— and Mullarney, K. 1989. The New Approach to Identification. Peter Grant, Kent.

Hachisuka, M. 1931-1935. The Birds of the Philippine Islands, with Notes on the Mammal Fauna. 2 vols in 4. H.F. & G.Witherby, London.

Hancock, J. and Kushlan, J. 1984. The Herons Handbook. Harper & Row Publishers. New York.

Harashima, M. 1991. Identification of Herons, Egrets and Bitterns. Nihonno-Seibutsu 5(5): 4-11. Bun-ichi Sougou Shuppan, Tokyo.

Harris, A., Tucker, L. and Vinicombe, K. 1989. The Macmillan Field Guide to Bird Identification. Macmillan Press, London and Basingstoke.

Harrison, P. 1985. Seabirds: An identification guide (Revised ed.). Croom Helm, London.

—— 1987. Seabirds of the World: A·Photographic Guide. Christopher Helm, London.

Hayman, P., Marchant, J. and Prater, T. 1986. Shorebirds: An identification guide to the waders of the world. Croom Helm, London & Sydney.

Howard, R. and Moore, A. 1991. A Complete Checklist of the Birds of the World. (2nd edition.) Academic Press, London.

Ishida, K. 1992. Ecology, Distribution and Form of Amami Woodcock Scolopax mira. Investigation of Special Birds: 43-85. Wild Birds Society of Japan, Tokyo. (in Japanese)

Johnsgard, P.A. 1978. Ducks, Geese and Swans of the World. University of Nebraska Press, Lincoln.

—— 1981. The Plovers, Sandpipers and Snipes of the World. University of Nebraska Press, Lincoln.

—— 1983. Cranes of the World. Indiana University Press, Bloomington.

Jonsson, L. 1992. Birds of Europe with North Africa and the Middle East. Christopher Helm, London.

—— and Grant, P.J. 1984. Identification of stints and peeps. British Birds 77: 293-315. Bedford.

Kahl, M.P. 1987. The Royal Spoonbill. National Geographic 171(2): 281-284.

Kameya, T. 1991. How to identify waders. Birder 5(9): 4-13. Bun-ichi Sougou Shuppan. Tokyo. (in Japanese)

Kaneda, H. 1991. Duck Watching. Nihon no Seibutsu 5(2): 4-25. Bun-ichi Sougou Shuppan, Tokyo. (in Japanese)

Kanouchi, T. and Hamaguchi, T. 1991. Yama-kei Field Books; Wild Birds. (Yacho).Yamato-Keikoku Sha, Tokyo. (in Japanese)

Kaufmann, K. 1990. A Field Guide to Advanced Birding. Houghton Mifflin, Boston.

Kennerley, P.R. 1989. Birds new to Hong Kong; Relict Gull at Mai Po, the first record for Hong Kong. Hong Kong Bird Report 1989: 80-91. Hong Kong Birdwatching Society, Hong Kong.

———— and Bakewell, D.N. 1991. Identification and status of Nordmann's Greenshank. *Dutch Birding* 13: 1–8. Amsterdam.

King, B., Woodcock, M., and Dickingson, E.C. 1975. *A Field Guide to the Birds of South-East Asia*. Collins, London.

Knystautas, A. 1987. *The Natural History of the USSR*. Century Hutchinson, London.

Kuroda, N. (ed.) 1984. *Definitive Edition for Large Pictorial Guide of Living Things: Birds. (Ketteiban Seibutu Dai Zukan; Chourui)*. Sekai-Bunka Sha, Tokyo. (in Japanese)

Lane, B.A. 1987. *Shorebirds in Australia*. Nelson Publishers, Melbourne.

Lekagul, B. and Round, P.D. 1991. *A Guide to the Birds of Thailand*. Saha Karn Bhaet, Bangkok.

Lewington, I., Alström, P. and Colston, P. 1991. *A Field Guide to the Rare Birds of Britain and Europe*. Harper Collins, London.

Lindsey, T.R. 1986. *The Seabirds of Australia*. Angus and Robertson Publishers, NSW, Australia and London.

McCaskie, G., Dunn, J.L., Roberts, C. and Sibley, D.A. 1990. Notes on identifying Arctic and Pacific Loons in alternate plumage. *Birding* 22: 70–73. American Birding Association, Colorado.

Mackinnon, J. 1988. *Field Guide to the Birds of Java and Bali*. Gajah Mada University Press, Yogyakarta.

Madge, S. and Burn, H. 1988. *Wildfowl: An Identification guide to the ducks, geese and swans of the world*. Christopher Helm, London.

Marchant, S. and Higgins, P.J. (eds.) 1990. *Handbook of Australian, New Zealand and Antarctic Birds*. Oxford University Press, Oxford.

Medway, L. and Wells, D.R. 1976. *The Birds of the Malay Peninsula*. Vol. 5: Conclusion and survey of every species. H.F. & G. Witherby, London and Penerbit University Malaya, Kuala Lumpur.

Nakamura, N. 1984. *Little Referentially Pictorial Guide of Birds: Waterfowl. (Yacho Kensaku Zukan; Mizube no Tori.)* Kodansha, Tokyo. (in Japanese)

———— 1986. *Introduction to Reference: Pictorial Guide of Wild Birds. (Kensaku Nyuumon Yacho no Zukan.)* Vols. 1 and 2 Hoikusha, Osaka. (in Japanese)

Olsson, U. 1987. The identification of snipes. *International Bird Identification;* 25–27. International Birdwatching Center Eilat, Eilat.

Phillips, J.C. 1986. *A Natural History of the Ducks*. Vol. I and II. Dover Publishers, New York.

Prater, A.J., Merchant, J.H., and Vuorinen, J. 1977. *Guide to the Identification and Ageing of Holarctic Waders*. British Trust for Ornithology, Tring.

Pratt, N.D., Bruner, P.L. and Berrett, D.G. 1987. *A Field Guide to the Birds of Hawaii and the Tropical Pacific*. Princeton University Press, Princeton.

Pringle, J.D. 1985. *The Waterbirds of Australia*. Angus and Robertson Publishers, NSW, Australia and London.

———— 1987. *The Shorebirds of Australia*. Angus and Robertson Publishers, NSW, Australia and London.

Ripley, S.D. 1977. *Rails of the World*. David R. Godine, Boston.

Roberts, T.J. 1991. *The Birds of Pakistan*. Vol. 1. Oxford University Press, Karachi.

Schauensee, R.M. 1984. *The Birds of China*. Oxford University Press, Oxford.

Shigeta, Y. 1991. How to identify Grey-tailed Tattler and Wandering Tattler. *Birder* 5(9): 46-49. Bun-ichi Sougou Shuppan, Tokyo. (in Japanese)

———— 1992. Little Tern; its taxonomy and distribution. *Birder* 6(7): 18-21. Bun-ichi Sougou Shuppan, Tokyo. (in Japanese)

Shirihai, H. 1988. Pintail Snipe in Israel in November 1984 and its identification. *Dutch Birding* 10: 1-11. Amsterdam.

Simpson, K. (ed.) and Day, N. 1984. *Field Guide to the Birds of Australia: A Book of Identification*. Christopher Helm, London.

Slater, P., Slater, P. and Slater, R. 1986. *The Slater Field Guide to Australian Birds*. Rigby Publishers, Australia.

Sonobe, K. 1985. New hints on bird identification; Bitterns. *Yacho* 50(8): 6. Wild Bird Society of Japan, Tokyo. (in Japanese)

Sonobe, K. (chief ed.) 1982. *A Field Guide to the Birds of Japan*. Wild Bird Society of Japan, Tokyo.

Soothill, E. and P. Whitehead. 1978. *Wildfowl of the World*. Blandford Press, London.

Symithies, B.E. 1981. *The Birds of Borneo* (3rd ed.). The Sabah Society and the Malayan Nature Society, Sabah.

Takano, S. 1981. *Birds of Japan in Photographs. (Nippon san Chorui Zukan.)* Tokai University Press, Tokyo. (in Japanese)

———— 1985. *Yama-kei Fine Pictorial Guide; Wild Birds of Japan. (Yama-Kei karaa Meikan; Nippon no Yacho.)* Yamato-Keikoku Sha, Tokyo. (in Japanese)

———— 1991. *A Field Guide to the Birds of Japan* (enlarged ed.). *(Fiirudo Gaido Nihon no Yacho, Zouho-ban.)* Wild Bird Society of Japan, Tokyo. (in Japanese)

Terres, J.K. 1980. *Encyclopedia of North American Birds*. Alfred A. Knopf, New York.

Ujihara, O. and Ujihara, M. 1992. *Identification Guide of Gulls. (Kamome Shikibetsu gaido.)* (special ed. of 'BIRDER'). Bun-ichi Sougou Shuppan, Tokyo. (in Japanese)

van den Berg, A.B. 1988. Identification of Slender-billed Curlew and its occurrence in Morocco in winter of 1987/88. *Dutch Birding* 10: 45-53. Amsterdam.

Viney, C. and Phillipps, K. 1989. *Birds of Hong Kong* (4th edition.). The Government Printer, Hong Kong.

White, C.M.N. and M.D. Bruce. 1986. *The Birds of Wallacea. An Annotated Check-list*. British Ornithologists Union, London.

Wild Bird Society of Japan (ed.). 1992. *Field Selection; Waterfowl. (Mizube no Tori.)* Hokuryuukan, Tokyo. (in Japanese)

Wu, J.S., Yang, H.Y., Taniguchi, T., et al. 1991. *A Guide to the Birds of Taiwan*. Taiwan Wild Bird Information Center, Taichun. (in Chinese)

Yamashina Institute for Ornithology, Department of Bird Banding. 1988. Identification of 4 species in *Gallinago*. *Manual for Bird Banding*. Yamashina Institute for Ornithology, Abiko. (in Japanese)

Yamashina, Y. 1934. *A Natural History of Japanese Birds. (Nippon no Chourui to sono Seitai.)* Azusa-Shobo, Tokyo. (in Japanese)

INDEX Scientific and English Names

The page numbers in the index refer to the text. The illustration appears on the opposite page.

MAP OF ASIA

INSIDE THE THICK LINE IS THE GEOLOGICAL REGION
WHICH COVERED BY THE FIELD GUIDE.